The Irish Novel
1960–2010

The Irish Novel
1960–2010

GEORGE O'BRIEN

CORK UNIVERSITY PRESS

First published in 2012 by
Cork University Press
Youngline Industrial Estate
Pouladuff Road, Togher
Cork, Ireland

© George O'Brien

British Library Cataloguing in Publication Data
A CIP catalogue record for this book is available from the British Library.

ISBN-978-185918-495-0
Printed in the UK by CPI
Typeset by Tower Books, Ballincollig, Co. Cork
www.corkuniversitypress.com

Contents

Acknowledgements

I have the great good fortune to have friends like John Evans, Eamon Grennan, Vincent Hurley, Máire Kennedy, Tim Meagher, Denis Sampson and Terry Winch. Many grateful thanks to them for all their hospitality, encouragement, help and support over the years. Terry's input early on was just what I needed. And special thanks to Denis, who made a timely intervention at a dark hour.

To my family – Pam, Ben and Nick – love and thanks, as ever.

Jonathan Williams was invaluable; many thanks to him.

Thanks, too, to Donna Even-Kesef, Office Manager of the Department of English, Georgetown University, for answering my dumbest questions with cheerful good grace. Finally, a warm word of thanks to all at Cork University Press with whom it was a pleasure to work and whose caring editorial attention and high production values have done so much to enhance the original typescript.

I am also indebted to everyone at the Joseph Mark Lauinger Memorial Library at Georgetown University, particularly Jill Hollingsworth, Jeff Popovich and the Interlibrary Loan staff, who were unfailingly helpful and obliging.

Introduction

If there is one literary landmark more prominent than another in Irish culture over the past fifty years, it is the growth and development of the novel. Half a century ago, Seán O'Faoláin could note, with some justification, 'the comparative failure of the Irish novel'.[1] No such statement could be made today. The intervening period has seen a remarkable flowering of the Irish novel on all conceivable fronts. Genre literature such as crime fiction, 'chick lit' and fantasy, once largely overlooked as forms for the Irish novelist's imagination, have proliferated. The Northern Irish novel has come into its own. The novel has been instrumental in making distinctive contributions towards the demarcation of gay and feminist literatures and to their histories and traditions within an Irish context. As the present study's bibliography shows, a considerable body of commentary and analysis by a large corps of Irish, British, North American and European academics – and others from further afield – has emerged, the focus of which has been, at least in some degree, to account for the manner in which the contemporary Irish novel exemplifies global critical discourses. Commercial success and literary awards received have increased media interest in Irish novelists and their work. In general, it is difficult to dispute the argument that the contemporary Irish novel and the careers of contemporary Irish novelists are integral to and illustrative of the country's recent history.[2]

These developments seem to place that remark of Seán O'Faoláin's well and truly in a bygone age. And indeed at the time it was made, the kinds of initiatives which would result in the novel becoming such an expressive resource and cultural bellwether were already taking place. Beginning with the early novels of Edna O'Brien, John McGahern, Brian Moore and John Broderick, and including Aidan Higgins's *Langrishe, Go Down* (1966), a decisive shift of tone and focus in the Irish novel can be detected, a move away from what has been called 'the all-too-familiar lachrymose dithyrambic beat of the old stuff'.[3] This departure was so unforeseen and unwelcome that most of the works embarking on it were banned under the Censorship of Publications Act (1929).[4] By officially silencing and disowning the authors concerned, the application of this antediluvian and philistine piece of legislation declared that its own antiquated moral and ideological landscapes were the only tenable imaginative terrain. In opposing new voices and fresh perspectives on Irish life and experience, censorship – one of the voices of the state – appeared not so much to dismiss possibilities as to deny them. The effect was to highlight the fact that change – the need for it, the inevitability of it, the difficulty of attaining it – was the primary interest of the proscribed works. Indeed, over the range of these authors' early novels, banned and otherwise, the primacy of this interest in change may be gathered from the variety of ways in which it is negotiated, contemplated, interrogated and internally debated.

Over and above the particularities of how individual novels handle change as a theme, a more general sense can be discerned of the form itself changing in order that the theme in all its complications receives full imaginative rein. Among the most fundamental of these formal changes is a closer focus on individual experience. This new focus sees the individual in the context of his or her inviolability, even – or especially – when the adequacy of that context is placed under stress by either the threat or the actuality of violation. (Figures whose depersonalising authority is based on orthodox, socially sanctioned codes of power and legitimacy are the typical source of the real or potential mistreatment.) Contrasting with and, in effect, opposing such codes are a particular character's distinctive inner life, a consciousness made up of memory, dreams and desires, from which arises an awareness of the validity of its own needs and which articulates its oppositional energies in conceptions of personal freedom in a secular world. This individual answers to his or her own self, not to the repressive expectations of precedent and convention. It is as though the issues that once were major themes in the story of the nation coming into being – self-determination, sovereignty, affirmation of the right to difference – have been redeployed in the contemporary Irish novel with the view to claiming and clarifying the value and potential of the individual's hopes and expectations.

Beginning with Edna O'Brien's *The Country Girls* (1960), the new focus may be seen to greatest advantage when embodied by youthful female protagonists.[5] As in the novel generally – as *Pamela*, *The Red and the Black*, *The Adventures of Huckleberry Finn*, and *The Magic Mountain*, for instance, show – young protagonists continue to be the rule in the Irish novel, one of the comparatively few lines of continuity that the form as a whole maintains throughout its history (the present study concludes with *Skippy Dies* (2010), whose cast of characters is largely the same age as Edna O'Brien's Cait Brady and whose collective title might be 'the suburban boys'). Youth and newness seem obviously associated, and in its role as a standard-bearer of change, youth personifies the novelty which prompts the type of news that the novel – not just the contemporary Irish novel – seeks to convey. But though the young perceive their own novelty, how best to commission that knowledge in the pursuit of fulfilment and a sense of social worth typically remains a matter of trial and error.

In the contemporary Irish novel, error tends to be judged before trial. The bonds between the young and the rest of the world consist less of trust than of obedience, particularly when the world in question is intimate, personal and private. The new generation finds itself to be subject to a command emotional economy, in which the rates of exchange on the part of dependants is exorbitantly high in view of what they receive in return. The novels of John McGahern have been rightly prized for the attention and intensity with which they portray distorted relations between fathers and sons, particularly *The Dark* (1965). And these novels also point to one of the major characteristics of the contemporary Irish novel, namely the considerable extent to which its stories originate in the split, the departure, the disruption, the rejection. Such storylines also present themselves in terms of such structures of thought and feeling as the nature of a disputed present and an unavailing past. This sense of rupture is in part because of inherited narratives – particularly those of the national and the confessional variety – having outlived their usefulness. In addition, the steady internationalisation and urbanisation of Ireland as a society and as a polity have not been accompanied by narratives with the same credibility and cultural appeal as those with which they are competing for attention. More starkly, it may also be that its origins lie in the belief that '[t]here is no society in Ireland as there is elsewhere; no sense of continuity, tradition, legacy, except one that is jagged, broken'.[6] This central sense of breakage and shapelessness identifies the narrative challenge which the contemporary Irish novel takes up and also marks the individual protagonist as not only the embodiment of that challenge but also the answer to it.

Emphasising the individual obviously affects the representation of those structures that the individual typically inhabits – the family and the nation. Here, too, there are significant changes. Home life is portrayed as either feckless or coercive, a sphere whose capacity for nurture has been replaced by an intimacy that is damaging, or at the very least counterproductive. The home no longer seems a viable site of continuity and inheritance, and its state of internal disrepair makes it the counterpart of the home of the gentry, the Big House, the story of whose succumbing to change continues to haunt the contemporary Irish novel, as though it still has historical and psychological truths to reveal. (Another house to experience eclipse is that of God. The religious spirit has not disappeared from the Irish novel, but the institution of Catholicism no longer exerts any imaginative appeal to speak of – priests are among the most obvious of the contemporary Irish novel's missing persons.)[7] And the withering away of the home of the citizenry, which often indicates the end of life on the land, is also frequently marked by the death of one or other parent, which is not only an unnerving deprivation for members of the younger generation but a manifestation of change contrary to those to which they aspire. Death is also a definitive instance of a break, and while it is a change that can initiate individuation, that development can be so beset by the pain and perplexity of discontinuity that its value is difficult to grasp. Moreover, death can also be a trope connoting losses that are less visceral and immediate but which are no less decisive, as is borne out by, for instance, Patrick McCabe's *The Dead School* (1995).

When the dead parent is a mother, the connotations include not only a Mother Church that is no longer available but also Mother Ireland and the ideas of care, sustenance, belonging and protection which such an entity might be thought to represent and which are also fundamental to the nature of the rights and entitlements a social contract might provide.[8] But by the 1960s, the icon's lustre was beginning to look irremediably faded, and sagas devoted to the birth of the nation as *Thy Tears Might Cease* (1963) and, in a somewhat different vein, *Strumpet City* (1969) conclude on notes of defeat and disappointment which belie the inspiration and energy that these novels' protagonists bring to the historical moment.[9] Indeed, such notes usher in a new phase of the Irish historical novel, in which it is not merely on the national story or Irish history that a cold eye is cast, but on the phenomenon of history itself.[10] The ensuing critique of history as essentially an experience of transience generated by an unmeaning demiurge with neither conscience nor object, destroying and preserving at will and without any discernible – much less predictable – pattern or tempo, is given comprehensive treatment in J.G. Farrell's *Troubles* (1970), though a case might be made that its conception of the historical, or of life in times of historical upheaval, owes something to the treatment of time in *Langrishe, Go Down*.

Higgins's novel arguably looks over its shoulder at such mordant meditations on the fate of being a child of time as those of Flann O'Brien's *The Third Policeman* (1967) and Samuel Beckett's *How It Is* (1964). In the former, the living experience of time as a progress to death is replaced, but not improved, by the afterlife experience of time as a series of eternally recurring repetitions. And the notion of time as a measure of progression is effectively derided in *How It Is* through the use of a form that is both randomised and self-referential, the effect of which is to suggest the impossibility, and the apparent irrelevance, of differentiating between the most common expressions of progression – before, during, after, and the like. And as *Troubles* goes to considerable lengths to demonstrate, historical narrative is under no obligation to represent the experience of the historical in terms of reliability, correctness or stability. On the contrary, an adequate rendering of the historical must incorporate the contending perspectives of the many different participants in, witnesses to and instigators of the events in question and reactions to those events, including those with the same outlook and loyalties.[11] If, from an objective standpoint, what history factually amounts to is a sequence of contingencies, the manner in which history is subjectively taken in will perforce be uncoordinated and inconsistent. And attempting to make one's peace between objective conditions and a personal reaction to them, as Willy Dunne wishes to do in Sebastian Barry's *A Long, Long Way* (2005), results in that state of bereftness which is one of the manifestations of the mourning mind that typifies the isolated modern subject.[12] With regard to the national story, disillusion began to be replaced by a revised and expanded sense of historical reality, a more discriminating imagining of the events and personages of the past. Here again – as Neil Jordan's *The Past* (1980) shows – the ground for such a revision is individual reaction, which serves as a deviation from, and thereby a corrective to, the simplistic Manichaeism of the inherited narrative. The attempt in this novel to articulate both the distance and intimacy that denote the past's somewhat ghostly existence ends up conveying how difficult it is to identify and trust the truth of any one view of the circumstances depicted.

The interest in jettisoning history's familiar though impersonal para-phernalia of domination, violence and ideology is clear. A fresh, less reductive start is desired. If a sense of the past is necessary, and if the past has anything to teach, surely its narratives of destruction (Stephen Dedalus's nightmare of 'shattered glass and toppling masonry')[13] are not the most desirable lessons. There are other histories – of beauty, of dis-interested action, of individual endeavour.[14] The appeal of choice figures in the novels of John Banville, which from the outset – in *Night-spawn* (1971) and *Birchwood* (1973) – express pronounced reservations regarding the potential for meaning of the historical scenarios that are their pretext. This scepticism is consolidated through being elaborated upon in *Doctor Copernicus* (1975) and *Kepler* (1981), where the disinte-grative consequences of political unrest are contrasted with the renovations and clarifications of free and original scientific thought. The two eponymous astronomers' restorative projections are not only immense achievements in their own right, triumphs of method and mind. They also confound the orthodoxies of their day, particularly rigidities of the confessional variety, the imposition and maintenance of which are such powerful justifications for history's depredations. The astronomers' willingness not only to imagine counter-positions but to formulate and publish their visions is on one level tantamount to civil disobedience, heresy or an offence against the concept of a divine, or hierarchical, cosmic order. But at another level it affirms that history also shows that thought, singular events in singular consciousnesses, is the most productive path to change.

But however history, in the sense of coherence rather than destruc-tion, is imagined, and whether better prompts to doing so are to be found in times and places in the story of European intellectual life instead of those closer to home, as Banville's 'Revolutions Trilogy'[15] sug-gests, Irish history as a concern of the contemporary Irish novel does not just fade away. As John McGahern's *Amongst Women* (1990) reveals, the fate of Irish history's old soldiers, as embodied by the patriarch Moran, has remained one that continues to overshadow not just the present but the attempts of the novel's other characters to abide by the nature of the present. This capacity for presentness, this affirmation of the limited but tolerable character of the here and now, is represented by the attentiveness and supple-mindedness of the women amongst whom Moran's last days are spent. And it is not only the dying man's own allotted time that is ebbing away, but the time that his youth as a fighter for Irish freedom represents. Or rather, not so much that time as Moran's having remained something of a hostage to it. The historical change that he helped to bring about did not inspire him to make other changes. On his death bed, he seems a monument to the immobility of mind and spirit which has weighed down, but also secured, his narrow life as a man and father – his natural life, as it were, in contrast to his brief and implicitly unnatural adventure as a historical agent. Only time's attrition can lift the burden that Moran is to others and to himself. Rather than representing the nature of historical legacy by such an inert and menacing presence, a more disarming strategy is to choose an artefact to signify legacy and to give the object in question its place of rest in collective memory by displaying it in a museum. This is what happens to the pikestaff retrieved from its traditional site of conceal-ment in the thatch of a rural home in Colm Tóibín's *The Heather Blazing* (1992). Such a move ratifies the historical dimension's inherently sym-bolic value while at the same time enclosing that value within a very specific contemporary cultural setting and assigning to it a limited cul-tural utility. The idea of now and then formally coexisting, each in its own right, each out of the other's shadow, seems to have gained a certain amount of ground in the recent Irish novel. By a suggestive coin-cidence, the Irish historical novel has been making a comeback following the cessation of major hostilities in Northern Ireland, though with notably revised perspectives in its two most significant works.[16]

Whether the impetus is to put the past in a safe place or to tidy up the native (or even the nativist) ground, it reflects an undoubted desire to dislodge the inherited collective narrative and its supposedly formative powers and commanding loyalties. The complexities of what is at issue are articulated to a critical degree by Francis Stuart's autobiographical novel *Black List, Section H* (1971). In his ties to the foundational events and historical personages, the protagonist is a link with the past. But in his over-active subjectivity, he also embodies what amounts to an ethos of splitting, always taking the path his own instincts point to, regardless of – and indeed humbly priding himself on – the abjection and obloquy that result. The apparent mastery of history depicted – not only survival against the odds, but rebirth of a kind with integrity enhanced as a result of those odds – struck an artistic nerve among some of the younger generation of contemporary Irish novelists. And Stuart's example can be regarded as another instance of the prevailing interest in talking back to authoritative structures, whether it is the past, the patriarchal family or the dictatorial church.

Yet to reject an inherited collective narrative is also to deny part of the make-up of memory, so that the realisation of the need to move on takes place in a fitful, unsychronised, tonally varied and increasingly iconoclastic manner. Nevertheless, one of the results of creating a critical distance between origins and outcomes, between the faith of the fathers and the scepticism of the inheritors, has been to open an increasingly wide discursive space for 'the individual mood, however trivial, perverse and fleeting'.[17] Change, obviously, is not merely a matter of endings, but also of beginnings. And the invention of privacy, as the development of this space might be described, and its exploration and cultivation, has arguably been the most substantial expression of a new start that the contemporary Irish novel articulates. Inasmuch as the a-historical discourse of personal life – that is life now, life unprecedented – may be thought of as a space, a clearing, it posits an alternative to time-driven narrative. Inasmuch as the discourse deals with mood, which seems a deceptively simple term for the nexus of vagaries and compulsions that typify individual consciousness, its subject is a sphere that is essentially ungovernable. If the 1960s' generation of novelists brought an end to what has been called 'the era of inhibitions',[18] this accomplishment is complemented by the stories of novelists who came to the fore during the 1980s and '90s seeking to end the era of atavism.

How much such a change of focus may be seen as a response to the civil strife in Northern Ireland, and the image of Irishness that thirty years of war conveyed, cannot be determined here. It is clear, however, from the work of Northern Irish novelists like Glenn Patterson, Deirdre Madden and Bernard MacLaverty that images of some other way of life besides that dictated by the Troubles – the life of the living, so to speak – need to be imagined and communicated. Understated, domestic, highlighting characters who are self-motivated, these stories of difference – Patterson's *Burning Your Own* (1988), Madden's *Nothing is Black* (1994) and MacLaverty's *The Anatomy School* (2001) – find their tone and orientation matched by those of the novel south of the border. By century's end, the themes of the Irish novel tend for the most part to dwell on the modern person's choices. This person's native country is the present, a state not defined by a national territory but rather characterised by many different opportunities for new domiciles and fresh affiliations. This private citizen's identity is no longer indebted to what he or she has been told but to what he or she thinks and feels, for all the vulnerability that comes with the freedom to do so. Asked what he is going to be, the anonymous young protagonist of *The Dark* replies, 'Whatever I'm let be, I suppose'.[19] That kind of answer – and even that kind of question – is pretty much unimaginable forty years later, partly because protagonists of the contemporary Irish novel in its later phases, from the 1990s on, are more likely to live in worlds of their own than in shared worlds.

Exceptional public and private circumstances, such as the World Trade Center bombings in Joseph O'Neill's *Netherland* (2008) and the Vietnam War in Colum McCann's *Let the Great World Spin* (2009), can lead to barriers of race and class being set aside and mutual interests embraced. Continuity, renewal, beginning again with some degree of integrity and purpose after a violent visitation from history are among those interests, collapsing the distance between the themes that have emerged at home and those from abroad. Abroad, however – the novels just mentioned are both set in New York City – expressions of solidarity are much more obviously an aspect of the news each novel wishes to convey. In a setting as ostensibly homogeneous as Irish society is represented as being, where race and class have made comparatively little impression on the imagination, living with another, much less living *for* another, is a much more difficult undertaking. Works as distinct from each other as Dermot Healy's *A Goat's Song* (1994), which in one sense deals with the personal dimension of cross-border relations, and Anne Enright's *The Gathering* (2007), which focuses on family troubles and the kind of relations that result from it, are two instances of the complications arising out of knowing one's own mind and believing oneself to be free to act in accordance with such knowledge. Such iterations of attachment and loss, hope and risk, make the world of one's own essentially a realm of mourning. The quality of consciousness that realm makes available is in the nature of a seismograph, registering the misgivings that isolation produces and the equally disturbing turbulence of intimacy.

The world outside the self, the social and material world beyond the borders of intimacy, is, not surprisingly, more problematic as a potential source of personal meaning. In rare cases, most notably that of Roddy Doyle's Barrytown, identity and community dovetail. The Rabbitte family and Paddy Clarke *are* where they live. Yet for this to be the case, it is evidently necessary that the characters in question have very little to do with the metropolis as a whole. Unlike the youngsters whose stories comprise Dermot Bolger's *The Journey Home* (1990), the natives of Barrytown do not consider themselves 'the children of limbo'.[20] But the disorientation and dislocation to which the modern city subjects Bolger's youngsters is more typical of the experience of modernity. And as Keith Ridgway's *The Parts* (2003) indicates, it is impossible to retain a sense of the whole where the city is concerned, given its multiplicity and its transitoriness. These characteristics seem to recapitulate the sense of the contingent attributed to the experience of the person in history by *Langrishe, Go Down* and *Troubles*.[21] In many respects, emotional as well as social, characters' youthfulness maintains them at a level of being. The possibility of becoming remains latent, which makes it seem as if it must be deferred. And the hard-won freedom to inhabit the present is troubled by the discovery that one of the present's fundamental characteristics is that 'all that is solid melts into air'.[22]

The last page of *Amongst Women* is a snapshot of some members of the late patriarch's extended family dawdling along the road – a picture of openness and informality, to be sure, but one that also displays a lack of decorum, an absence of self-possession and an air of drift, as though those concerned were so many particles, incapable of forming a nucleus of their own. The picture forms a striking contrast with the rigidities of the past. But its lack of structure suggests that the contrast is too great. There is an implication that the centrality of the homestead, Great Meadow, is no longer sought, and its status as home and country abandoned. McGahern retrieves this state of affairs in his final novel, *That They May Face the Rising Sun* (2002), where people and place are reunited, respect is shown for the dead (as the title indicates), and a strong sense of the ebb and flow of life under heaven, as it were – life that is not entirely shaped by social contaminants – is registered. Yet, this imagined community does not entirely supplant the view of Moran's heirs and successors as apparently aimless travellers.

In the light of such a view, it is not surprising to find the term 'post' prefixing a good deal of the critical discussion that the contemporary Irish novel has attracted. Post-national, post-colonial, post-Catholic are among the most familiar of these usages, all of which seem to speak of a present that is most helpfully thought of in terms of its belatedness. Even if it does reflect the increasing institutionalisation of literature, this critical terminology clearly has its uses.[23] At the same time, assuming that characters and plotlines have discharged their imaginative function by living up to such terms risks too prompt and assured a comprehension, or even a rationalisation of the uncertainties – the interplay between state of desire and quality of awareness – that gives so many contemporary Irish novels their vividly unfinished, or not quite consummated, character. This characteristic is an expression of beginning again, even if how to and towards what end necessarily remains unclear. On the other hand, 'post-' looks back. Yet, perhaps the differences between critical and imaginative discourses may be regarded as yet one more enactment of the *agon* of becoming endemic to change and typical of the rapid and to a considerable degree leaderless shifts in the identities of self and world which Ireland has seen over the past fifty years.

An important ground for identity that has gained in prominence as the collective national and confessional narratives have substantially given way to the private, the personal, the inward, is sexuality – or - sexualities. An obvious sphere of self-realisation, its salience also denotes isolation and a lack of fulfilment, a biological imperative whose emotional rewards can be unexpectedly problematic and disappointing. Sexuality undoubtedly denotes individuation, but it can also be a zone where other thematic structures – the split, problems with bonding, continuity, the potentially adversarial nature of the other – present themselves in acute form. Nevertheless, the liberating experience (and resonances) of sexual activity is certainly seen as having much to recommend it.[24] And the social psychology of sexuality is also significant imaginative territory. The manner in which Northern Irish novelists have adapted this field to dismantle identities ostensibly imposed by demographic standing and confessional affiliation is shown to probing effect in the novels of Eoin McNamee and Maurice Leitch, particularly with regard to their sense of male pathologies. The unmaskings carried out in the latter's *Stamping Ground* (1975) and the former's *The Blue Tango* (2001) enact arresting social critiques.[25] Neither Northern nor Southern novels suggest that there is any necessary incompatibility between sexual identity and membership of society, as may be seen from both Colm Tóibín's *The Blackwater Lightship* (1999) and Glenn Patterson's *The International* (1999) – unless, like the protagonist of Emma Donoghue's *Hood* (1995), one thinks there is. A greater change from the way the homosexual in society is depicted in John Broderick's *The Waking of Willie Ryan* (1965) is difficult to imagine.

In addition, a developing awareness of how experience is inflected by characters' sex has produced many varied and not infrequently alarming narratives concerning motherhood, paternity, the complementarity and contradictions between nature and nurture, and the social and cultural meanings of both the feminine and maleness. Ways in which these personal domains are distorted and rendered sterile through the arrogance of power and victims' lack of recourse and resource are also the basis for some necessarily outspoken narratives, such as Dorothy Nelson's *In Night's City* (1982) and *Tar and Feathers* (1987), the latter an instance of 'the modern style' of Irish writing, the aim of which is to 'show a world where virtually nothing is secure'.[26] The plight of the victim forms the worst possible world of one's own.[27] The increased volume and broadened range of contemporary Irish women's novels have displayed a particular sympathy for the typically excluded and forgotten victim.

More generally, it might even be argued that sexuality is the major marker of difference in the contemporary Irish novel, carrying out the same discursive function as race and class do elsewhere in the naming and claiming of identity. As the bearer of sex, the body becomes an important imaginative territory, private but contested, sovereign but exploited, site of abjection and haven of dreams. Women's bodies exemplify the tensions between these and many other sets of properties, as the novels of Edna O'Brien, Caroline Blackwood and Anne Enright, to mention three very different authors, attest. And even in novels where class is a significant component – those of Dermot Bolger are a notable example – sex has a central role in character formation, with particular attention being paid to male characters' consciousness of it in themselves and others. Here, as elsewhere, the choices that behaviour deriving from sexuality exemplify, and the critique to which those choices are often subjected, constitute one version of a need shared by many contemporary Irish novelists to handle as many fresh contours in the moral landscape as they can discern. Doing so is a means of keeping faith with their characters, in recognition of and in solidarity with the isolation and vulnerability those characters typically embody.

One other effect of the diversification occasioned by valorising individual experience is that it challenges the traditional idea of the Irish people as a monolithic entity. The familiar poster children for this idea – peasants, rebels, Gaels, the faithful – are essentially missing from the contemporary Irish novel.[28] And although it would not be accurate to say that the cultural standing of such representative figures has been entirely usurped, it is also the case that members of the diaspora and other ostensible outsiders have become equally worthy embodiments of Irish experience. This development has led to exile becoming not only a theme but a more complicated imaginative structure.[29] The representation of the Irish abroad – in Colum McCann's America and Colm Tóibín's *Brooklyn* (2009); in Carlo Gébler's and J.M. O'Neill's England (and the rather different place of the same name depicted in the mid-career works of Edna O'Brien) – imparts some of the imagination's saving grace to worlds hitherto treated with a strange, if not total, silence.[30] And part of McCann's output has ventured further afield to reclaim different exiles in stranger contexts, highlighting his interests in reclaiming in such novels as *Dancer* (2003), a fictional biography of Rudolf Nureyev, and *Zoli* (2006), the story of a Roma poetess set in wartime Europe. Other noteworthy, though quieter in tone and more intimate in setting, works in this vein are those of Hugo Hamilton. The Germany in which his first three novels are set is a place of 'surrogate' experiences. Berlin life in *Surrogate City* (1990) evokes parallels, overlaps and resonances with life in Dublin, while in *The Last Shot* (1991) one generation's experience of the Second World War are echoed, imperfectly but unmistakably, by the succeeding generation's more private conflicts. These novels, and others with international settings such as Vincent Banville's *An End to Flight* (1973) and the works of Aidan Higgins, Julia O'Faoláin and to a certain extent Deirdre Madden, form a counterweight to an exceptionalist view of Irishness and to the cultural nationalism in which it has traditionally been enshrined.

Whether at home or abroad, however, the protagonists of the contemporary Irish novel share one condition: an apparently inescapable solitude affects them. This is the result of making the break, of having freedom of access to their own personalities and needs, of locating themselves in the here and now. Yet these accomplishments also require the endorsement of others, asks for the sanction and tolerance of somebody else's similar experience, wishes for partnership, community, some restructured sense of trust, mutuality, neighbourliness, commonality. It is as though, assured at last of life and liberty, protagonists can now begin on the pursuit of happiness. Change has been experienced, but it still wishes for ratification. Such preoccupations declare themselves in the various ways in which love is a central issue for many contemporary Irish novelists. Love can take the form of agape in the novels of William Trevor, or it can be full of passionate intensity in Aidan Higgins's *Balcony of Europe* (1972) and *Bornholm Night-Ferry* (1983). In the novels of Desmond Hogan, love can be the primal place of denial and rejection. However it is represented, love largely appears to be a subject of recurring difficulty, and its many psychological, sexual and spiritual connotations bring into focus not only various problems of individual personalities but also more general issues regarding autonomy, belonging and continuity. In that general sense, the desire for personal attachment can be understood as the need, or hope, for a public ethic which has at heart the possibilities of equilibrium and reciprocity between self and other. Such an aspiration is another aspect of a change from the past, one that echoes the kind of change Leopold Bloom suggests when he defines love: 'I mean the opposite of hatred.'[31] It may not necessarily be the case that, as the opening sentence of Robert McLiam Wilson's *Eureka Street* (1996) claims, 'All stories are love stories'.[32] But many Irish stories over the past fifty years do seem to wish that it were so.

Changes in theme and range are accompanied by changes in the art of the contemporary Irish novel. Yet, although throughout the period under review narrative concerns deal increasingly with the modernisation of the individual sensibility, formal developments show little interest in replicating, much less in adding to, the innovations that earned the modernism of Joyce and Beckett its international eminence. Indeed, another way of thinking about the present inhabited by the protagonists of contemporary Irish fiction is that it is a site where modernisation as a set of material and cultural events is tolerated even as the intellectual and ideological constituents of modernity encounter resistance. From the standpoint of artistic practice, the example of the masters has been, in effect, internalised, with the contemporary Irish novel typifying what might be described as the domestication of modernist texts' idiosyncratic representations of time–space relations. The consciousnesses of individual protagonists may mix memory and desire at a rate resembling that of their modernist avatars, but the manner in which their doing so is represented usually eschews high modernism's self-conscious formal devices. The artistic ambitions that such devices underwrote attained epic proportions. But the contemporary Irish novel is on the whole narrower in scope, inclining towards a sense that the form is more a dramatic poem than anything Homeric.

Yet a comparative formal conservatism, consisting mostly of modest modifications of pre-modernist models, is perhaps the most appropriate method by which to illustrate those departures from convention which individual feeling and behaviour undertake. And although the idea of an Irish novel tradition still calls to mind something in the nature of a collage rather than a more lapidary entity, it is also the case that one of the achievements of Irish novelists over the past fifty years has been to create a body of solid, reliable, character-centred stories. By doing so, they have exhibited the confidence to be ordinary. It would be entirely beside the point of their focus and interests to lament their works' tendency towards mainstream models of the novel. On the contrary, it could be more justly argued that the mainstream model is a means of keeping faith with the reader and of mediating between privacies, those of the text and those of individual readers. Irish novelists, in short, 'have noted that the novel has survived its destruction by the Irish modernists, and that it remains oddly adequate for their own contemporary purposes'.[33] And the mode in question facilitates concentration on protagonists' arrival at moments of intensity – of pain, recognition, resistance, recollection – which are deployed with a view to authenticating the arduousness of their own personal process of becoming.

The pursuit and enactment of the authentic is, for the most part, carried out in a plain prose. Very few Irish novelists aspire to the performative flair of the experimental international style. The kind of verbal elaboration found in *Ulysses*, for instance, has become *passé*, although it is noteworthy that John Banville, whose novels recurringly express misgivings regarding what constitutes authenticity, is also an exponent of a refined, aesthetic, artificial style, which on occasion achieves exceptional levels of visual representation. In the main, however, stylistic energies are reserved for performances in the demotic, as exemplified by, for instance, Roddy Doyle's *The Woman Who Walked into Doors* (1996) and Patrick McCabe's *The Butcher Boy* (1992).[34] Ever since the publication of Maria Edgeworth's *Castle Rackrent* (1801), voice has been a narrative resource in the Irish novel, and it is not surprising that the developing focus on personal histories is reflected in the spontaneity, irreverence and syntactical imprecision of direct speech. And use of voice is also an acknowledgment of the speaker's entitlement to his or her own story, particularly when the story in question is one that society at large has either not heard or ignored, as in the two more recent novels just mentioned. But there are also other voicings, with much studied suppleness underlying the seemingly unexceptional surfaces of many a novel – here, too, McGahern is a representative figure.

With respect to genre, there have been two noteworthy developments. One is the appearance of the double narrative, exemplified in different ways by such novels as Dermot Bolger's *The Journey Home*, Hugo Hamilton's *The Last Shot* and Anne Enright's *The Gathering* (2007). This flexible form can parallel a third-person story with a first-person one or it can alternate between a first-person narrative of the present and an attempt by the same narrator to reconstruct key events from either his or her own past or that of some significant other. Such a structure is not only an effective means of representing memory but, more importantly, of showing memory's limitations, the nature of which can lead the narrator to a sense of never being fully informed but also, by the same token, to not being a hostage to the past's immutability. Individual consciousness can only know so much and, as such, is vulnerable to those feelings of uncertainty and disconnectedness which typify the modernist mode of experiencing and knowing. Yet, for the sake of its own freedom and well-being, individual consciousness need only know so much. More than a means of conveying relevant information, the double narrative tacitly explores ideas of balance and reconciliation, even as it leaves the choice of how to take responsibility for making use of those ideas to its protagonists.

The second important development in genre has been the emergence of a sub-genre – the biographical novel. Although not entirely unknown to the Irish novel,[35] this form has undergone significant renovation by contemporary novelists. The biographical novel was initially given a fresh look by John Banville in his astronomer novels, and he has made further use of it in such later works, as *The Untouchable* (1997) and *Shroud* (2002) confirm, even if in *The Newton Letter* (1982) he has subjected the biographical and its forms of perception to a rather sly critique.[36] Part of the biographical novel's significance is that it typically features a departure not only into international settings but into the lives of others. By doing so, it marks both a break and an aftermath. As novels of the diaspora make clear, other places and other people are relevant to Irish novelists. The sub-genre's interest in the individual is a passport to different cultures – Eliza Lynch's nineteenth-century Paraguay in Anne Enright's *The Pleasure of Eliza Lynch* (2003), Berlin during the teens of the twentieth century in Mary Morrissy's *The Pretender* (2000), and eighteenth-century England in Brian Lynch's *The Winner of Sorrow* (2005) are cases in point. Such landscapes were largely unimaginable in the Irish novel before now, and their representation is a sign of an unwonted artistic confidence. In addition, the interest these works reveal in unfamiliar histories and personalities extends the contemporary Irish novel's openness, range of sympathy and worldliness. Serving as a complement to first-person narratives by ostensible outsiders, the biographical novel brings home the reality of otherness, affirming its sovereignty, ratifying its incorrigibility and, above all, perhaps, paying tribute to its struggles for integrity, fraught though these may be.

But to regard the kind of imaginative freedoms exemplified by the biographical novel as the last word on half a century's work would be a distortion. The finality implicit in such a conclusion misleadingly connotes one single trajectory of development over the years, success after failure and the latest thing being the most important. Any body of work is bound to be more complicated than that. And in any case, it is not its last words that are characteristic of the contemporary Irish novel but its interest in overtures, revisions, unexpected angles and fresh tonalities. Yet it seems appropriate to embark on a survey of the past fifty years of Irish novel-writing on a note of imaginative expansion. Freddie Montgomery, the notoriously amoral protagonist of John Banville's *The Book of Evidence* (1989), confesses that, with regard to his murder victim:

> This is the worst, the essential sin, I think, the one for which there will be no forgiveness: that I never imagined her vividly enough, that I never made her be there sufficiently, that I did not make her live. Yes, the failure of imagination is my real crime, the one that made the others possible. (215)

The violent change that Freddie wrought results in a denial of freedom – his own and another's. In contrast, the work of the imagination is one notable way in which to express freedom – the idea, that is, which inspires change, or at least the type of creative, forward-looking change which is the theme and moral, the hope and focus, of the Irish novel's story between 1960 and 2010.

In method and intention, *The Irish Novel 1960–2010* participates in and reflects upon the idea of change as it pertains to the contemporary Irish novel. That is one of the reasons for its chosen approach. By writing an essay on one particular novel from each of the fifty years covered – not an especially original idea, as it happens[37] – change itself is a built-in component of the attempted overview. In addition, the arrangement also allows for a good deal of flexibility. Instead of suggesting ways in which different texts may be shown to support one particular perspective, as monographs tend to do, different aspects of different texts can be highlighted. Critical monographs obviously have their place and their undoubted uses, and the contemporary Irish novel has benefited in many ways from their various perspectives. The choice here has been to represent works by allowing for a view of the relevant context in the case of one of them, for a sense of formal innovation in the case of another, a perspective on its cultural significance with regard to a third, and so on. In many cases, it has been possible to indicate something of these three concerns, and indeed others, in the course of discussing one novel. This eclectic approach is a response to the contemporary Irish novel's range. But the intention also is to give the reader as much access as possible to a given work. For that reason, additional sources of information and criticism have been provided following each essay (the bibliography at the back of the book is meant to be a preliminary guide to criticism covering the field of the Irish novel since 1960).

Confining the choice of texts to one per author is also intended to give as broad an idea as possible of range and diversity. No attempt has been made to produce a hierarchy of 'greatest' works. The goal throughout has been to offer a representative view. Well-known novelists will not have their reputations unduly diminished if their best-known works are not included here. And the opportunity to include some lesser-known novels seems worthwhile not only from a critical standpoint but also bearing the reader in mind. In addition, the form of *The Irish Novel 1960–2010* aims to suggest the difficulties presented by the contemporary Irish novel to canon formation and to the idea that there is one specific notion of tradition that the novel, or any other literary form, should maintain. Those difficulties can be resolved, but doing so can exert a type of institutionalising pressure on the individual voice and on the pre-eminence of individual experience that that voice maintains. Noting after each essay some of the other titles published in the year in question not only provides useful information. It also gives readers an opportunity to create their own canons and consider how ideas of continuity, tradition, individual authors' careers and literary history are composed – or imagined.

In a word, the operating principle throughout has been openness. At the same time, no book can maintain an absolute ideal of openness or the encyclopaedism such an ideal enjoins. But a sense of inclusivity has been thought to be not only discursively desirable but in tune with such valuable aspects of the subject matter as its venturesome energies, its democratic instincts, and its willingness to engage with the fascination and the fallout of becoming modern. This engagement is at times defensive, at times tentative, and for the most part ambivalent and uncertain on the part of storyteller and story alike. Such reactions to change are as revealing as they are inevitable. And by imparting to them coherent narrative form, the contemporary Irish novel bears invaluable witness to the spirit of its time, portraying in the midst of all the many developments in Irish life the most essential one, that of a country in the throes of wanting to change its mind.

Notes

1 Seán O'Faoláin, 'Fifty Years of Irish Writing', *Studies*, vol. 51, no. 201 (Spring 1962), pp. 93–105, at p. 102.

2 See R.F. Foster, *Luck and the Irish: A Brief History of Change from 1970* (Oxford: Oxford University Press, 2008), especially Chapter 5.

3 Aidan Higgins, 'Tired Lines, or Tales My Mother Told Me', in John Ryan (ed.), *A Bash in the Tunnel: Irish Writers on Joyce* (Brighton: Clifton Books, 1970), pp. 55–60, at p. 57.

4 For the reactions of Edna O'Brien, Brian Moore, John McGahern, John Broderick and Maurice Leitch, among others, to having their work banned, see Julia Carlson, *Banned in Ireland: Censorship and the Irish Writer* (Athens, Georgia: University of Georgia Press, 1990).

5 The focus is not necessarily a feminist one and is not confined to women novelists, as is shown by novels such as John McGahern's *The Barracks* (1963), Brian Moore's *I Am Mary Dunne* (1968), Colm Tóibín's *The South* (1990), William Trevor's *Felicia's Journey* (1994) and Roddy Doyle's *The Woman Who Walked into Doors* (1996), to mention some noteworthy examples.

6 Colm Tóibín, *Martyrs and Metaphors* (Dublin: Raven Arts, 1987), p. 8.

7 Two notable exceptions are Richard Power's *The Hungry Grass* (1969) and Michael P. Harding's *Priest* (1986). Tensions between the institutional church and individual faith are exemplified in different ways by the clerical protagonists of Brian Moore's *Catholics* (1972), *Black Robe* (1985), *The Colour of Blood* (1987), *No Other Life* (1993) and *The Statement* (1995).

8 Some of the judgments issued by Justice Éamon Redmond in Colm Tóibín's *The Heather Blazing* (1992) indicate the imbalanced relationship between state and citizen and between authority and need.

9 A harsher note in the same key of disillusionment is sounded in Anthony Cronin's *The Life of Riley* (1964), a satire of Dublin's terminally tiresome post-war intellectual life.

10 Thomas Flanagan's *The Year of the French* (1979) treats some of the events of the 1798 Rebellion as a basis for the type of critique of history in question. What few contemporary Northern Irish historical novels there are do not regard history in the same way – see Sam Hanna Bell, *A Man Flourishing* (1973), set in the Belfast of the 1790s, and his *Across the Narrow Sea* (1987). Seamus Deane's *Reading in the Dark* (1994) may be read as an exception. See also David Martin's *Dream* (1986), set in the years leading up to the First World War.

11 For a multi-perspectival approach to the historical novel, see Flanagan, *op. cit.*, and William Trevor, *Fools of Fortune* (1983) and *The Silence in the Garden* (1987).

12 The protagonists of Barry's other recent novels – *The Whereabouts of Eneas McNulty* (1998), *Annie Dunne* (2002) and *The Secret Scripture* (2008) – are also orphans of history, not least in the sense that their stories have not been previously included in the repertoire of Irish experience.

13 James Joyce, *Ulysses* (New York: Vintage, 1986 [1922]), p. 20.

14 With the exception of Thomas Kilroy's *The Big Chapel* and its treatment of nineteenth-century sectarianism and clerical power, the thought that events in the Irish past might offer an instructive perspective on current conditions has not been taken up.

15 As the one-volume paperback edition of *Doctor Copernicus*, *Kepler* and *The Newton Letter* (1982) was entitled (London: Picador, 2001).

16 The works in question are Roddy Doyle's *A Star Called Henry* (1999) and Jamie O'Neill's *At Swim Two Boys* (2001). Joseph O'Connor's *Star of the Sea* (2002) and *Redemption Falls* (2008) also revive the historical novel with the aid of a good deal of pastiche *à la* Flanagan. John Maher's *The Luck Penny* (2007) is a thematically interesting treatment of Ireland in 1849.

17 Colm Tóibín, 'Introduction', in Tóibín (ed.), *The Penguin Book of Irish Fiction* (London: Viking, 1999), p. ix.

18 Maurice Harmon, 'The Era of Inhibitions: Irish Literature 1920–1960', in Masaur Sekine (ed.), *Irish Writers and Society at Large* (Gerrards Cross: Colin Smythe, 1985), pp. 31–41.

19 John McGahern, *The Dark* (London: [Faber & Faber, 1965] Panther, 1967), p. 19.

20 Dermot Bolger, *The Journey Home* (London: Viking, 1990), p. 7.

21 A related sense of the city occurs in Barry McCrea's *The First Verse* (New York: Carroll & Graf, 2005).

22 This phrase is the title of Marshall Berman's noted study, *All That is Solid Melts into Air: The Experience of Modernity* (New York: Simon & Schuster, 1982).

23 The kinds of rhetorical structures invoked in Gerry Smyth's *The Novel and the Nation* (1997) and Linden Peach's *The Contemporary Irish Novel* (2004), in illustrating new modes of reading and re-reading, are themselves participants in the cultural change that their subject exemplifies.

24 See, for instance, the London sequence of John McGahern's *The Leavetaking* (1973) and Freddie Montgomery's trysts with twins in Berkeley, California, in John Banville's *The Book of Evidence* (1989). And sexual love is a strong component of the relationship at the heart of Deirdre Madden's *Authenticity* (2002).

25 The plot of Leitch's first novel, *The Liberty Lad* (1965), revolves around the then taboo subject of homosexuality, while McNamee's *Resurrection Man* (1994) is a dense, dark meditation on the intersection of sexuality and violence in members of the Shankill Butchers sectarian murder squad.

26 Aidan Higgins, *Windy Arbours: Collected Criticism* (Champaign, Illinois: Dalkey Archive, 2005), p. 189.

27 See Jennifer Johnston, *The Invisible Worm* (1991), Lia Mills, *Another Alice* (1996) and Edna O'Brien, *Down by the River* (1996).

28 What some of these figures represent is the subject of the broad satire of Arthur Mathews's *Well-Remembered Days* (2001).

29 For a sketch of some of the implications of this structure, see George O'Brien, 'The Aesthetics of Exile', in Liam Harte and Michael Parker (eds), *Contemporary Irish Fiction: Themes, Tropes, Theories* (Basingstoke: Macmillan, 2000), pp. 35–55.

30 A particularly resounding shattering of that silence occurs in Patrick McCabe's *Breakfast on Pluto* (1998).

31 James Joyce, *Ulysses* (New York: Vintage, 1986 [1922]), p. 273.

32 Robert McLiam Wilson, *Eureka Street* (London: [Secker & Warburg, 1996] Minerva, 1997), p. 1.

33 Fintan O'Toole, 'Future Fictions', *Princeton University Library Chronicle*, vol. LXII, no. 1 (Autumn 2010), pp. 407–18, at p. 409.

34 Frances Molloy's *No Mate for the Magpie* (1985) is a graphic display of Northern Irish demotic.

35 One earlier instance is Francis MacManus's trilogy on the life of the eighteenth-century poet Donnacha Ruadh Mac Conmara: *Stand and Give Challenge* (1934), *Candle for the Proud* (1936) and *Men Withering* (1939).

36 Other noted contributions to this sub-genre include Mary Morrissy, *The Pretender* (2000), Anne Enright, *The Pleasure of Eliza Lynch* (2003), Colm Tóibín, *The Master* (2004) and Brian Lynch, *The Winner of Sorrow* (2005).

37 A not dissimilar plan is used by Anthony Burgess in his *Ninety-Nine Novels: The Best in English since 1939* (London: Allison & Busby, 1984) and Carmen Callil and Colm Tóibín in *The Modern Library: The Two Hundred Best Novels in English since 1950* (London: Picador, 1999). Gerry Smyth's *The Novel and the Nation* has a modified version.

1960

Edna O'Brien, *The Country Girls*

Banned in Ireland on publication and burned in the author's native County Clare, The Country Girls *was followed by the equally provocative* The Lonely Girl *(1962; reissued as* Girl with Green Eyes *(1964) – the protagonist of* The Country Girls' *eyes are 'a curious green'). A third novel,* Girls in their Married Bliss *(1964), follows the girls to England, though their story does not finally conclude until 'Epilogue', first published in the 1986 one-volume edition of the trilogy. O'Brien (b. 1930), the author of fourteen novels as well as a large number of short-story collections and a good deal of non-fiction, has throughout her career returned to the landscape of* The Country Girls, *critically in* A Pagan Place *(1970), controversially in* In the Forest *(2002) and most autobiographically in* The Light of Evening *(2006). The setting is also central to* The Eleventh Summer *(1985), the first novel by Edna O'Brien's son, Carlo Gébler.*

This novel's principal events consist of breakdown, rejection, leave-taking and abandonment. Punctuating Caithleen (Cait) Brady's childhood and adolescence, these discontinuities map onto the known world a private landscape of loss. Her feckless father – who, in his fondness for gambling and drink, is something of a throwback to characters familiar from the Irish novel of an earlier time – acts with a confused and irresponsible disregard for both his property and his family, and eventually has to forego the former and forsake the latter. Cait's long-suffering mother is accidentally drowned while seeking refuge in her parents' house from her husband's excesses. Such a pattern of experiences suggest a rupture between land and people which makes the rural environment a habitat where nature seems incompatible with nurture, thereby complicating the traditional cultural and ideological status of the land as site and source of Irish authenticity. In addition, her family history deprives Cait of such formative influences and valuable developmental resources as a stable family structure, a sense of heritage and of a past that amounts to something, so that conceptions of continuity and direction become unexpectedly problematic. By the time she is fourteen, Cait is effectively on her own and is starting over, although she cannot act as though she is. And in many ways her inevitable

1

cluelessness is a reflection of the largely misguided choices and standards of her immediate community.

Even before her mother's death, Cait has adopted the live-in farmhand, Hickey, to fill a nurturing role. Hickey may not be a model as far as carrying out his agricultural and domestic duties are concerned, but he does – before eventually making the conventional departure of emigrating to England – supply Cait with something of the attention and amusement needed to distract her from family affairs. Attention of a different kind comes from the pawky Jack Holland, a mother-dominated shopkeeper and self-styled author with an artificially decorous manner through which he advances his pretensions to sensitivity. But his manner is unable to disguise the grasping mentality by which he eventually secures the Brady land. Jack's emotional gombeenism blends with the more familiar economic kind to characterise a local status quo to which Hickey is obviously marginal and in which Cait has standing only on the basis of her vulnerability.

In addition to her family circumstances, the gauche body language and dreamy disposition typical of teenagers also make Cait aware of being different. This awareness is reinforced by her best friend, Baba Brennan. Brash, in contrast to Cait's timidity, outpoken while Cait is tongue-tied, crude and pushy where Cait is polite and deferential, Baba is an alternative version of a country girl. Her unconventionality and bumptiousness, her preoccupation with fashion and her insistence in getting her own way make Baba not merely a foil to Cait but a parody of adult independence and maturity. Egotistically, she seems to need to have a 'right-looking eejit' (21) such as Cait to play off. But Baba's egotism is essentially imitative, and if it is the obverse of Cait's wallflower demeanour, it is also more obviously childish in its attention-seeking clamour. But Baba's family, too, is unhappy in its own way, as becomes clear when Cait temporarily joins it. Indeed, the Brennan household is a mirror image of the Brady's, with Baba's mother restless and extravagant while her veterinarian father is dutiful and patient, even if there does seem something rather incongruous about his proposing himself as a father figure to Cait. But this family's ramshackle way of life is no more than one more instance of the inadequacy of all the duly constituted structures that Cait encounters. And public institutions are no more reassuring than private ones, as the girls' experience of boarding school reveals. Cait's academic gifts do not help her to withstand Baba's impatience with school and study.

The latter's contrivance of their expulsion leads them to the independence in Dublin which Baba has craved, though in the event she remains the country girl, while Cait, for all her misgivings and self-consciousness, responds to the city's modernity, not only in being 'restless for crowds and light and noise' (142) but in her implicit comprehension of its prompts to desire and its endorsement of loneliness.

Cait's urban self-fashioning is based on her acknowledgment of her sexuality, and in this she is both more independent and more needy than her friend. In contrast, the fate of Baba's body turns out to be contracting tuberculosis. Cait's embrace of her womanliness has had its tentative origins down home in the crush she developed on Mr Gentleman, as locals call him, a Dublin businessman of reputedly French origins who maintains a home for his mentally ill wife in the neighbourhood. Whether or not he should know better than to play the seductive father figure for the impressionable Cait is a question which a more moralistic novel than *The Country Girls* would be apt to ask. Here – as, for instance, Cait's father indicates – the rights and wrongs of personal actions lag a long way behind more fundamental psychological spheres such as appetite and need. Cait cultivates her romantic attachment to Mr Gentleman as a means of having something, or someone, of her own, as a means of realising her difference, and in due course as a basis for her incipient understanding of sexuality as a key to autonomy, and to that 'living at last' that Baba so often mentions but never quite seems to manage.

As with just about all this novel's juxtapositions and affiliations, the pairing of Cait and a much older beau has a marked incongruity about it. Yet it is this very quality that shows the imbalanced emotional economy of the world the novel is depicting. Incongruity's combination of the excruciating and the preposterous results in an instructive perspective on the various landscapes from which Cait makes her departure. And if Mr Gentleman does, predictably, decline to fulfil Cait's romantic longing for him, this let-down is not merely meant to mock the truth of need and desire as the young woman has acknowledged and experienced them. A Cait who knows exactly who she is and what she is doing is the opposite of the risk-taking, naive, unrehearsed protagonist the author has in mind. But as the story makes plain, such a personage, uneducated in the ways of the world as she might be and with little in her favour other than her complicated and conflicted emotional reality, is as entitled to life, liberty and the pursuit of happiness as anybody else. Where such a life might be had remains open to question. And its remit appears to be beyond the pale of conventional belonging, deprived as it is of the usual contexts of place, family, home, community, church and school. But the possibility of realms beyond the fatherland, and of personalities to which neither the father nor the fatherland can credibly lay claim, are not to be denied. The flux of Cait's inner life and her ultimately knowing no more than to abide by its mutable nature – plausibly rendered by the novel's loose structure and informal style – delineate something of those realms and of the subjective energies necessary to arrive at them.

Supplementary Reading

Raymonde Popot, 'Edna O'Brien's Paradise Lost', in Patrick Rafroidi and Maurice Harmon (eds), *The Irish Novel in Our Time* (Villeneuve-d'Asq: Publications de l'Université de Lille III, 1976), pp. 255–83

Berenice Schrank (ed.), *Canadian Journal of Irish Studies*, vol. 22, no. 2 (Edna O'Brien Special Issue) (December 1996)

Lisa Colletta and Maureen O'Connor (eds), *Wild Colonial Girl: Essays on Edna O'Brien* (Madison, Wisconsin: University of Wisconsin Press, 2006)

Declan Kiberd, 'Growing Up Absurd: Edna O'Brien and The Country Girls', in Nicholas Allen and Eve Patten (eds), *That Island Never Found: Essays and Poems for Terence Brown* (Dublin: Four Courts Press, 2007), pp. 107–21

Also Published in 1960

Eilís Dillon, *The Head of the Family*; Benedict Kiely, *The Captain with the Whiskers*; Janet McNeill, *As Strangers Here*; Brian Moore, *The Luck of Ginger Coffey*

1961
Sam Hanna Bell, *The Hollow Ball*

A noted presence in Northern Irish culture at mid-century, Sam Hanna Bell (1909–90) was born in Glasgow, but is regarded as a native of Belfast, where he was reared. His four novels – the others are December Bride *(1951),* A Man Flourishing *(1973) and* Across the Narrow Sea *(1987) – constitute an informal social history of Ulster Protestant mores. The last two titles are set in the Belfast of the United Irishmen and the time of the Ulster Plantation, respectively, while* December Bride *takes place on the culturally resonant ground of the Ards Peninsula.*

Belfast is depressed, and life there tends to run in narrow channels. Work is scarce and opportunity rare. Economic insecurity is endemic and breeds various repressive forms of social diffidence and passivity. In most minds, the need to hold a job is paramount. So, when sixteen-year-old David Minnis starts his three-year apprenticeship in Hamilton's clothing store, all concerned ensure that he bears in mind how lucky he is – his widowed mother, scrimping to make ends meet by taking in sewing, in addition to his co-workers and his workplace superiors. But David's strongest sense of obligation is to himself. His is the story of a youngster with an overwhelming drive to live up to his own image of who he is. Under a carefully rendered veneer of realism, this novel is ultimately a moral tale – in certain respects a parable – calling on the reader to ponder the claims and costs of vanity, egotism and ambition, even as David's own sensitivity to such concerns fails to mature.

As embodied by David's downtrodden mother, the conventions of the boy's lower middle-class background view thoughts of self-realisation as a snare and a delusion. David's goal of making a name for himself as a star soccer player is replete with both risk and frivolity. Its implicit independence conflicts with prevailing social hierarchies. And as the widow of the late Pastor Minnis, David's mother is keenly aware of how antithetical her son's ambition is to her low church vision of life's earnest struggle. The nurturing shelter of the faith into which David was born is irreconcilably at odds with the demands of his natural athletic ability. Though his mother more than once reminds David that 'we're made for better things than kicking a hollow ball' (64), the nature of those things seems to David as at best abstract and in practice repressive. In striking out for himself, he embodies not only such socially and culturally resonant themes as individual choice, a fresh start and self-belief, he also introduces a more substantial idea of conflicting loyalties. This idea permeates the course of his career, and makes of David not merely a typically selfish and callow young man but somebody whose choices, by virtue of their individuality and their strictly secular and material contexts, make him an unwitting figure of protest – a Protestant of a non-traditional stripe.

In certain respects, it is David's own indifference to the forms of protest available to him which substantiates the sense of difference and singularity he conveys. He has no interest whatever in Northern Ireland politics, even though his native city has recently witnessed political violence (the novel does not directly identify the time period in which it is set, though not only its treatment of economic conditions but its brief evocation of republican casualties, its portrait of working-class radicalism and its awareness of soccer's burgeoning mass appeal all point to the period being the 'hungry 1930s'). More to the point, he also rejects the union activity of Boney McFall, his friend, co-worker and prospective brother-in-law. Boney – named by his loyal Orange mother for English politician and opponent of Irish Home Rule, Andrew Bonar Law – initially comes across as a good-natured, obliging, unexceptional employee. His home is in a more obviously blue-collar street, and if anything in even less enviable economic circumstances, than David's, but it is a livelier, more colourful place. Its vitality comes from the rambunctious Mrs McFall, and also from Boney's father, in many ways an embarrassing failure, but one whose weaknesses are mitigated by the goodwill of his left-wing leanings.

The McFall home is not a sentimental portrait of cheerful working-class amity. Indeed, in time, this household also fractures, like David's, with Boney pursuing his own form of self-fashioning as a radical. Initially, the McFall household's accommodation of differences offers David an appealing contrast to his own conflicted home, an appeal that is deepened when he begins dating Boney's sister, Maureen. Boney's radicalism is home-grown, not only in deriving from his father but in its engagement with local and immediate issues. And echoes of radicalism past are also made audible by the author – meetings take place in Spinners Hall, a name that brings to mind dissident Northern tradesmen of an earlier age. The issue that sets Boney on his political path is the attempt by some workers at Hamilton's to organise a trade union. Those involved are fired, among them Boney, in an incident that does much to sharpen the differences between him and David, since it is at about the same time that the latter has his first success, and receives his first earnings, from playing soccer.

Motivated by confused, though essentially insincere, feelings of loyalty to Boney, David does attend an abortive meeting at Spinners Hall and encounters there some European radicals now resident in the city (a tribute to Belfast's generally unacknowledged cosmopolitanism). But such meetings have little effect on David's soccer career, much less on his developing a social conscience. All that concerns him when signing for a top-flight English soccer club is how much money he will earn. Boney, on the other hand, leaves home for a life devoted entirely to political activity. The two young men part in an awkward and unaffected tableau which represents not only their incompatible interests and opposing loyalties but also a sense of mis-giving regarding the future and the quality of change upon which the new generation is embarking. Neither team nor union is capable of altering prevailing social and economic conditions. David's success in England merely enables him to abandon a way of life from which he had always dissented, the psychological cost of which may be assessed from his callous rejection of Maureen. Boney's violent end as a member of the IRA is the price exacted by a dead-end idealism. Whether loyalties are forsaken or intensified, whether life is conceived of in terms of selling or of sacrificing oneself, the outcome hardly seems of much value.

Boney's death in the name of nationalism takes place just as David, after a protracted absence, returns to Belfast, having been selected to play for Northern Ireland. As he pays his respects to Boney's father, the latter acknowledges (somewhat vaingloriously, perhaps) that he sacri-ficed his son 'to my own vainglory' (248). The same judgment applies to David's career. And it also draws attention to the status of fathers in *The Hollow Ball*. In addition to the novel's abundance of inadequate father figures, neither the late Pastor Minnis nor the feckless Mr McFall manage to hand down very much morally or politically. Such failures suggest that the younger generation are heirs to a past that merely repeats itself. Loyalty to such a heritage strikes both David and Boney as a life-denying waste of their energies and abilities. But the search for alternative identities leads these two city boys astray, an outcome which sounds a comprehensive note of hollowness.

Supplementary Reading

Sam Hanna Bell et al., 'The War Years in Ulster (1939–45): A Symposium', *Honest Ulsterman*, no. 64 (1979), pp. 11–62

Douglas Carson, 'The Antiphon, the Banderol, and the Hollow Ball: Sam Hanna Bell, 1909–1990', *Irish Review*, no. 9 (Autumn 1990), pp. 91–9

Seán McMahon, *Sam Hanna Bell: A Biography* (Belfast: Blackstaff, 1999)

Fergus Hanna Bell (ed.), *A Salute from the Banderol: The Selected Writings of Sam Hanna Bell* (Belfast: Blackstaff, 2009)

Also Published in 1961

John Broderick, *The Pilgrimage*; Michael Campbell, *Across the Water*; Flann O'Brien, *The Hard Life*; Paul Smith, *The Stubborn Season*

1962

John Broderick, *The Fugitives*

Author of a dozen novels, John Broderick (1924–89) was born in Athlone, the setting for a good deal of his fiction. An anatomist of market-town sensibilities and tribal ties, his major themes of sexuality and hypocrisy are most evident in such novels as Don Juaneen *(1963),* An Apology for Roses *(1973) and most tellingly, perhaps,* The Trial of Father Dillingham *(1982). Broderick's sharp eye for hypocrisy makes him a connoisseur of bad faith, while his treatment of sexuality includes an acknowledgement of homosexuality that, for all its ambivalence, shows – in* The Waking of Willie Ryan *(1965) – courage and cultural awareness.*

The London assassination by the IRA of the Northern Ireland Under Secretary makes fugitives of Lily Fallon, her brother Paddy, who was one of the assassins, and Hugh Ward, Paddy's IRA handler. Immediately following the murder, Paddy seeks out Lily, instead of following instructions, an early indication not only of his unpredictability but of the novel's focus on aftermath, dislocation and problems of continuity and starting anew. All three end up in the Fallon family home, a pub-grocery in an Irish midlands town. This establishment is now run by the vigilant, taciturn Hetty, stepmother of Paddy and Lily, both of whose parents are deceased. The household is completed by Aunt Kate, an ascetic-looking, chain-smoking failed nun, who for years has been at loggerheads with Hetty and who confines herself to her single, cell-like room, as though she too is a fugitive. While the assassination is ostensibly a blow for Irish independence, its political and ideological implications are of far less significance than the ties and tensions it creates between Lily, Paddy and Ward. The increasing intensity of their fraught interdependence plays out against a backdrop of the town's unchanging attitudes and rituals, typified by malicious gossip, affectations of piety and a preoccupation with 'the time-honoured hieratic movements of the national *danse macabre*' (17) which the final days of a cancer-stricken young neighbour sustain.

One of the intensifying elements is that, as a cover story for his presence, Ward is said to be Lily's fiancé. As a former actor, handsome and silver-tongued, he has no trouble in playing the part, even if doing so complicates the emotional mix. Paddy, whose instability is being aggravated by excessive drinking, reacts with characteristic hysteria, disputing the fabrication's plausibility by attempting to take Lily from Ward, so to speak, with a passionate kiss. Ward wishes Paddy were kissing him, and treats the unhappy youth with unwonted tenderness in the hope of securing a love that will not be fugitive – an aspiration that throws an intriguing sidelight on the Republic their violence intends to re-establish. And to complete the realignment of male and female roles, thirty-six-year-old Lily reverts to the maternal attentions which she bestowed on Paddy – ten years her junior – while they both still lived at home. Indeed, Paddy has a surfeit of mothers, with Aunt Kate the self-appointed guardian of his moral state, while the more down-to-earth Hetty keeps him physically safe and sound.

An additional twist is Lily's falling for Ward. As well as being a pretext for a series of grating pronouncements on the putative nature of women by both the narrator and Ward, the emotional development in question also focuses the novel's variations on themes of dependence and independence. The need for attachment, which in London led Lily to a life of being a kept woman, is exacerbated by the limitations and uncertainties of her clandestine, fugitive return home. On the one hand, there is now nobody to trust; on the other, she has never had a greater need to trust somebody. Her London lover is no longer available to mask her utter isolation, and left to her own resources she can come up with only an 'impossibly romantic' (124) notion of safety and security. Ward both understands Lily's emotional needs and repudiates them as being beside the point of his supposedly revolutionary politics. For him, concern for the lives of others is essentially self-serving or, at best, a means to an end. Love is a far less potent expression of possibility than violence and, for all his attraction to Paddy, the prospect of that young man sacrificing himself for the cause attracts him far more than anything Lily can offer. All that keeps Paddy going, meanwhile, is a narcissistic identification with the once and future Republic, his awareness of others occluded by tantrums, drunkenness and prolonged spells of deep sleep.

It is from the conditions and impositions of their own natures that Paddy and Lily are on the run. Circumstances have conspired to reveal the crisis of belonging and direction which their irresolute, fearful and dependent personalities have in common. The fallen Fallon children's susceptibility to Ward's 'satanic cunning' (164) portrays them as orphans in more than the familial sense. They are would-be historical actors whose awareness has withered owing to psychological starvation. Trapped in their home town's 'stifling atmosphere of unreality' (151), they do not belong anywhere else either. Their cultural and confessional birthright provides neither understanding nor sanctuary, leaving them with nothing but nerves. To be so comprehensively alienated and superfluous is perhaps an indictment of the Ireland of their generation – the first generation of citizens born in an independent Ireland. They are the children of a country that Ward lambasts as 'A smug little corporation run by a gang of professional politicians who have no interest except self-interest' (163).

Broderick also, however, shows Lily and Paddy trapped between love and death, which enlarges the range of *The Fugitives*, though it also leads to the narrator tendentiously dilating on the frailty of human nature. As a means of concentrating on the siblings' position and the trio's interdependence, the novel's culminating scenes forsake town for that primal Irish landscape, the bog. In this abandoned, a-social place they wait for the police to close in, Paddy in particular insisting on staying put, although the bog's labyrinthine pathways, known to him from boyhood, are a sure means of escape. The authorities duly arrive. Lily's last-minute challenge to Ward fails. She ends up disgraced, her London love life a matter of public knowledge. Paddy, in ironic contrast, is mythologised as another martyr for Irish freedom, to Hetty's great satisfaction. She now turns her attentions to the dying Aunt Kate. This final combination of feelings – Hetty's embodiment of charity and illusion, her contradictory expressions of family loyalty – represents the unchanging keeper of the house's staunchness. But it is also a reflection on what the members of the younger generation were on the run from and on the sense of change they had created without knowing what to do with it.

Supplementary Reading

Michael Paul Gallagher, SJ, 'The Novels of John Broderick', in Patrick Rafroidi and Maurice Harmon (eds), *The Irish Novel in Our Time* (Villeneuve d'Asq: Publications de l'Université de Lille III, 1976), pp. 235–43

Klaus Lubbers, 'John Broderick', in Rüdiger Imhof (ed.), *Contemporary Irish Novelists* (Tübingen: Narr, 1990), pp. 79–91

Madeline Kingston, *Something in the Head: The Life and Work of John Broderick* (Dublin: Lilliput Press, 2004)

Madeline Kingston (ed.), *Stimulus of Sin: Selected Writings of John Broderick* (Dublin: Lilliput Press, 2007)

Also Published in 1962
Walter Macken, *The Silent People*; Brian Moore, *An Answer from Limbo*; Paul Smith, *The Countrywoman*; Jack White, *The Devil You Know*

1963

Michael Farrell, *Thy Tears Might Cease*

Drawing on the author's boyhood and youth, Thy Tears Might Cease is perhaps the most thorough chronicle available of provincial Irish society in the early years of the twentieth century. Farrell (1899–1962), a native of Carlow town, was a noted radio personality and cultural commentator. His writing career consisted largely of a regular column – 'The Open Window' by Gulliver – in The Bell. The author's only novel, Thy Tears Might Cease was long completed and accepted for publication before Farrell's death but appeared posthumously only in an edited version prepared by his friend Monk Gibbon.

The opening part of *Thy Tears Might Cease* is entitled 'The White Blackbird', and that is a fitting description of the protagonist, Martin Matthew Reilly. But the phrase might also be applied to the town of Glenkilly, whose variegated social and political populace is depicted with painstaking relish. At its centre stands Martin's solid Catholic bourgeois family, an embodiment of the town's 'citizen merchant' (25) class. Confident, comfortable, respected, these burghers give little indication of being a subject people, nor are they impatient to attain separation from Britain. 'We must mix' (79), Martin's Aunt Mary says, explaining her barely lukewarm attitude to the issue. Noticeably absent from Glenkilly are the Gaelic League, the Gaelic Athletic Association and similar contemporary manifestations of Irish Ireland – indeed proponents of such organisations are regarded as 'them Gaelic brats in Dublin' (33). Yet the Reillys' nationalist credentials are not in doubt, as their adherence to John Redmond, the leader of the Home Rule movement, demonstrates. A narrow post-independence nationalism reconstructed earlier conditions along polarised lines, but the elaborate description by which the author documents his vanished Edwardian world rejects such a revision.

As a Reilly, Martin is a member of this settled community, but he is also an exception within it, a 'half-and-half' (520), as he calls himself, being the offspring of a liaison between a married English Protestant and Matthew Reilly. His mother has died in childbirth, and his father drowned himself shortly thereafter, leaving Martin to be reared by his aunt and uncle. An obvious air of tragic romance surrounds such origins, and this follows Martin throughout his youth. But it is also possible to read in his parentage a story of Parnellite sexual rebellion, complete with modernist overtones of dislocation and downfall. Not too much is to be made, perhaps, of the fact that both parents are buried in Paris, but it does emphasise that their story is not Glenkilly property. In any event, these beginnings give Martin a complex heritage – Anglo and Irish in cultural terms, passion and loss from a psychological perspective, singularity and doubt when it comes to loyalties and causes. One of the conventions of a *Bildungsroman* such as *Thy Tears Might Cease* is that, as the protagonist makes his way, his experiences teach him to know his place in the order of things. But as Martin's history unfolds, it reveals an increasing difficulty in establishing where he belongs, culminating in a realisation that 'No rightful name belonged to him, no family, no Church, no country, no sweetheart' (531). As a result he decides to take a position in Cochin-China, although typically enough that is no future for him – nor is there any other.

One unavoidable sign of Martin's difference are his feminine features, detailed in his eyes, his frequent blushing, his highly strung temperament and his fondness for the company of young women. Millie, the working-class girlfriend he acquires when he becomes a medical student in Dublin, comments on the girlish quality of his behaviour with her. In boarding school he develops a crush on Norman Dempsey, while also receiving the sexual attentions of one of the school's priests. Yet, despite Martin's troubled reactions to these experiences, his sexual identity is not ultimately the point at issue. Rather, his femininity points to the refinement and incorruptibility of his inner nature. 'Romantic Martin Reilly!' (476) he is called, derisively, but in his idealism and ardour he not only embodies a young man's typical quest for something to believe in but also elements of the spirit that animated his parents.

Boarding school leaves him only with the ambition of founding a periodical entitled *The Atheist's Torch*, and his medical studies at university in Dublin do not engage him. He has also by now experienced the appeal of his mother's family, having been a guest in Keelard, his Aunt Kathleen's Big House. But that connection also comes to grief when he breaks with his aunt's daughter, Sally, over the national question. Yet, Martin's own relation to that question is typically unresolved.

The day the Easter 1916 Rising breaks out is spent with Millie on their first date, although, en route to meet her, Martin's path crosses that of a detachment of Irish Volunteers who remind him 'of a description of Washington's army, which he had lately read' (272). After the Rising, Martin and Millie visit London, whose sights he finds to be 'intimately part of his connective tissue' (332). He coldly rejects one of his university professor's beliefs that 'A man's first duty is to himself' (341). But Martin is also troubled when a rebel friend espouses the public imposition of a puritanical brand of Catholicism, while his idealistic nature nevertheless draws him to the rebels. But that leads to imprisonment, Martin's ultimate reversal of fortune. There his story ends.

One of Farrell's epigraphs is a phrase of Falstaff's: 'tush man, mortal men, mortal men'. This supplies a universalising perspective to the historical specificity of the novel's action, and regards it in the same light that prompts a star-gazing Martin to wonder 'if it could be something more than mere human foolishness to see in that formal display up there the assurance of a universal harmony' (398). Such lofty thoughts no doubt do the young man credit, and are a moving expression of his romantic yearning, of his solitary spirit and of his need for guidance. His hopes of wholeness, belonging and reassurance have been aggravated by the friable character of the historical context in which he has come of age. By birth and temperament he has proved unsuited to this context, and it has failed to furnish him with the faith in life he seeks. From that point of view, *Thy Tears Might Cease* can be thought of as another of those expressions of disappointment typical of Irish fiction in the immediate post-independence period. Unlike much of that literature, however, this novel forgives Martin's disappointment by regarding it from Falstaff's long perspective, thereby dissolving it into the common mortal lot. The gap between aspiration and achievement is not merely in ourselves, but in the stars.

Such a view glosses over the modernity that the narrative invokes. In doing so it is consistent with some of the novel's other features. Its leisurely pace, somewhat starry-eyed tone, its affirmation of innocence are reminiscent of work from the period in which its early action is set – William O'Brien's *When We Were Boys* (1890) comes to mind. Yet, despite the author's intentions, *Thy Tears Might Cease* also cannot help but speak to the stories of its own day, when the tensions in Irish culture and society between tradition and modernity could no longer be palliated.

Supplementary Reading

Anthony Cronin, 'Bitter Emeralds', *The Times Literary Supplement*, 21 November 1963

Brendan Kennelly, Untitled Review, *Hermathena*, vol. XCIX (Autumn 1964), pp. 94–5

Peter Costello, *The Heart Grown Brutal: The Irish Revolution in Literature from Parnell to the Death of Yeats 1891–1939* (Dublin: Gill & Macmillan, 1977)

Thomas Kilroy, 'The Autobiographical Novel', in Augustine Martin (ed.), *The Genius of Irish Prose* (Cork: Mercier Press, 1985), pp. 65–75

Also Published in 1963

John Broderick, *Don Juaneen*; John McGahern, *The Barracks*; Brian Moore, *An Answer from Limbo*; Iris Murdoch, *The Unicorn*; Anthony C. West, *The Ferret Fancier*

1964

Samuel Beckett, *How It Is*

Although it tends to be overshadowed by his plays, Beckett's fiction is arguably a more substantial body of work, not only with regard to its size but also its aesthetic challenges, verbal inventiveness, formal innovations and philosophical demands. The centrepiece of his fictional output is the renowned trilogy consisting of Molloy (1955), Malone Dies (1956) and The Unnameable (1958). A pendant to, and critique of, that trilogy's final work, How It Is, in its preoccupation with voice and its reliance on rhythm and patterns, can also be regarded as the seedbed of a later trilogy of novellas – Company (1979), Ill Seen Ill Said (1981) and Worstward Ho (1983). All these works were originally written in French; dates given here are those of first English editions. Beckett (1906–89) was born in County Dublin. He was awarded the Nobel Prize for Literature in 1969.

While retaining identifiable links with his other post-war fiction, *How It Is*, true to Beckett's restlessly innovative imagination, also breaks new ground in form and language. Such is this work's novelty, indeed, that an approach to it which relies on plot summary and character analysis will fall well short of being an adequate accounting. In many respects, *How It Is* is an attack on such familiar aspects of the novel. What passes for plot does follow the convention of having a time sequence – 'before Pim with Pim after Pim' (7). But the familiar sense of plot as an exposition of causes and effects does not at all obtain, even if happenings of different kinds, mental and physical, are consistently in evidence. And where character is concerned, the entity referred to as Pim may have some sort of existence apart from the narrative voice, although both voice and entity seem in the mud-bound surroundings to exist at the level of species rather than as individuals, and both seem too indebted to an aesthetic of 'bits and scraps' (20) to be characters in the usual sense.

Even in attempting the rudimentary task of describing *How It Is*, then, it must be noted that the text itself formally indicates that it cannot be thought of in categorical terms. Although what the narrative voice reproduces has a random and disconnected quality, each separate utterance appears in a layout resembling how the verses in the Bible appear. But these brief paragraphs are discrete in looks only. Their contents cross-refer with, and leach into, each other. The same is the case with the narrative's three phases. The pre-, during- and post-Pim sections are explicitly differentiated, but their content does not comply with the formal divisions. The seemingly concrete and definitive connotations of this work's title are reproduced in its formal narrative arrangements but are contradicted by its narrative data. And on the basis of this antinomy between storytelling's elementary ingredients – form, which serves stasis, and content which enacts flux – *How It Is* addresses its many other far-reaching concerns with the experience of time, the nature of memory, the composition of identity, and knowledge of the other.

In keeping with this sense of contrariety, the work's two aspects of continuity also appear to be in opposition. One is the voice – 'how I'm told this time' (12) – the other the inky mud which is the speaker's unvarying environment. The voice itself represents a further disjunction, for while it is the speaker's, what it says appears to be dictated ('I say it as I hear it' (7)). The life it provides is evidently a fresh iteration of an obviously irrecoverable past, although its new details make no difference other than suppressing the old ones. It is as though any life is conceivable to the virtually disabled one currently being endured. 'Images' (8, 10, 15) from the world of light, the world above ground, impinge on the speaker, though the language in which they do so is not syntactically ordered like writing but has an onrush typical of speech, unreflecting and bearing merely intermittent evidence of an engaged, presiding consciousness. This unreconstructed speech is one means of indicating the distance between the speaker and the source of what he says, a distance underlined by the few calls that occur for a witness. In that sense, the pre-Pim phase is that of utter isolation, with only a coal-sack full of tins as the voice's objective correlative.

Whatever Pim might be – he may well be the speaker's invention – he is a medium through which presence may assert some sort of validation: 'with somebody to keep me company I would have been a different man more universal' (67). So, for instance, Pim is a reason for the speaker to assume a name of his own, Bom (though the names and the notion of identity they signify soon change to Pem, Bim and numerous similar variations). The uses to which Pim is put are excruciating, and a kind of trench warfare is carried out between the two, with Bom the source of the aggression. Being another makes Pim a candidate for torture, and the responses attributed to Pim fail to relieve his plight. And if there is one other, the possibility of many others is introduced, which brings with it notions of lineage (Bom acquires parents), partnership (he has been married to Pam, or Prem), a history which is in the keeping of an archivist. Yet such witnesses pretty much disappear as soon as they are revealed, as though life in relation to others ultimately bears no comparison to the speaker's current state and the certainty imposed by that state's limitations. Though an antithesis to the opening solitary phase, the Pim time may also be regarded in terms of the speaker's recurring refrain of 'something wrong there' (9).

The third part – life after Pim – is not, however, a return to how it was before Pim. Or rather, there is a return, since the possibility of anything changing, or of change being a source of meaning, is unthinkable. But now there is the additional burden of the consciousness of others, and this proves as difficult to shake as the dictating voice, even when the thought of others is given depersonalised acknowledgment in the speaker's extravagant arithmetical treatment of them. These mathematical exercises in themselves convey consciousness's unremitting character – 'one can't go on one can't stop put a stop' (90). But inasmuch as that statement is a conclusion, it contradicts itself. The only option is to dismantle the whole apparatus that the text – the voicing – has availed of, supplanting it with a bare animal perception of the minimalism delineated by darkness and virtual immobility, as though only the conditions of the afflicted flesh – embodying as they do the coexistence of victim and tormentor – can attest to how it is.

Thematically expansive and stylistically compressed, identifying the universal in the particular, deconstructing the properties of the human even as it invokes them, this novel (to use the most convenient if not necessarily the most accurate classification) is yet one more remarkable demonstration of Beckett's intellectual range and aesthetic control. But it may not seem to have very much to do with Irish writing. This view, however, seems shortsighted. To speak generally, there is obviously no reason to think of Ireland being beyond the pale of such a work's interests. More specifically, however, some of the themes and structures of *How It Is* are also among those to which contemporary Irish novelists, in their own very different ways, have directed their attention. Among these are the availability of a usable past, the possibility of living outside of history, the aesthetics of voice, the utility of 'old words' (134), the resources of memory and journeys through certain buried spiritual and psychological terrain. Not to reduce the imaginative domain of *How It Is* to that of a quaking sod, but its discursive interests are not quite so alien as they appear, surprising as that may seem.

Supplementary Reading

Hugh Kenner, *Samuel Beckett: A Critical Study* (Berkeley: University of California Press, 1968, 2nd ed.), pp. 187–99

John Fletcher, *The Novels of Samuel Beckett* (London: Chatto & Windus, 1970, 2nd ed.), pp. 209–18

Gary Adelman, 'Torturer and Servant: Samuel Beckett's *How It Is*', *Journal of Modern Literature*, vol. 25, no. 1 (Fall 2001), pp. 81–92

Edouard Magessa O'Reilly, *Samuel Beckett:* Comment C'est/How It Is: *A Critical-Genetic Edition* (New York: Routledge, 2001)

Also Published in 1964

Anthony Cronin, *The Life of Riley*; Janet McNeill, *The Maiden Dinosaur*; Edna O'Brien, *Girls in their Married Bliss*; Flann O'Brien, *The Dalkey Archive*; Richard Power, *The Land of Youth*; William Trevor, *The Old Boys*

1965

Brian Moore, *The Emperor of Ice-Cream*

This is the third of a trio of novels – the other two are Judith Hearne *(1955) and* The Feast of Lupercal *(1957) – dealing with Moore's boyhood and youth in his native Belfast. Prior to its publication, novels such as* The Luck of Ginger Coffey *(1960) and* An Answer from Limbo *(1962) had already begun to draw on his post-Belfast life, most of which was spent in North America. But Moore (1921–99) continued to keep his origins in mind, as his prolific output indicates by, among other elements, its interest in religious matters. Works as superficially different from one another as* Cold Heaven *(1983),* Black Robe *(1985),* The Colour of Blood *(1987) and* No Other Life *(1993) return to the subject. The air-raid described in* The Emperor of Ice-Cream *took place on 15 April 1941. Over 900 people died in the seven-hour attack.*

Seventeen-year-old Gavin Burke is a failure. This is not only how he sees himself. So does his family. He has failed his exams and will not be following in the footsteps of his father and his brother Owen in reading law at Queen's University, and he is only notionally studying for an alternative exam which may secure him university entrance. This exam he also fails. His relationship with the pert but very sensible Sally Shannon, a student nurse, is on-again, off-again. And he has enlisted in the ARP (Air Raid Precautions), an official British organisation established to assist the civilian population in the event of air raids. Gavin's father, whose unreconstructed brand of Irish nationalism has been fortified by Hitler's initial military success, regards his son's enlistment as a particularly deviant departure. Nobody whom Gavin knows thinks that in joining the ARP he is making a declaration of independence or even that a life of one's own is conceivable beyond the narrow confines of conventional bourgeois activities, attainments and institutions. And Gavin himself has only a hazy sense that he is taking a step towards a life of his own. In his view, adulthood consists of the male entitlements to drink and wench to one's heart's content, supposed freedoms in which his peers indulge as a means of transgressing the cultural limitations of their class and the puritanical ethos of their Catholicism.

The world of the ARP post appears to be less an antidote to Belfast's typical rigidities than a microcosm of them, with sectarianism, sexism and bureaucratic overkill its prevailing social features. Yet, these features are most in evidence at the administrative level, and there is also a collective spirit of resistance to the petty restrictions to which the rank and file are subjected. Most of Gavin's colleagues are the type of people with whom he has hitherto had no social contact. His ability to hold his own in their company shows that the appetite for experience which he wishes his enlistment to satisfy has not been misleading. In particular, the friendship he quickly forms with the anti-authoritarian, 'independent Marxist' (21) Freddy Hargreaves is critical to his development (they share a taste for modernist poetry, their favourites being Eliot, MacNeice, and somewhat precociously perhaps, Wallace Stevens).

Not only is Freddy's penchant for speaking out and stepping up a more highly evolved version of Gavin's independent-mindedness, his taking the youngster in hand reveals a more diverse Belfast – 'a grown-up world' (76), inhabited by gay clergymen, Jewish refugees and left-wing theatre – than Gavin ever suspected.

In view of Freddy's ideological leanings, it probably is unfair to consider him a big brother. As is very often the case with Moore's characters, there is a marked element of staginess about him (and about Gavin, too). But even if Freddy is affecting a worldliness that he does not really command, he is for Gavin a welcome and influential model of non-compliance, the value of which is enacted in their joint efforts at the novel's climax. Here, in volunteering to coffin the bodies of the blitz's victims, they show themselves to be a pair of exceptions whose common humanism rises above the pettiness all around them. Acting in the spirit of the moral sense that they share, 'They had never been better friends' (183). Nor had Gavin ever seemed more clearly the older man's equal. The youngster's growth is confirmed when he visits his bombed-out home to find that his worried father has returned from Dublin, where he went with the rest of the family to escape the destruction. Now it is the hitherto masterful Mr Burke who seems unable to cope, and it is his teenage son who comforts him.

Gavin has outgrown the world of the father with its concerns about career and security and predictable forms of citizenship. He has also outgrown his infatuation with Sally, who has told him he is a 'hero' (180) yet who denies him a parting kiss when one of her superiors is present. This conventionality leaves Gavin cold, as does the simplistic moral schema, featuring a White Angel and a Black Angel, whom he has employed to arbitrate over his choices. By his own efforts, Gavin overcomes some of his adolescent uncertainties and in choosing not to accompany his family to the safety of Dublin shows his capacity for a more level-headed appreciation of the things that matter to him.

Moreover, Belfast itself has not been able to remain unchanged, a marginal outpost formally at war but according to complacent local opinion too distant from hostilities to be menaced by them. Provincialism turns out not to be protected by geography. In contrast to conventional wisdom, Gavin's view has been that 'war was freedom' (10), a freedom that he believes will be in sharp contrast to the quality of life ushered in by the war of Irish independence. 'The terrible beauty was born aborted' (105), Gavin thinks, amending Yeats. Certainly his experience of the air-raid itself has a liberating effect, making him feel 'like a knight in some ancient romance' (159). But such an adrenaline-induced reaction is replaced by the raid's sombre aftermath, whose sobering effect is brought home by the ineffectuality of the whiskey dispensed to help the workers face all the dead. It is in carrying out that secular, civic and dramatically unconventional undertaking that Gavin proves himself as a person of value, tireless, focused and unself-conscious. 'The world and the war had come to him' (151), and they did not find him wanting.

'Sally Shannon would never change' (185). This is Gavin's last word on his former girlfriend. It is also a tacit commentary on the consequences of his experiences. Not only has Gavin changed, but he has done so by choice; and by his choices he has consistently allowed himself to be drawn to the disruptive historical forces of the modern moment. To do so, he has had to disentangle himself from his family's traditional roles and expectations, he has had to make himself vulnerable, he has had to dress up in a funny, initially ill-fitting, uniform. But he has been led to have faith in himself, rather than in the unchanging, paternalistic and politically reactionary modes which he could have thoughtlessly inherited. In his self-reliance, his capacity for growth, his unmourned homelessness, his youthful forwardness, Gavin Burke becomes something of a poster-child for an imperium of ice-cream.

Supplementary Reading

John Wilson Foster, *Forces and Themes in Ulster Fiction* (Dublin: Gill & Macmillan, 1974), pp. 122–30

Jo O'Donoghue, *Brian Moore: A Critical Study* (Dublin: Gill & Macmillan, 1990), pp. 71–4

Denis Sampson, *Brian Moore: The Chameleon Novelist* (Dublin: Marino, 1998), pp. 150–5

Patricia Craig, *Brian Moore: A Biography* (London: Bloomsbury, 2002)

Also Published in 1965

John Broderick, *The Waking of Willie Ryan*; Eilís Dillon, *Bold John Henebry*; Iris Murdoch, *The Red and the Green*; William Cotter Murray, *Michael Joe*; Edna O'Brien, *August is a Wicked Month*; William Trevor, *The Boarding House*

1966

Aidan Higgins, *Langrishe, Go Down*

Higgins (b. 1927) is the author of five novels, including Balcony of
Europe *(1972; revised edition, 2010),* Scenes from a Receding Past
(1977), Bornholm Night-Ferry *(1983) and* Lions of the Grünewald
*(1993). In these, interactions between love, time and memory are
explored with an artistic sensibility which recalls such modernist prede-
cessors as Marcel Proust and Samuel Beckett. Much of Higgins's work
has an autobiographical dimension – Springfield House in* Langrishe,
Go Down *has the same name and location as the house near Celbridge,
County Kildare, in which the author was born and raised – and he has
written three admired volumes of autobiography,* Donkey's Years
(1995), Dog Days *(1998) and* The Whole Hog *(2000). These
appeared in a one-volume American edition entitled* A Bestiary *(2004).
His other works include a volume of short stories, two books containing
his travel writing, journalism and uncollected short fiction, and collections of both his book reviews and radio plays.*

The novel opens in 1937, and 'The world was in a bad way' (10). In
Spain, the Civil War is going poorly for the Republican side. That much
is public knowledge. Helen Langrishe learns it in the evening paper as,
feeling almost suffocated and beset by the grinding noise of the bus's
wheels, she travels home to Springfield House from Dublin. But Helen
also has news of her own, the personal and imponderable nature of
which adds to her claustrophobia, social alienation and feeling of being
ground down. The news from Spain is of military positions falling, and
Helen's news is also of a fall – 'the old impossible life was ending' (18).
The family home can no longer be maintained, and the future of Helen
and her two sisters, Lily and Imogen (another, Emily, has already died),
seems inevitably set to follow the descent into deterioration and decay
already evident in their birthplace.

With this opening, not only the discursive but the aesthetic terms of
Langrishe, Go Down are set. There is obviously no direct connection
between Springfield and Spain, or between a bleak outlook and a
crowded bus. But all these phenomena, carefully delineated and differentiated though they are, exist in the same plane, their condition
one of contiguity without entailment. Later, when the affair between
Imogen and her lover, Otto Beck, is disintegrating, the thought occurs
to Imogen that '*We are like figures come loose out of a frieze*' (239). And
that artistic form is one way of thinking about how this novel depicts

the human condition, its characters confined to limited postures. At another level, though, the characters cannot be motionless; their actions continually slide into one another, as in a modern painting in which perspectives and tonal values interact to articulate restlessness and to blur boundaries.

The narrative's pervasive sense of slippage and helplessness, illustrated all too plainly by Springfield's slovenliness and dereliction, is also borne out by Helen's failure to convey adequately her news from the family's Dublin lawyers. Perhaps there seems little point in her trying, given her sisters' indifference and remoteness. Yet, although Helen is the only member of the 'rank sisterhood' (79) to grasp their present circumstances, she turns aside from current concerns to visit her parents' grave. This interlude is notable for its integration of memory and loss, for its juxtaposition of personal, local and national history – all distinct from each other and all united in their common moribund state – and for leaving Helen with the feeling that 'History begins and ends in me. In me, now, today' (76). Back in Springfield, Helen also revisits the past in its documentary form, foraging among Imogen's letters to Otto, the emotions of which she regards with distaste, as she does the reprehensible Otto himself. Imogen too has been reading through her past life, though to her the affair comprised 'the two happiest years of my long and insignificant existence' (67).

Helen concedes that she has 'never known the love of the body or of the heart' (79). It is just such knowledge that Imogen received from Otto, with his fox's face and poacher's disposition. The affair between the thirty-nine-year-old Imogen and the German 'poor scholar' (217) four years her junior, which comprises the body of the novel, has taken place five years earlier, in 1932 (a year remembered in Ireland as that of the Eucharistic Congress, though obviously memorable here for sexual congress). As a youth, Otto served in the First World War, and his subsequent career has been erratic, so that he seems a member of a lost generation, wandering Europe with no obvious purpose other than to take what he can get. He has a son he has never seen, and his lack of conscience about this makes his taking advantage of the inexperienced Imogen hardly a surprise. To her, Otto's attentions – 'never have I lived more in my senses' (179) – are a welcome relief from the respectable tedium that has been her social destiny. But the ways in which Otto contrasts with Imogen – he is worldly, unhygienic, intellectual, imperious – ensures that she is no match for him.

And true to his wandering history, he takes up with another local woman. As the final confirmation that the affair has no issue, Imogen gives birth to Otto's stillborn child.

Their relationship is, in its own way, an expression of the absence of control, the slither towards dissolution, the insidious entropy concealed in an ostensibly stagnant time. To these impersonal agents of erosion, the immediate, local world, the distant, geopolitical world, and love itself are prey. Otto, with his allusions to Husserl and Heidegger, his anti-Nazism and intellectual faddism, brings to the backwater of Springfield a touch of Europe. But the Europe he embodies is one that has been defeated, is in 1932 in an in-between state, lacks direction and is destined for downfall. If Imogen thinks Otto is her future, then that future is no more promising than bankrupt Springfield's. But Imogen is not thinking. The affair drifts along, an uneven string of moments, some delightful, others humiliating, some fulfilling, others enraging. It, too, is a transit towards terminus. In the end, Otto is not to be managed, any more than Springfield is. The novel concludes in the year after it began with a brief account of Helen's funeral and of Imogen wandering alone through her increasingly squalid and decrepit home.

Because Springfield has such an emblematic presence, *Langrishe, Go Down* has been viewed as a Big House novel, or as an example of a modern revision of that genre. Such a view tends to downplay both the work's European backdrop and its modernist aesthetics. The former places such national resonances as there are in a much broader framework, a departure whose implications are echoed in many different ways in numerous later Irish novels, foremost among them Higgins's own. And the complicated usages of time and space in *Langrishe, Go Down*, which deploy both dimensions in a manner that seems both unpredictable and ineluctable, are not only central to its composition but convey an unsettling disconnection between cause and effect. Indeed, the fall of the house of Langrishe might be described as the story of a house that is not big enough, a structure that is insufficiently flexible or capacious to absorb the visitations of love and death, subjective illusion and objective decline – the underside of history, as it were – that time imposes. Such a narrative also has many class and cultural implications for this novel's Irish context.

Supplementary Reading

William Eastlake/Aidan Higgins issue, *The Review of Contemporary Fiction*, vol. 3, no. 1 (Spring 1983), pp. 106–224

Vera Kreilkamp, *The Anglo-Irish Novel and the Big House* (Syracuse: Syracuse University Press, 1998), pp. 235–47

Aidan Higgins, *Windy Arbours: Collected Criticism* (Champaign, Illinois: Dalkey Archive, 2005)

Neil Murphy (ed.), *Aidan Higgins: The Fragility of Form* (Champaign, Illinois: Dalkey Archive, 2010)

Also Published in 1966

Patrick Boyle, *Like Any Other Man*; Edna O'Brien, *Casualties of Peace*; William Trevor, *The Love Department*

1967

Flann O'Brien, *The Third Policeman*

After Joyce and Beckett, and quite different from both, O'Brien (1911–66) is the third most noted twentieth-century Irish novelist. Flann O'Brien is one of two pseudonyms used by Brian O'Nolan, a native of Omagh, County Tyrone; the second is Myles na gCopaleen, under which he wrote his celebrated Irish Times newspaper column, 'An Cruiskeen Lawn'. O'Brien's five novels include At Swim-Two-Birds (1939), The Hard Life (1961) and The Poor Mouth (1973; a translation of his Irish-language satire, An Béal Bocht (1941)). Written in the early 1940s, a complicated publishing history resulted in The Third Policeman appearing posthumously, preceded by The Dalkey Archive (1965), which recasts some of the earlier work's material. A number of compilations of his newspaper column have been issued, among them The Best of Myles (1968). His later fiction is a less impressive showing of the imaginative originality, formal resourcefulness, conceptual playfulness and stylistic flair on which his national and international reputation is based.

In Ernest Hemingway's 1936 short story 'The Snows of Kilimanjaro', the dying protagonist, Harry, observes that the banal image of 'two bicycle policemen' can connote death as readily as the traditional scythe and skull. Imagine, then, the effect a third policeman might have. So it is that towards the end of this uncanny narrative, Policeman Fox, hitherto an all but invisible presence, puts the finishing touches to the accomplishments of his two colleagues, Sergeant Pluck and Policeman MacCruiskeen. Their efforts have been arresting enough, as they repeatedly demonstrate how in their custodial realm traditional forms and commonplace images shed their purchase and reliability, and death changes from being a fact of life to being a whole new and unnerving sensorium which challenges consciousness and comprehension.

Life yields to afterlife, its distorted, unnatural but not unmeaning complement. This sphere is a landscape seemingly contiguous to the one from which the deceased narrator has departed, restlessly patrolled by Fox, as befits his predatory name. In addition to its topographical properties, this space also has its own arts, supervised by MacCruiskeen, and sciences, which are in Pluck's keeping. But these familiar forms of knowledge and apprehension are no longer subject to the principles by which they are usually known. And the same is the case for such essential categories as time, space, matter, mass and dimensionality. In a typically witty development, even the policemen's speech exhibits certain modifications in syntax and vocabulary, and ordinary words – 'pancake', for instance – become synonymous with mystery. Not surprisingly, the narrator finds the miraculously elasticated but at the same time denatured state of things to be frightening in its operation, as well as in the rather sadistic playfulness with which it carries out its continually surprising ambushes on his powers of comprehension. In a word, this is hell.

Yet, if the mental pain of shock, alarm, uncertainty and dislocation of various kinds are now the version of hell's torments that the narrator must undergo, there does seem to be a perverse justice to it. It is in the nature of his altered circumstances that he cannot overcome an awareness of his limitations. But it is by exceeding his limitations in the first place that he has fallen into his present condition. Although the statement by Cassius in *Julius Caesar* which is the novel's epigraph – 'Since the affairs of men rest still uncertain,/Let's reason with the worst that may befall' – at least concedes the availability of reason, it is not easy to have faith in its utility, given the way things are in the infernal police state. Yet a connection is at least implied between the narrative's primal event, the narrator's murder of Philip Mathers, and where he ends up. Such a connection is reinforced by the fact that the crime was committed in order to further the narrator's promotion of the philosophy of de Selby, the study of whose works has been for the narrator 'more important than myself' (11), his life otherwise being an impoverished, isolated affair.

This savant's works and days are substantially footnoted throughout *The Third Policeman*. Like the theories on which the policemen premise their activities, de Selby's ideas possess a laughably entertaining, daft consistency, and the non-natural experimentation common to both renders them complementary. The tendency in de Selby's thought is to atomise, while for the policemen the exact opposite is the case, signified by their production of the 'inutterable substance' (188) known as omnium. The likely outcome of de Selby's revisionary conception of direction are said to be 'New and unimaginable dimensions' (95). An idea of what these might be are reproduced in the time/space relations of the 'strange country' (39) to which the narrator is confined.

The novel's comedic inventiveness is its most striking feature, and the pleasures it affords are hardly to be denied. Yet, there are reminders throughout that this feature's context consists of dark deeds, excruciating constraints, the threat of execution and widespread cognitive dissonance. Theory is given a risible character, but that does not disguise its denaturing subtexts, and the fun is undercut by the narrator's frequently abject dread, as well as by the arrogant and self-serving murder, the commission of which is highlighted by a needless excess of violence. Most obviously, there is the monitory undertone that the novel's sense of the cyclical carries with it. The chief law-enforcement concern of Pluck and MacCruiskeen is with bicycles and is carried out by bicycle. When the narrator is under the illusion that he is escaping, it is by means of a bicycle so fine as to provide him with many a tender, sensory thrill. Appropriately for a location to which change is alien, the policemen's work is a neverending cycle, and the conclusion that eternity is repetitive by definition is confirmed by the outcome of the supposed escape.

This confirmation comes indirectly from the third policeman. It is from his encounter with Fox that the narrator thinks he can return to his former life. But no amount of back-pedalling will result in such a reversal. And Fox makes the link between the missing proceeds of the Mathers murder and the dreaded omnium, with which he is 'calmly making ribbons of the natural order' (188). In its hostility to that order, omnium – whatever else it might be – may be regarded as the opposite of gatherum, from which the natural order, in its highly differentiated heterogeneity, is composed. Some of the novel's most pleasing passages are those depicting the Elysian countryside through which the narrator makes his way to the police station, imagining – self-deceiving materialist that he is – that there he will be assisted in recovering the Mathers booty. On the eve of his execution, he

contemplates the possibility that death will make him 'free and innocent of all human perplexity' (159), and that his post-mortem
existence might be as a wind, 'Or perhaps a smaller thing like movement in the grass on an unbearable breathless yellow day' (ibid.). At
any rate, he envisages being at one with the natural order, in contrast
to his former life when he acted in violation of it.

A playful but by no means superficial disquisition on the vanity of
human wishes; a satire on learning; a self-reflexive piece of post-mod-
ernism *avant la lettre*; a pastiche of those middle-Irish romances about
voyages to the other world, updated for the atomic age – *The Third
Policeman* seems quite capable of living up to these and other seemingly incompatible accounts of its contents and method, including a
sustained expression of scepticism regarding the power of the imagination itself. More basically, given the status it accords creation's
natural make-up, the novel also appears to take a dim view of human
agency and of the cupidity with which it typically operates. The narrator may hardly be considered very well-off before the murder, but
clearly the crime only changes things for the worse. In what is
perhaps the most unnerving instance of the dialectic that keeps the
narrative cycle revolving, the ludic latitude of *The Third Policeman* is
counterbalanced by a pessimistic conservatism. Each of these components is a critique of the other, and both are expressions of modernist
misgivings about such concerns as the limits of freedom and the adequacy of the human subject for a world made in his own image.

Supplementary Reading

Benedict Kiely, 'Fun After Death', *The New York Times*, 12 November 1967
Anne Clissmann, *Flann O'Brien: A Critical Introduction to His Writings* (Dublin: Gill
& Macmillan, 1975), pp. 151–81
Anthony Cronin, *No Laughing Matter: The Life and Times of Flann O'Brien* (London:
Grafton, 1989)
Keith Hopper, *A Portrait of the Artist as a Young Post-Modernist* (Cork: Cork
University Press, 2009, 2nd ed.)

Also Published in 1967

Michael Campbell, *Lord Dismiss Us*; Janet McNeill, *The Small Widow*; Bernard Share,
Inish

1968

Anthony C. West, *As Towns with Fire*

Born in County Down, Anthony C. West (1910–88) spent his childhood in rural County Cavan, a time and place which recur in his novels Rebel to Judgment *(1962) and* The Ferret Fancier *(1963). The landscapes of these works are rich in natural detail, and are also the setting of primal experiences of love and violence, blood and soil, possession and isolation. A lush style and an attraction to archetypal intellectual frameworks distinguish West's handling of his material. His rather small output also includes a collection of short stories and a fourth novel,* The Native Moment *(1961), set in bohemian Dublin.*

During the Second World War, West was a member of the Royal Air Force and saw intense action in the bombing of German cities as a navigator in the Pathfinder squadron led by Guy Gibson of 'Dambusters' fame. This experience provides *As Towns with Fire* with a number of impressive action sequences, as well as with notable tributes to the romance of aviation. Yet, even though this work is centrally concerned with questions of identity and of the standing of the individual at a time of collective crisis, it is only a contribution to the Irish autobiographical novel in a limited sense. For while the protagonist, Christopher MacMannan, is a native of the same part of Northern Ireland as West, and like him is an aspiring writer as well as, eventually, an RAF navigator, such items of personal history comprise only one component of his complex presence. As well as being an individual, MacMannan is also portrayed – and indeed is much given to thinking of himself – as man in history, a figure who has difficulty in retaining his individuality in the face of the historical moment's compelling claims, resisting change even as he succumbs to it. His acute awareness of living at the intersection of personal desire and historical obligation not only highlights some key aspects of Northern Irish identity but also maps the cultural, psychological and existential components that make up the spirit of the wartime age. And it is typical of the author's imaginative perspective that MacMannan is a navigator both literally and figuratively, in search of himself in a series of unpropitious places – with 'one foot in Tir na nOg and the other up to the hock in nowhere' (81), as one of his various descriptions of himself has it.

The novel opens in London on New Year's Eve 1939, a year that sees the aimless MacMannan achieving very little other than the bedding of a succession of women who, in addition to putting up with his sexism, take him to various social gatherings where different views of the international situation are rehearsed. These set-pieces (which include a soirée at the home of Irish writer James Stephens) show MacMannan's resistance to prevailing orthodoxies, his detachment from incipient war fever, and his commitment to thinking for himself. Speaking his own mind makes him appear awkward and out of place, showing him to be not only 'an individualist' (77) but to possess an alternative cultural identity to that of his metropolitan acquaintances, one formed by his rural Northern Irish childhood. From this background he retains a strong feeling for the natural world, a taste for English Romantic poetry, an appreciation of innocence and of outsiders who embody it, and a desire to transcend the bigotry fostered by institutional rigidity.

When war eventually breaks out and his home place of Kilainey offers a retreat for himself, his wife Molly and their twin boys, MacMannan rejects it, though he is quite prepared to move to Ireland for the duration. The failure of a plan to live in Donegal leads to a sojourn in Belfast which not only includes an account of the 'terrible beauty' (270) of the city being bombed but also reports on the numbers from south of the border coming north to enlist – a fact not widely acknowledged when *As Towns with Fire* was first published. Life in Belfast is uncongenial – 'this wee toun's a Third Reich for years' (279) – and soon becomes untenable. Broke, with an ailing marriage, his writing ambitions in ruins, MacMannan decides to join up, motivated more by the prospect of a steady income on which his family could live than by the call of loftier loyalties.

Yet it is these loyalties which consume a good deal of his attention once he is in uniform. Stationed eventually in rural Lincolnshire, with Molly and the children housed nearby, it is in a sense as though MacMannan has returned to the scenes of his childhood with, on the one hand, the bounty of nature all around, and on the other the fallibility of man, particularly man in an institutional context. Time and again, MacMannan tries to think through the meaning of the war as far as it concerns him personally, maintaining in arguments with his comrades and his copious inner reflections that sense of protest and exceptionalism which has been characteristic of him from the outset. Such philosophical flights complicate the official view of the war as a simplistic struggle between good and evil, as well as denoting

MacMannan as a querulous dissenter, necessary but alone. He is the one who most keenly recognises war's bitter paradoxes of gain through loss and victory by destruction – 'As towns with fire, so won, so lost . . . Seems to be my theme song – or epitaph, he said. Biron [sic] in *Love's Labours Lost*' (205).

Yet, seeing through the prevailing outlook, by declining to be at peace with the war effort, threatens to leave MacMannan in no man's land. As a participant in a modernity he can neither repudiate nor endorse, he is continually in two minds as to his identity. This duality has numerous exemplifications, beginning with his name, with its combination of the Christian and the pre-Christian (Manannán is the Celtic god of the sea), and including his allegiance to certain aspects of both Ireland and England, as well as a marriage in which his wife is the earth-mother opposite of MacMannan's ungrounded self. While he is emblematic of the cultural, spiritual and existential challenge of his time, his personal perspective tends towards the transhistorical, expressed in 'mystical adumbrations' (191) and 'amateur theories about the continuous evolution of human consciousness' (97). Intellectually, his relation to the order of things is based on an autodidact's composite of world mythologies in which blood lines have a disquieting prominence. Physically, his engagement with life is sensual, a celebration both of sexuality and of 'nature, the only constant' (376). An erratic mixture of the Quixotic and the Icarian, MacMannan's imagination, by which he aspires 'to see Time without any of the freely provided blinkers' (165), finds a necessary counterpart in his ultimate fate, the fall which takes him down to earth and confirms his mere mortality. This interplay of rise and fall also recapitulates in individual terms the contrariety alluded to in the novel's title. MacMannan's deliverance costs him everything.

Such a conclusion may not be particularly original, but that should not detract from the novelty of *As Towns with Fire*. Even thinking of it as simply another novel of the Second World War attests to its inventiveness in the context of the Irish novel. And it is also a noteworthy addition to the rather sparse literature of the Irish diaspora in England. But its ambition exceeds the constraints of genre, even if the genre is that of epic, since in a manner typical of almost its every feature, *As Towns with Fire* is both at the service of the sense of quest and conflict inherent in epic and resistant to that sense. Rather, in keeping with the most ambitious Irish novels, it is an epic of consciousness, seeing in the maelstrom of historical circumstances a need for sharpened and more urgent assessments of identity. These revaluations are based on questions such as the viability of difference, the substance of independence and the credibility of modernity, which have a particular cogency for the development of the Irish novel.

Supplementary Reading

John Wilson Foster, *Forces and Themes in Ulster Fiction* (Dublin: Gill & Macmillan, 1974), pp. 263–8

Aubrey S. Eyler, 'Piques in Darien: Anthony C. West and His American Publishers', *Éire-Ireland*, vol. 27, no. 3 (Fall 1992), pp. 49–66

Aubrey S. Eyler, *Celtic, Christian, Socialist: The Novels of Anthony C. West* (Rutherford, New Jersey: Fairleigh Dickinson University Press, 1993)

Also Published in 1968

Kevin Casey, *The Sinner's Bell*; Benedict Kiely, *Dogs Enjoy the Morning*; Brian Moore, *I Am Mary Dunne*

1969

James Plunkett, *Strumpet City*

The three novels of James Plunkett Kelly (1920–2003) – Farewell Companions (1977) and The Circus Animals *(1990) are the other two – comprise an informal social history of fifty years of working- and middle-class life in the author's native Dublin. A careful style, leftward political leanings and thick description provide these works with a solid grounding in realism, though perhaps the later novels are slowed by a dearth of dramatic material. Plunkett also published two noted short-story collections, some non-fiction, and a play which draws on the same historical background as* Strumpet City.

The flags are out and the crowds are cheering as the whole of Dublin welcomes King Edward VII. The year is 1907, and the kingdom is peaceful.

This is how *Strumpet City* begins. Seven years later, the novel ends in the place where the king arrived, but now there is little to celebrate. Fitz – the central character, Bob Fitzpatrick – is shipping out for England, where he plans to join the army. This outcome is a far cry from the opening picture of unity and amity. Fitz's leaving of his wife and children marks a breach in his family circle, a personal defeat. But his departure also marks a public defeat, brought about by the 1913 Lockout's crushing effect on the Irish Transport and General Workers' Union (founded in 1909). Fitz had been a committed union member. And added to these losses is the reader's awareness of what 1914 has in store.

Yet, if the conclusion is bleak, *Strumpet City* seeks to redeem it through its detailed and devoted narrative of the struggle in Dublin between the city's leading employers and its brutalised working class. Drawing on the historical record, as it does, risks making the novel seem largely a work of commemoration and homage. And its lengthy timespan, its broad social overview, its thorough inventory of material conditions, as well as the sheer ambition of integrating its hetero-geneous episodes and scenarios, also lend the work a certain monumental standing. Part of *Strumpet City*'s importance, therefore, is as a cultural document preserving facsimiles of significant events. In that regard, it can be read as a supplement to, or even a revision of, the narrative of nationalistic attainment celebrated by the fiftieth anniversary of the 1916 Rising. The refrain of Yeats's 'September, 1913' – 'Romantic Ireland's dead and gone' – is tacitly echoed and, in passing, endorsed.

Not that the national – and nationalist – dimensions of the Lockout and related events are overlooked. When those dimensions show up, however, their generalised rhetoric and abstract claims tend essentially to reinforce the pre-eminence of the local. Freedom and suchlike ideas are all very well, but it is the material reality and direct experience of this place and this time that furnish the grounds for the story. Even the novel's title (from a speech given by Robert Emmet as he surveys the city from the Dublin mountains in Denis Johnston's 1929 play, *The Old Lady Says 'No!'*) sounds the local note in its backhanded compliment to 'dear, dirty Dublin'. And that note is sustained throughout by the placing of city and citizen to the fore. The interaction between these two produces another revisionist perspective by showing Dublin to be the scene of endeavour and aspiration – the direct opposite of James Joyce's designation of it as 'the centre of paralysis'. In terms of literary history, *Strumpet City* marks the restoration of the capital to a degree of visibility it had not enjoyed since Joyce himself made its name, a visi-bility it has retained.

It is in Chandler's Court, the slum where Fitz and the other working-class characters live, that both the image and the ethos of the local may most clearly be grasped. Chandler's Court has a cut-off, back-street air, but its apparent isolation seems conducive to the intimate interdependence and communal sense of values practised by those living there. Yet what might be called the Court's inner life, morally rich though it appears to be, is also notoriously constrained by the impoverished quality of its inhabitants' material circumstances. Labour implicitly affirms the interconnection between body and soul and its aim is to create a more equitable and sustainable balance between them. The record shows that the employers resisted this aim, and had the resources and the institutional support to come between the citizen and his needs. This resistance also relied on a propaganda coup which effectively stifled the necessary translation of what workers understood as personal needs into what society at large might perceive as human rights.

The denial of such a perception is demonstrated in the reactions to the conflict of choleric Arthur Bradshaw, *rentier* and stockholder, expostulating on the need to maintain the *status quo*, regardless of the human cost, a disregard that extends to his own home and in doing so notably enhances the story's feminine interest. Not every stockholder is a Bradshaw, though, and the gentlemanly Yearling quite sees, at length, the workers' point of view. But his capacity for change is limited and despite his liberal sympathies he ultimately proves himself to be more an embodiment of the Edwardian era on the wane than a greeter of a brave new world. The employers' remorseless obduracy and pride in their own power suggest that for all its comprehensiveness – its honouring of history, its graphic action set-pieces, its attempts to integrate the panoramic and the intimate – *Strumpet City* is concerned with one fundamental question: what is owed? Employers' narrow fixation on a financial answer to the question comes as no surprise, though in maintaining it they reveal their hostility to any idea of a social contract, an idea on which society's good order relies. Freedom without responsibility is what the bosses seem to practise, as is confirmed by their expectation that those who depend on them must practise the reverse.

The novel's action very readily makes clear that economic preoccupations diminish other, more essential conceptions of value – those upheld in the idea of justice, for instance. And it is to articulating and exemplifying some of those other values that the clergy might be expected to contribute, using the power and authority of its pastoral mission as a counterweight to the muscle of Mammon. The crucial question, after all, is basically one about charity, the cornerstone of the faith. But the Church sides with the employers, preaching to its flock a doctrine of turning the other cheek and denying the power of moral imagination that the concept of charity inspires. The vacillating, craven Father O'Connor highlights this denial by reading the travails of his Chandler's Court parishioners in the light of his own middle-class conditioning, which the Church's and employers' hierarchical thinking both substantiate. And this weakling priest's failure is seen to be symptomatic of the clergy's self-inflicted moral impotence, as O'Connor's drunken parish priest, Father Giffley, crudely confirms. In contrast, *Strumpet City* wears its secular, humanistic heart on its sleeve, not only appealing thereby to an image of a sensitive, fair-minded common reader but conjuring up such an image. This reader is perhaps an ideal, but his cultural value can be appreciated by imagining the manner of enlightened citizenship that he represents.

Notwithstanding where its heart is and the appeal its concerns with rights, responsibilities and the common good makes to the reader's better nature, *Strumpet City* is an old-fashioned novel. Many of its characters are two-dimensional. Men tend to be weak and women long-suffering, and there is a surplus of stock types, from the good-natured whore to the whiskey priest. It is not the author's fault that the basic conflict is in black and white, but the outcome is predictable. An air of inevitability hangs over even the very few days when it is not raining. Nevertheless, there is something iconic about the departing Fitz. His recent history and his immediate future depict him as a man in the middle. Not only is he between an end and a beginning and in transit from his native country to a foreign one, he is also between one version of who he is and another. The collective endeavour typifying his experience has not rewarded the faith he placed in it, while his future offers only antithetical forms of allegiance. This image of Fitz shows him undertaking the passage from type to individual. Like any other modern man, he finds himself, for better or worse, obliged to relinquish the secure identity provided by group effort for the isolation and uncertainty of an individual destiny. Individuality and its vulnerabilities seem to be regarded as poor compensation for the changing times. Such a conclusion also gives *Strumpet City* an old-fashioned feel, not least because it is on the individual and the character of his public and private engagements that the contemporary Irish novel has focused its attention.

Supplementary Reading

Hanna Behrend, 'James Plunkett's Contribution to Democratic and Socialist Culture',
  Zeitschrift für Anglistick und Amerikanistik, vol. 27, no. 4 (1979), pp. 307–26
James Cahalan, *Great Hatred, Little Room* (Syracuse: Syracuse University Press,
  1983), pp. 179–90
James Plunkett, *The Boy on the Back Wall and Other Essays* (Dublin: Poolbeg, 1987)
Jochen Achilles, 'James Plunkett', in Rüdiger Imhof (ed.), *Contemporary Irish
  Novelists* (Tübingen: Narr, 1990), pp. 41–57

Also Published in 1969

Elizabeth Bowen, *Eva Trout*; Tom MacIntyre, *The Charollais*; Richard Power, *The
  Hungry Grass*; William Trevor, *Mrs Eckdorf in O'Neill's Hotel*; Terence de Vere
  White, *The Lambert Mile*

1970
J.G. Farrell, *Troubles*

*Born in Liverpool to a family with Irish connections, Farrell (1935–79)
spent his early youth in the Dublin area. He had published three novels
before the appearance of* Troubles, *but it is on this novel and the two
that followed it –* The Siege of Krishnapur (1973) *and* The Singapore
Grip (1978) *– that his reputation rests. These works comprise his
'Empire trilogy', an ambitious, prize-winning treatment of the fall of the
British Empire. And seeing post-First World War Ireland in the light of
an imperial, rather than a Celtic, twilight is an ironic reversal of perspective typical not only of this novel but of the trilogy as a whole. Some
details of* Troubles *contribute to the texture of one of the most highly
regarded contemporary Irish poems, Derek Mahon's 'A Disused Shed in
Co. Wexford', which is dedicated to Farrell.*

The year is 1919. Major Brendan Archer has survived the First World
War – in a manner of speaking. Released from hospital, though still psychologically frail, he makes his way to the Majestic Hotel, an enormous
pile of over three hundred rooms, on the shores of the Irish Sea at
Kilnalough, County Wexford. 'These days he was only at ease in the
company of strangers' (10) is one reason for his taking this step. But the
major also has the vague understanding that he is engaged to Angela
Spencer, whom he met while on leave during the war and with whom
he has been corresponding since. She is the daughter of Edward, owner
of the Majestic, and sister of Ripon and of the twins Faith and Charity
(there is no Hope). Angela's letters have been distinguished by an

absence of sentiment and excessive attention to the history and lineage of the family's dogs as well as to the minutiae of hotel life. She turns out to have little or no interest in the major, and not long after his arrival she sickens and dies.

The suddenness of this event inaugurates a pattern of adverse action for the rest of the novel. Things continue to fall apart in every conceivable manner. The Majestic's untended Palm Court becomes a parodic heart of darkness; wild cats have the run of the place; Edward's management style veers between the high-handed and the slovenly; the hotel's permanent population of old ladies grows increasingly grotesque and *distrait*. This entropic indoor realm has its counterpart in the chaotic conditions beyond the pale of the hotel grounds. These conditions are the Troubles – the War of Independence, sometimes known as the Anglo-Irish war (the novel's timespan roughly approximates that conflict's duration). On a visit to Dublin, Archer witnesses the 'absurd' (100) killing of an elderly man by paramilitaries. Meanwhile, the news from farther afield is no more reassuring, as the inclusion in the text of newspaper reports of bizarre and unsettling events from around the post-war world confirms. Although 'the country's vast and narcotic inertia' (39) is noted, news of guerrilla activity gives rise to wild rumours and exaggerated fears on the part of the Majestic's residents.

Perhaps this pervasive state of disorder, which appears to be remote and difficult to take in, while at the same time adding a palpable layer of neurasthenia to an already dense local atmosphere, immobilises the Major. Yet, though he hardly feels at home there and never succeeds in overcoming his initial sense of 'How very foreign, after all, Ireland is!' (57), he seems in thrall to the place. But there is also a personal reason for his remaining at the Majestic, namely Sarah Devlin, daughter of the Kilnalough bank manager, for whom Archer finds himself falling. Again, however, his actions are not altogether clear, so that attachment to Sarah is the private counterpart to his problematic continuation at the hotel. Owing to his nerves, and also because of the anachronistic pre-war gentlemanliness that still informs his manner, the major finds it difficult to know his own mind, to find a direction for himself or to make a decision. His confusion, partly the legacy of the war and partly the result of changed, unpredictable post-war conditions which he fails to grasp with any certainty or reassurance, makes him an emblem of the times. Indeed, Archer may be regarded as a portrait of modern historical man, caught in the flux of events that he is unable to control or understand yet which he also, quixotically perhaps, feels compelled to confront. On the one hand, he does not espouse the belief of bombastic and assertive Edward Spencer that order reflects God's purpose – without which 'our life here below would be nothing more than a random collection of desperate acts' (41). On the other hand, Archer's behaviour does not quite bear out the fatalistic view of Ryan, the local doctor, that 'people are insubstantial, they never last' (314). Sometimes, the major acts with Edward's position in mind; at other times, Ryan's outlook seems to guide him. He is forever uneasily and comically teetering between affirmation and misgiving.

In Catholic Sarah Devlin and himself, however, Archer does apparently see the possibility of a new order, a harmonious union to withstand the news of menace and disintegration. A precedent for such an outcome has been established by the marriage of Ripon Spencer to the daughter of the local mill-owner. But for the major, Sarah is something of 'a girl in the head' (to quote the title of a 1967 Farrell novel), one who proves difficult to remove, reject him as she may. Elfin, elusive, wilful, unpredictable, she seems an embodiment of the spirit of the out-of-joint times perversely at odds with his own. And perhaps she represents the foreignness that both attracts and alienates the major. It turns out that she has been having an affair with Edward. And she eventually tells Archer that he is not man enough for her and instead marries Bolton, a member of the Auxiliaries, a division of the police recruited by the major's former fellow-officers. Bolton informs Archer that the Irish are 'More like animals than human beings' (275), and according to gossip, beats Sarah. He has previously distinguished himself by eating a rose. Two other Auxiliaries try to rape the Spencer twins. One of these officers has a public school background and Archer has initially thought him to be a gentleman.

Inevitably, old enmities find a new lease of life, some arising from Edward's imperious disregard for native sensibilities, to which he adds by shooting a local IRA man. The major almost loses his life in a most unpleasant fashion, until rescued, rather implausibly, by some of the Majestic's permanent regiment of widows and spinsters. A visiting architect declares the hotel to be in fine condition – 'One might just as well expect Dublin Castle to fall down' (410). But Dublin Castle does fall, symbolically, and nothing can save the Majestic, though the latter's incineration is caused by an employee whose republican sympathies seem to owe more to paranoia than to ideological high-mindedness.

But although the terminal, the violent, the deliquescent and the delinquent are all very much part of the story *Troubles* tells, the novel is not merely a monitory treatment of either the birth of an independent Ireland or of the old order passing. The work's significance lies not only in its presentation of the narrative materials, impressive and pleasing as that is, particularly its various set-pieces. Nor does its importance solely lie in its vision of Irish history in the light of an imperial world system, or in its sense of Archer's fate being symptomatic of a radically demanding modernism, though its treatment of these considerations is of obvious cultural importance. The focus of *Troubles* is less on events themselves than on the reactions of its characters to those events. Archer's and the others' negotiations with the blind will of change, however, are less occasions of dark despair than of excruciating comedy. Staging that comedy requires considerable aesthetic resources of timing, pace, tone and style. These the novel exhibit with a consistency that counteracts, even as it discloses, its puppetry of disarray, futility and flux.

Supplementary Reading

Lavinia Greacen, *J.G. Farrell: The Making of a Writer* (London: Bloomsbury, 1999 (2nd revised ed., Cork: Cork University Press, 2012))

John Banville, 'Introduction', *Troubles* (New York: New York Review Books, 2002), pp. vii–xi

Lavinia Greacen, *J.G. Farrell in His Own Words: Selected Letters and Diaries* (Cork: Cork University Press, 2009)

Robert F. Garrett, *Trauma and History in the Irish Novel: The Return of the Dead* (New York: Palgrave Macmillan, 2011), pp. 19–36

Also Published in 1970

Christy Brown, *Down All the Days*; Brian Moore, *Fergus*; Edna O'Brien, *A Pagan Place*; Julia O'Faoláin, *Godded and Codded* (US title, *Three Lovers* (1971))

1971

Francis Stuart, *Black List, Section H*

The enfant terrible of modern Irish letters, Stuart (1902–2000) is as famous for his non-literary activities – including becoming Maud Gonne's son-in-law and broadcasting from Berlin during the Second World War – as for his writing career. Born in Australia but raised in Ireland, he is the author of over twenty novels, in addition to a number of plays and volumes of poetry. His fiction deals recurringly with the fate of an outsider persona. Among his later novels are Memorial *(1973)*, A Hole in the Head *(1977) and* The High Consistory *(1981), works dating from Stuart's re-emergence in Irish cultural life. A divisive presence, his influence is detectable among some of the young writers of the 1980s.*

One of Irish fiction's most important sub-genres is the autobiographical novel, to which *Black List, Section H* makes a significant contribution. Taking the reader from the author's early years to his complicated situation *nel mezzo del camin* in the aftermath of the Second World War, its significance at one level derives from the people and places with which Stuart associated himself. Detailing encounters and relationships with noted personages, among them W.B. Yeats, George Russell (Æ), Maud Gonne and Liam O'Flaherty, the story also revisits his participation in historical events, most notably the Irish Civil War and the Second World War, as witnessed from Berlin. Marriage at eighteen to Iseult Gonne makes him susceptible to 'the magic of Yeats's shadowy world' (18) and he also reports much that is unflattering about the great poet, to whom he seems to set himself in opposition. Equally, his resistance to the antipathy of Iseult's mother towards him produces a sharp-etched portrait of her and a criticism of 'her easy assumption on the absolute rightness and moral purity of the nationalist cause' (21). Although Stuart counts among his early heroes the men of 1916, he also honours the Russian poets Esenin and Mayakovsky, less on account of their artistic attainments, with which he admits he was not familiar, than because they were revolutionaries and, 'above all [for] having suffered calumny and derision' (21).

Judgments and recollections of these early years in Dublin are communicated in a style of unassuming forthrightness, and the same is true of the parallel account of his inner and private life. It seems a point of honour to recall that on a mission to Belgium for the purchase of arms, he also buys contraceptives, and that 'they seemed at least as important as the guns' (76). Stuart's depiction of his sexual life with Iseult is treated with similar candour, and he also records his various love affairs, the fast life he lives in London, his consuming interest in horse racing and his various forays into spirituality, which include time spent as a stretcher-bearer at Lourdes. In certain respects, this phase of Stuart's career resembles, in its restless pursuit of intensity, behaviour typical of the many First World War veterans, particularly ex-officers, who experienced considerable difficulty in finding a sense of direction in the interwar period. In Stuart's case, however – or at least in the case of his persona H (the initial of the author's first given name, Henry) – his behaviour is prompted by a sense of rebelliousness dating from his childhood, and expressed by a thorough indifference to the opinions or expectations of those around him.

This combination of dissent and intensity – which, as he notes, might have led him to Moscow – eventually brings him to Berlin. Initially accepting a 1939 invitation to make a lecture tour of the country, H goes on to spend the war in the German capital – 'the most intense five years of his life' (365). One reason for this choice is that his imagination, he believes, will benefit from the challenge and novelty of the situation. This rationale seems to be a sublimation of the political in the aesthetic, which allows H to differentiate himself from those who served the Republican cause in the Spanish Civil War. Those volunteers acted on their political beliefs, whereas for H, 'the Ebro wasn't his destiny, wasn't, that is, the place where the risk and hardship were of the kind that he needed for his imaginative growth' (247). Not that artistic expression is necessarily a value-free zone; and H's description of an SS man giving a Heil Hitler salute – 'hand extended as if releasing a dove' (257) – does not seem to be merely aesthetic in content. It may or may not be the case that 'the true purpose of fiction was the moving in on unoccupied areas by the imagination and their incorporation into small new aspects of reality' (261). But, quite apart from the essentialising nature of this claim and the militaristic echoes of its phrasing, it is not entirely clear why such an artistic manoeuvre benefits from being carried out in close proximity to territorial expansion of the historical kind. In both the style of argument and the nature of the case, there are here indications of the pursuit of the singular and the deviant which, as the novel's title indicates, typifies H's trajectory.

Acknowledgment is also made of the Berlin broadcasts, in keeping with the novel's overall confessional air, though less attention is paid to them and to contextualising them than to increasingly difficult physical conditions in the city. H ends up experiencing fully Berlin's destruction from the air and the abject human conditions that ensued, sharing the latter with Halka, one of his students. In this way, questions of ideological affiliation are deferred in favour of how H felt about his situation, the state of the Reich and the plight of its citizens: 'In the case of a German disaster . . . having thrown in his lot with the losing side would certainly turn out to be of immense value in his growth as an imaginative writer' (317). When the disaster takes place, H becomes a displaced person, a historical ratification of his unsettled spirit. Not even his own country, Ireland, is willing to repatriate him, and in the cell where the reader has a last sight of him, H only knows that he is suspended between past and future, his present reality as indeterminate as ever, open in its uncertainty and closed in its physical constraints.

Indeterminacy has been characteristic of H all the way through. Its origins lie in his extreme sensitivity to mood, nuance, atmosphere, feeling, instinct, sensation and other manifestations of pre-conscious awareness. Such mental events characterise the brief flares of reaction which occasion his youthful *gaucherie*, his impulsiveness and the intuitive intelligence he brings to his assessment of persons and events. To relate to the world by means of the signals and impressions these surges of neurological energy provide is to know one's own mind in a unique, unconditional sense. Psychological events such as these seem to obey nothing but themselves, and perhaps because of this, the conduct to which they give rise will also have a strong non-conforming dimension. H seems to be most himself when disobeying and transgressing, when offending against orthodox morality and the received idea. Not surprisingly, as a writer Stuart has little or no time for tradition (which, coincidentally, may be one of the reasons for his latter-day appeal). As a fledgling author, H 'was embarked on a private war which he hoped might cause a few cracks in the walls erected by generations of pious and patriotic Irishmen around the national consciousness' (80). The appropriateness of the term 'war' is borne out by the lengths to which he goes to demonstrate the unimpeachable quality of his own oppositional integrity.

It is not merely the primacy of the subjective elements in H's makeup – his independence, his risk-taking, his pursuit of change, his association of critique with self-dramatisation, his impenitent and even helpless dissidence – that make *Black List, Section H* a singular testament. It is also H's frank avowal of those elements, which together with the work's temporal, geographic and historical range makes this work another modern Irish epic of consciousness. And like Joyce and Beckett, Stuart also invokes European avatars – 'Baudelaire . . . Dostoevsky, Proust, or Kafka' who 'acting on ultra-responsive neurological systems, had been driven beyond the place where the old assumptions are still acceptable' (223). Such literary associations are an additional measure of this novel's ambitions. They also provide the basis for a perspective on the singular and challenging status of *Black List, Section H* as a cultural document and generic artefact in the canon of Irish modernity.

Supplementary Reading

W.J. McCormack (ed.), *A Festschrift for Francis Stuart on his Seventieth Birthday* (Dublin: Dolmen, 1972)

F.C. Molloy, 'A Life Reshaped: Francis Stuart's *Black List, Section H*', *Canadian Journal of Irish Studies*, vol. 14, no. 2 (January 1989), pp. 37–47

Geoffrey Elborn, *Francis Stuart: A Life* (Dublin: Raven Arts, 1990)

Brendan Barrington, 'Introduction', *The Wartime Broadcasts of Francis Stuart 1942–1944* (Dublin: Lilliput Press, 2000), pp. 1–60

Also Published in 1971

John Banville, *Nightspawn*; Thomas Kilroy, *The Big Chapel*; Edna O'Brien, *Zee & Co* (US title, *XY & Zee*)

1972

Jennifer Johnston, *The Captains and the Kings*

Author of fifteen novels, Jennifer Johnston (b. 1930) tends to focus on the need for, and difficulty of, reconciliation. Her minimalist scenarios, limited characters, understated language and watercolourist's touch present positions which seem to be helplessly in opposition to each other. Parents and children, husbands and wives, upper class and lower class are the conflicted parties which recur in her work, and their conflicts are often set in the context of broader social and historical frameworks – the First World War *in* How Many Miles to Babylon? (1974), *the* Northern Irish Troubles *in* Shadows on Our Skin (1977) *and* The Railway Station Man (1984). *Later works such as* The Invisible Worm (1991), Two Moons (1998) *and* Foolish Mortals (2007) *situate the opposing forces in more intimate settings. Johnston is also the author of a number of plays.*

Charles Prendergast is an old soldier who is fading away in Kill House, the County Wicklow property he has inherited from his family, though he has never felt at home there. Not that he has felt at home anywhere else, his career following service in the First World War having been essentially one of travel, though his neglect of his English wife, Claire, and their daughter, Sarah, indicates that Charles has been as unsettled emotionally as he has been geographically. Now a widower, and estranged from London-based Sarah, he passes the time drinking, playing the piano, reading, and dealing with his alcoholic gardener, Sean Brady (a rather heavy-handed portrait in shades of Caliban).

Apart from being the choir-master at the local Protestant church, Charles's interactions with the local community are reluctant to the point of being minimal. Yet, the successful reduction of his life to a series of elementary, repetitive gestures in time and space has also made Charles prey to memory. Not only is he at the mercy of involuntary recollections of soldiering and of his neglectful marriage, he is also haunted by the image of a weak father, an imperious mother and of a brother, Alexander, by far their mother's favourite, who was killed in the war that Charles not only survived but did so with medal-winning honour. From such presences, too, Charles wishes to cut himself off, though he can neither suppress nor come to terms with them. His wilful solitariness is part of a larger intention to 'have spent my life trying to avoid trouble' (66). But this way of life has resulted in a scepticism of others and the worlds they inhabit whose most obvious manifestation is a self-destructive diffidence and passivity. Loss of faith in attachment, loyalty and, particularly, love has made of Charles a hollow man, one for whom masculinity itself has proven to be corrosive. Marginal and etiolated, his personification of aftermath, together with his numerous family ghosts, the disused state of the house and its increasingly untended garden furnish this work with many of the generic elements of the Big House novel. But *The Captains and the Kings* declines to comply with generic expectations, for in Charles Prendergast's apparent end there is a potential beginning.

The new element – the fresh ingredient of change – comes in the form of Diarmid Toorish, a village youngster, son of the local grocer and nephew of a former Prendergast maid. He initially approaches Charles in search of work, his parents – in particular, his bossy mother – having despaired of making a reliable grocer of the boy. Charles does not give Diarmid a job, but instead takes to him in more complicated ways by not dissuading him from spending time in the house and on the grounds when he is supposed to be in school, and entertaining him with mugs of instant coffee laced with whiskey and piano pieces by Chopin. And even if Charles, one of the 'people of privilege' (82), does refer to Diarmid as a 'Celt' (15), such barriers of age, race and class as there are between them are transcended by their human contact. Although perhaps Charles's assumption that his use of the tribal designation can only be meant playfully is an indication of the self-absorption that Diarmid initially relieves and then confirms.

The contact is consolidated by their being on the same side regarding Diarmid's future. His parents plan to send him to Dublin to become a grocer's apprentice, a fate both he and Charles abhor. To avoid it, Diarmid runs away from home and Charles shelters him, even though he is well aware that this sojourn can be only temporary. The games of toy soldiers they play in the nursery are the escapist antithesis to the communal battles whose lines they have now, however inno- cently, drawn. Vacillating Charles's one resolve is that 'I cannot throw the boy to the wolves' (111), but that is countermanded when Diarmid's parents, accompanied by a priest and a policeman, invade Kill House in the small hours and take the boy home with them. This forceful action, and the agents of judgment who assist in carrying it out, makes the youngster feel betrayed by Charles, and in his distress he tells the police that his would-be benefactor took advantage of him sexually. 'I'll do my last bit of fighting for you' (116), Charles has already told him, but he has neither the will nor the resources to resist village attitudes. The upshot is that Diarmid is taken into the care of the Christian Brothers, and Charles is to face charges, though he does not live to have his day in court.

Charles's innocence may be consistent with the right he claims for old age to be 'No longer bound by . . . conventions' (39). But his adult life has been lived in the same spirit of subjectivity and difference. In a sense, he has remained childish, as his apparently desexualised male- ness suggests. Also indicative of Charles's dubious maturity are the parallels between himself and Diarmid. The latter is also the child of unsympathetic parents, thinks himself a misfit, misguidedly hankers after a soldier's career, and obviously believes that he is at liberty to behave in ways unapproved by the community, limited to the point of stereotype though that community is. Neither Diarmid nor Charles has much regard for tradition or for the settled life by which it is main- tained and transmitted. To Charles, Diarmid is 'A bit of an original' (133). Diarmid wonders if Charles isn't 'a little bit touched or not' (116). If they are two of a kind, however – if together they represent a compatibility that overrides both the natural barriers of age and expe- rience and the nurturing contexts of confession and class – no issue can come of it. Reconciliation of the differences between them seems conceivable only in terms of childish interludes and forms of play. The real world – the narrative as a whole is framed by two policemen closing in on Charles for questioning – is a divided place, a realm of oppositions and antagonisms. Its codes, practices and ways of understanding people are based on facile judgments derived from received ideas and from taking appearance as reality. 'To tangle with the Church, the Law and the local grocer all over the head of one small boy' is, as Charles concedes, 'Ludicrous' (125). Yet to do so is a last-ditch attempt to affirm the individuality that he has spent his life fostering and to assert that his unworldly, cultivated values, which the house enshrines, might be the spring of useful action. Besides which, 'I loved the boy' (138). That, too, should count for something, even if part of what it signifies is a restored identification with the boy in himself. But love is unthinkable. And what the Big House might stand for – an open, secular, disinterested ethos – is undermined by too little faith on its inheritor's part and an excess of bad faith in the case of those who maintain Diarmid's heritage.

A word on the title. Music is an important compositional strand in the narrative, and is an economical means of sounding its subtext of memory and desire (Charles's failure to provide adequate accompaniment to the vocally gifted Alexander's performance of Schubert's 'Der Erlkönig' strikes a number of resonant psychological notes throughout). Johnston's title, however, is that of a song from Brendan Behan's *The Hostage* which crudely, though not unwittily, satirises England's imperial style and English self-importance. This satirical intent is not shared by *The Captains and the Kings*, however. Rather, Johnston's aim seems to echo the song's undercurrent of transience and faded glory. Diarmid and Charles are not each other's hostages. They are, instead, hostages to a time which makes them both seem superfluous and to spaces whose reality consists of apparent exclusiveness.

Supplementary Reading

Seán McMahon, 'Anglo-Irish Attitudes: The Novels of Jennifer Johnston', *Éire–Ireland*, vol. 10, no. 3 (Autumn 1975), pp. 137–41

Mark Mortimer, 'The World of Jennifer Johnston: A Look at Three Novels', *The Crane Bag*, vol. 4, no. 1 (1980), pp. 88–94

Shari Benstock, 'The Masculine World of Jennifer Johnston', in Thomas F. Staley (ed.), *Twentieth-Century Women Novelists* (London: Macmillan, 1982), pp. 191–217

Jürgen Kamm, 'Jennifer Johnston', in Rüdiger Imhof (ed.), *Contemporary Irish Novelists* (Tübingen: Narr, 1990), pp. 193–206

Also Published in 1972

Aidan Higgins, *Balcony of Europe*; Brian Moore, *Catholics*; Edna O'Brien, *Night*; Paul Smith, *Annie* (reissued in 1975 as *Summer Sang in Me*)

1973

Vincent Banville, *An End to Flight*

A native of Wexford town, Banville (b. 1940) is best known as both a crime writer and an author of children's books. His work in those genres has contributed to broadening the range and conception of Irish writing. In An End to Flight, *originally published under the pseudonym Vincent Lawrence, the author draws on four years spent teaching in Nigeria during the Biafran war (1967–70). The novel was reissued in 2002 with an ending rewritten to reflect the influx of Nigerian immigrants to Ireland and the continuing story of Biafra as embodied in the execution of the writer and activist Ken Saro-Wiwa.*

The town of Ogundizzy in Biafra (the former province of eastern Nigeria) may have a school, a hospital and the Welfare Hotel, but as a domicile – a place to settle in, a community with a future – it represents one of the senses of a dead end that the novel's title connotes. At least that is how Michael Painter, an Irish teacher at the town's mission school, has come to view the place. Yet the flight which brought him there from Dublin was not merely a matter of escape. It initially contained elements of uplift and a fresh perspective which produced in Painter a certain idealism and enthusiasm for his new responsibilities. But he has not been able to sustain this outlook. In familiar expatriate style, he keeps referring to Ireland as home, and retains such Irish practices as going regularly to Mass and dining in the sweltering noon on bacon and cabbage. Positive change has led to sameness and time's attrition. To Painter, his teaching has now become 'merely a job, something to occupy the hours between eight and one, an exercise to prevent the mind from succumbing to the green deliquescent fungus' (17).

Increasingly seedy, derelict in his professional obligations, and given to drink, Painter seems in the process of turning into a facsimile of one of Graham Greene's minor colonial functionaries or some similar version of that modern citizen of the world, superfluous man, conscious to just about the point of moral inanition of his dislocated state and of his incapacity to do anything about it. He is unwilling to share the things of the spirit available from the local priest, Cork-born Father Manton. And he seems unable to act on his interest in Anne Siena, an American nurse at the local hospital. Stranded between the spiritual and physical forms of service, ritual and social structure embodied by those two fellow-expatriates, it is hardly surprising when Ben Nzekwe, an Ibo friend from Painter's Dublin days, concludes, 'I think you have really reached a point of no return' (210).

The outbreak of war between the federal Nigerian government and the secessionist Ibo people of Biafra brings predictable changes to Ogundizzy. Eventually the town is evacuated. Anne and Father Manton both leave, and Painter is more obviously on his own than ever. His decision to stay put ignores the instructions of his superior, the local bishop, and he feels unmoved by the threat of those particularly intimate forms of violence and treachery peculiar to civil war. Indeed, he sees in the hostilities an opportunity to rekindle the spirit that brought him to Nigeria in the first place. Or so he claims in one of a series of extended, complicated and lacerating conversations with Ben in which his friend rejects Painter's plea 'to travel a road that is going somewhere' (210). In the course of these exchanges, Ben not only unsparingly exposes Painter's personal weaknesses but also associates him with the generally false and parasitical European presence in Nigeria and Africa as a whole. Although Painter claims that 'I have dreamed of freedom, just as you Ibos have dreamed of it. It is my war as much as yours' (220), he is plainly incapable of experiencing the war as Ben does. There is no indication that he detects in his friend's acceptance of bloodshed as a necessary prelude to nationhood, and in his understanding of the conflict as an expression of youth and power, echoes of the ideology of Ireland's 1916 rebellion.

In a sense, the social, historical and physical reality of the Nigerian civil war can only make more painfully clear to Painter his war with himself. His occupation of a marginal position between two sides underlines his lack of role or purpose, unlike Ben, who as an Ibo believes he has a duty to become involved. Witnessing the horrors of war suffered by the civilian population confirms Painter's sense of uselessness. And his encounters with the military additionally emphasise his dissociation, as when he tells the Biafran Colonel Ozartu that victory is impossible and that the war is 'a futile gesture' (50). The Federal officer, Captain Basanji, on the other hand, is a rather more unsettling presence, his virile and triumphalist personality – 'God is on my side because I am my own god' (120) he proclaims – a palpable challenge to Painter's incapacity to be anything more than a spectator. It is Basanji who brings the violence home to Ogundizzy, and the manner of his own murder marks the culmination of an inevitable intensification in gruesome atrocities that include the killing of Painter's houseboy, Jude, and of Father Manton, who has returned to the town on an errand of mercy. Even Painter recognises that things are irremediably falling apart and that staying on is not an option. With Ben's help, he is able to catch a flight that will take him back to Dublin.

Helping Painter make what he experiences as 'a wild flight' (222) to the airfield costs Ben his life, an event that not only functions as a perhaps predictable verdict on the waste of war but which also is related to the theme of sacrifice which runs through the novel. This theme adds a metaphysical dimension to the narrative and to the plight of characters who all, in different ways, are victims not only of war but of their own limitations. Natives and strangers alike are in the wrong place at the wrong time, without any indication that there is a better place, a better time. The road leading to something that Painter says he wishes to take turns out to be the road out of Biafra, the road on which Ben dies. And the Christian connotations of the sacrificial theme are further emphasised by the titles of the novel's three parts, 'The Last Supper', 'Gethsemane' and 'Golgotha'. But the enactment of the suggested passion play subverts Christian orthodoxy. There is little that is redemptive in its scenarios, little of mercy, grace or love. A bleak existentialism, centred on problems of freedom and choice in a degraded world, sets Painter's tone.

The novel's epigraph gives the source of its title phrase as a statement by General Ojukwu, leader of the rebel troops and Biafra's first president: 'Having crossed a line, we called it home. That is what Biafra is, an end to a journey and an end to flight.' These words place Painter's journey back to Dublin in an uncomfortably ironic light. For those not included in the tribal embrace of 'we', an end to flight is also a coming down to earth, a confrontation with ways of the world that are much more undermining than they are lofty, a crisis in direction and value. The precarious standing and fragile integrity of Painter's identity when obliged to face intractable, unknowable, death-dealing conditions add some original sombre colours to the palette of the Irish novel's internationalism. As well as being welcome in themselves, these additions are all the more arresting in representing a protagonist whose Irishness proves irrelevant to the circumstances in which he finds himself.

Supplementary Reading

'Pointed Questions', Unsigned Review, *The Times Literary Supplement*, 5 May 1973
Colm Tóibín, 'Back to a Dark Biafran Drama', *The Irish Times*, 21 December 2002

Also Published in 1973

John Banville, *Birchwood*; Sam Hanna Bell, *A Man Flourishing*; John Broderick, *An Apology for Roses*; Eilís Dillon, *Across the Bitter Sea*; Jennifer Johnston, *The Gates*; Edna O'Brien, *Night*

1974

Ian Cochrane, *Gone in the Head*

Northern Ireland's so-called 'Bible Belt' stretches across mid-Antrim, and Ian Cochrane (1941–2004) is the author who has uniquely brought it to fictional life. Born in Ballymena – the 'buckle' of the Belt – and reared in the surrounding countryside, Cochrane produced six novels, four of which, including Gone in the Head, *are set in his native territory, the others being* A Streak of Madness *(1972),* Jesus on a Stick *(1975) and* F for Ferg *(1980). Two other novels –* Ladybird in a Loony Bin *(1978) and* The Slipstream *(1983) – take place among London's marginal young Irish immigrants, whose seemingly structureless, peripheral lives do not greatly differ from those of their fictional brethren in Cochrane's Northern world.*

The Boodie family has just moved from rural Heathermoy to a new house in a housing estate on the fringe of an unnamed Northern Ireland village. The estate's location is so marginal that the road leading to it is unpaved, and like a lot of these public housing developments, North and South, the place is neither in the town nor in the country. This hybrid space at first seems an appropriate dwelling-place for Cochrane's social misfits and marginal personalities, and a suitable stage for the various dislocations and lapses in consciousness indicated by the novel's title to play themselves out. But such characters and conditions are also typical of the village, and in the event, the most shocking events are those concerning some of the most obviously established members of the community.

The Boodies are Ma, Da, and two teenage boys, Frank (the

narrator), aged fourteen, and his older brother Bobby, who is sixteen. Their father has a record as a petty thief, works in the local linen mill, is given to violent outbursts and has a clutch of stolen hens illicitly housed in the back yard coal shed. Ma has a weak heart, is besotted by religion, and spontaneously administers chastisement to her two boys. Soon after moving in, she appears to suffer a heart attack, brought on in part by one of her husband's physical onslaughts. As to Frank and Bobby, their changed surroundings is so strange and intimidating that they are initially afraid to go out. And when they do venture forth, estrangement becomes the hallmark of their experiences, as life in their new world presents not only the challenges and temptations to which teenagers in general are subject but treats them as strangers and scapegoats. In general, the moral atmosphere is bewildering. The village, too, seems gone in the head. Adjustment to such a habitat requires being able to negotiate its fragmentary – or, to use the colloquialism, 'cracked' – attitudes, and to think of dislocation as relocation. 'My name is Frank and I live in Ireland. Ireland is in the world and the world is in the universe, and the universe is in the . . .' (51). This incomplete and generalised revision of Stephen Dedalus's well-known attestation of his place and station in *A Portrait of the Artist as a Young Man* is one expression of both the narrator's being out of place and his inconclusive recognition of the fact.

The youngsters' confusion and estrangement also underline the quality of Boodie family life, its casual violence and emotional impoverishment. Frank acknowledges that 'where we lived before, our name was the lowest of the low' (40). It has sometimes occurred to Frank that his mother does not want him, although if he tries to express that worry, 'she just seems to cast her mind away somewhere else' (5). He is on unhappily familiar terms with Da's violence, and receives an unmerciful beating when, in a fit of rage and panic, he dispatches the ill-gotten hens. This beating is so severe that even his parents fear for his recovery, although when Frank does come round, 'I felt sorry for [Da] because he knew all the time he had hit me hard but he didn't even want to tell himself that' (55). And Ma pleads ignorance to excuse her husband's actions. A neighbouring couple, Gwen and Harold, befriend Frank, and when he sees them kissing, he reflects that he has never seen his parents do that. The crush he develops on Gwen is typical of how unbalanced his need is, even if it seems a model of self-possession compared to brother Bobby's stalking of six-year-old Rosie Jackson.

The crude and ill-mannered Bobby, in turn, is stalked by Hessie Hill, an irreligious cripple with an over-developed sex drive. Hessie is sufficiently gone in the head for others to notice, although the neighbours are unable, and the authorities unwilling, to help her. Her dark outlook – 'No God, no devil, no pope, no Jasus . . . and no world' (72) – has its ultimate expression in her murder of Rosie. When Frank lands a job in Jack Orr's overstocked and under-patronised hardware and general store, he preposterously humiliates himself by masturbating in the local graveyard. Yet that instance of abuse seems trivial to the manner in which he is hazed by three adult garage-hands who subject him to electric shocks to force him to drink poteen. This experience – 'a joke' (101) to the perpetrators, and a mirror to his father's senseless beating – leaves Frank thinking that 'maybe I was dead' (100), a thought that often crosses his loveless mind. Eventually Harold rescues him from the three bullies, for which Frank repays him by rifling his wallet.

Frank needs the cash to run away to London with pregnant, fifteen-year-old Sarah Knocks, daughter of a fire-eating lay preacher – and, coincidentally, another devotee of physical abuse. The fact that Sarah has given Frank a second look goes to his head, and in their first and only date, the novel's blend of pathos and comedy attains a particularly high level. During it, prompted by Sarah asking if he ever felt lonely, Frank is reminded that 'I used to think that I wasn't real and that maybe I was mad' (118). The more people he meets, however, the less of a grip on their lives they appear to have. Jack Orr is a case in point. Married with two children, he is the father of Sarah's child. As bankruptcy approaches, he spends his days in the back of the store losing at poker to some local youngsters. Unable to evade any longer what he has wrought, Orr drowns himself. In a typical instance of how events in the novel reflect each other, police find Orr's body near that of Rosie Jackson. Frank disposes of the money he has taken from Harold. Bobby is cleared of suspicion of murdering Rosie. By this time, the Boodies have a television set, so perhaps their name is no longer the lowest. Nor is the village as badly off as some places not so very far away, as is suggested by footage on the television news of 'people fighting about Jasus in Belfast' (90). Whether those images are intended to foreshadow a yet more cracked and riven future remains moot. For now, there are other, local, more elementary and equally imponderable reasons for Frank's conclusion: 'Maybe it would have been better if we never had gone out in the first place' (136). It is difficult to disagree with him.

The use of repetition in *Gone in the Head*, its sense of stalemate, the unwonted air of randomness and irresponsibility which permeates the action, the devalued state of the subject, all have the immediacy and the seemingly artless absence of perspective to be seen in a primitive painting. Such features are all the more striking for pertaining to Northern Irish Protestants. This social group's pride of possession and political superiority seem not to have had the desired effect on Cochrane's demographic. Instead of a chosen people, the villagers seem a lost tribe, their wandering internalised, their way of life marked by a lack of control and a surrender to impulse, and their impaired sense of belonging even to each other a sly satire on the idea of being loyal and whether or not it begins at home.

Supplementary Reading

Unsigned review, *The Times Literary Supplement*, 18 October 1974
Maurice Leitch, 'Obituary of Ian Cochrane', *The Guardian*, 23 September 2004

Also Published in 1974

Jennifer Johnston, *How Many Miles to Babylon?*; John McGahern, *The Leavetaking*

1975

Maurice Leitch, *Stamping Ground*

The setting of Stamping Ground *is that of rural County Antrim where the author was born and grew up. Leitch (b. 1933) has published nine novels, two short-story collections and the novella* Chinese Whispers *(1987). Beginning with* The Liberty Lad *(1965), these works focus consistently on the dark side of his Northern Irish characters' inner lives, with plots that probe obsession, sexual complications and violence. Among the most notable works of an* oeuvre *that has received less than its critical due are* Silver's City *(1981), set in Belfast;* Gilchrist *(1994), about a renegade Protestant clergyman; and* The Smoke King *(1998), which deals with racism in Northern Ireland during the Second World War. Leitch's other novels are* Poor Lazarus *(1969),* Burning Bridges *(1989) and* The Eggman's Apprentice *(2001).*

The Valley is the setting of *Stamping Ground*, a location evidently close to the County Antrim towns of Ballycastle and Ballyclare. It is summertime at mid-century (the year is 1950, which the nature of the action in this novel suggests is not as distant and unexceptional as simple chronology might indicate), and the living is easy. Or so it seems for the trio of young men who are the focus of the action – Harvey Gault, the son of a local landowner, 'a Clydesdale' (3) with respect to his physical bearing, though not his temperament; Mack McFarlane, a Gault employee and snake in the grass; and Frank Glass, a university student home on holiday (and the protagonist of Leitch's first novel, *The Liberty Lad*). These three are first seen making hay while the sun shines on the Gault family farm, the Craigs, or rather taking a break after a morning working at that very job. Now their time is pretty much their own and they can sport and caper, activities that amount to typically homo-social horseplay and teasing, revealing as it sublimates an equally commonplace undertow of homo-erotic tension.

The freedom the trio affects is no more than the sort of licence to perform claimed by cowboys when they come to town – there are a number of references to Westerns. Their behaviour seems rooted less in their own natures than in certain approved codes and rituals of maleness, so that when the Gaults' seventeen-year-old servant, Hetty Quinn, appears, nothing apparently will serve the occasion but the staging of her mock-rape. Just about every exchange between the three is primed to elicit embarrassment, outrage or the threat of appearing unmanned. Frank is fully aware of this rustic ballet of verbal slap and dig, finds it puerile and potentially malevolent, but knows that the bonds of this version of male culture are such that he is not allowed to reveal that he has outgrown them. Mack manipulates the exchanges' devious, destructive pleasure. And Harvey is ignorant. Not surprisingly, their maleness receives its comeuppance as events unfold in the course of the rest of the day and into the early hours of the following day (coincidentally or not, the duration of *Stamping Ground* is roughly the same as that of *Ulysses*, eighteen hours). The culminating action is Hetty Quinn's actual rape. Not all the three young men participate in this act, but by the complicity of each of them in it the question is raised as to whether or not it is possible for any of them to shed the façade of his generic behaviour, and the somewhat tribal brotherhood it promotes, in favour of moral agency, social responsibility and independent-minded individuality. Their fraternal ties, the nature of the common identity that they continually talk each other into substantiating, their membership of a community and the status of their youth as an emblem of that community's future, is based on concealment, repression and abuse. The change to Hetty seems unlikely to affect anybody but her.

The Valley, too, appears to be hidden. Despite its apparent proximity to a couple of local towns, *Stamping Ground* is careful to avoid giving its fields and woods a specific geographical position. The nearest village is Tardree, also a mid-Antrim place-name. But the village is no more than 'just a black hole in the middle of Ireland' (177), which does not exactly pinpoint it. Another local landmark is Hollybush House, but this too is a name possessing merely picturesque associations. Both names conceal, or overlook, that distinctive referential idiosyncrasy that tends to grace what homes and homelands are called. The Valley's natural features are conveyed with a keen appreciation of nature's variety and abundance, but the name's singular, unadorned and generic aspects remain silent about them. It is as though the environment possesses the same typicality or representative standing as its three young natives. Indeed, the word valley's connotations of enclosure and limitation reflect the sense of limitation the youths' moral sense conveys. In addition, however, the name also suggests a self-contained and undisturbed area, something in the nature of settlers' providential landfall – 'every bush, every stone, every barren corner of the Valley . . . the barest remove from that other Eastern landscape' (161). A promised land, then, even if the promise is now being somewhat blighted by the land surrendering its natural bounty to building interests. And if Frank, Mack and Harvey take the Valley as their stamping ground – 'haunt, or favourite place of resort', with the intimation of freedom that definition brings with it – it will require a strong act of will on their parts to retain that sense of place in view of what has happened to Hetty.

A sense of the locale's history and tradition are provided by Hollybush House and the two elderly characters associated with it. The house is the home of Minnie Maitland, and she lives there as a sort of latter-day Miss Havisham. Daughter of a repressive father, she has been jilted by the novel's other main elderly character, Barbour Brown. Almost the only person Minnie sees regularly is Hetty, whom she employs as a part-time maid and advises as to the ways of high fashion and gracious living. Star-struck Hetty – 'She had wanted to be Hedy Lamarr' (183) – keenly identifies with these instructions' image-changing potential. During the night in question, however, Hetty shows her naive susceptibility to images, as she walks through Hollybush House – where she has sought sanctuary from a violent father – 'acting the spoiled society lady' (183), and disrobing as she goes. Precisely when she is in her natural state, and at her most vulnerable, Mack, Frank and Harvey arrive. With Barbour Brown also present, having determined on 'this night of nights' (188) to secure Minnie's hand at last, Hollybush House ends up as a perverse stamping ground.

Barbour's futile aim is consistent with other attempts of his to redeem history. He has been engaged in compiling an archival 'book of the Valley' (30), and as a younger man he had archaeological interests. He also has to cope with a reputation for eccentricity, arising out of his failure to march to the First World War with all the other sons of Ulster. One source for this book of his are the papers of a Doctor Colville, an eighteenth-century divine, the language of which gives something of the chosen-people outlook of the Valley's Protestant occupants. (Leitch can uniquely deploy biblical tonalities to make orthodoxy sound as if it is challenging itself, and his use of scripture is a notable feature of his entire output.) The good doctor, however, was prey to human weakness. His fallen nature contradicts the putative integrity of settlement, security and singularity crucial to the newcomer's identity. The individual human subject reveals that back-sliding and breakdown are as unavoidable in the historical record as the triumphalism that seeks to mask them. And Barbour, too, resides within the web of distorted human contact which evidently typifies Valley life. Earlier in the novel his voyeuristic eye had Hetty in its sights. His passivity is the submissive counterpart to Harvey Gault's animal machismo – Harvey is the one who commits the rape. Mack proves to be impotent, to which Frank's inaction is the equal and opposite. And the violated Hetty's match is Minnie Maitland's brutalised emotional history.

In the aftermath of the climactic scene at Hollybush House, the narrative point of view begins to switch from one character to another, registering their different reactions. Regardless of what anybody thinks, however, there is no denying that a crime has been committed. Frank Glass and Barbour Brown are aware of this. For the former, especially, it goes without saying, but he also knows that this is exactly how it will go. Reporting what took place is unthinkable; on the contrary, 'alibis were needed, a good watertight conspiracy was the first essential'

(202). Even Hetty realises that she will have no redress, and offsets it by the recognition that she now has power of a sort over all concerned. To take the event further would require going beyond the collusive *mores* of the Valley. By a brutal paradox, the place's integrity as a charmed protectorate depends on complicity, silence, the absence of a civic sense, and indifference to the reality of others. Whatever you do, do nothing. The scene is Northern Ireland but, as many another Irish novel shows, the challenge to value and communal purpose which *Stamping Ground* presents is by no means unique to the Valley.

Supplementary Reading

Tom Paulin, 'A Necessary Provincialism: Brian Moore, Maurice Leitch, Florence Mary McDowell', in Douglas Dunn (ed.), *Two Decades of Irish Writing* (Cheadle Hulme: Carcanet, 1975), pp. 242–56

Linda Leith, 'Subverting the Sectarian Heritage: Recent Novels of Northern Ireland', *Canadian Journal of Irish Studies*, vol. 18, no. 1 (December 1992), pp. 88–106

Richard Mills, 'Closed Places of the Spirit: Interview with Maurice Leitch', *Irish Studies Review*, vol. 6, no. 1 (April 1998), pp. 63–8

Barry Sloan, 'The Remains of Protestantism in Maurice Leitch's Fiction', in Elmer Kennedy-Andrews (ed.), *Irish Fiction since the 1960s: A Collection of Critical Essays* (Gerrards Cross: Colin Smythe, 2006), pp. 247–61

Also Published in 1975

Ian Cochrane, *Jesus on a Stick*; Brian Moore, *The Great Victorian Collection*; Julia O'Faoláin, *Woman in the Wall*

1976

Caroline Blackwood, *The Stepdaughter*

Born in London and raised on the family estate in County Down, Northern Ireland, Lady Caroline Blackwood (1931–96) was the daughter of the 4th Marquess of Dufferin and Ava. Connected to the Guinness brewing family on her mother's side, she may be better known for her husband's than for her own writing. Her first marriage was to the painter Lucian Freud; her third to the poet Robert Lowell, in whose book The Dolphin *(1973) she is a central figure. The author of a number of non-fiction works –* For All That I Found There *(1973) contains autobiographical material –* Blackwood also wrote a number of well-regarded novels: Great Granny Webster (1977), The Fate of Mary Rose (1981) and Corrigan (1984). These are marked by outrageous characters, bad behaviour, dark humour and an incisive style, characteristics also shown* *to advantage in* The Last of the Duchess (1995), *an account of the later years of Wallis Simpson, Duchess of Windsor.*

J, the narrator of this offbeat epistolary novella, has immured herself in a Manhattan high-rise apartment with her four-year-old daughter Sally Anne, her stepdaughter Renata, and a French *au pair*, Monique. A kind of valedictory offering, Monique has been sent from Paris by J's former husband, Arnold, a lawyer. He has now established himself in the French capital with a girlfriend much younger than J, who is in her mid-thirties. J can hardly stand the sight of Monique – this is one expression of her currently 'irrational behaviour' (39) – and she is not much of a mother to Sally Anne, either. And the inevitable emotional turmoil that Arnold has left in his wake is compounded by Renata's unwanted presence and anomalous status.

Now thirteen – an awkward age (the novella seems to have the Henry James novel of that title at the back of its mind) – Renata appears to have nothing to recommend her. She is overweight, friendless, taciturn, an indifferent student in school – a general nuisance and embarrassment as far as J is concerned. The child's principal sources of sustenance are both addictions, one to the cakes she bakes from ready-mix packages, and the other to the television set in her bedroom. Already feeling 'in the position of a martyr' (17) for having taken Renata in two years earlier when Arnold's deranged and alcoholic first wife could no longer maintain their Los Angeles home, J now can see the youngster only as essentially symbolising Arnold's betrayal. He has not only left J. Adding insult to injury, he has left her with Renata. And J regards everything that Arnold did leading up to his departure, primarily his purchase of the splendid apartment in which J now feels herself trapped, to have been in order to consolidate Renata's tiresome, stolid and evidently immovable presence. All J can call her own is the apartment, whose spectacular views produce 'the illusion that I have been given control of New York City' (12). She has cut herself off from her friends, and is resistant to the feminist critique the best of these would make of her apparently disenfranchised condition. A painter of some talent, J has given up on that too. Rather than being in control of anything, J finds herself in 'a little human hell' (45). The fact that she knows she is one of its principal architects does not help and is one of the reasons she keeps on composing the letters in her head that comprise her cruel, unusual and ultimately shocking narrative.

After the obviously traumatic change brought about by Arnold's desertion, J finds it difficult to contemplate further change. But eventually she overcomes her 'customary inertia' (13) and resolves to pack Renata off to her father. To begin with, however, this solution will require that unheard-of event, an actual conversation between J and the girl. Things were bad enough while J did nothing. They get worse now that she has a plan. The first surprise is that Renata has long known that Arnold has deserted J. He told her himself that he was leaving. Moreover, it turns out that Renata is not Arnold's daughter, and that he feels he was tricked into marriage by his first wife, pregnant with Renata, telling him that the child was his. But though he has told Renata that he cannot be a father to her, he has saved her from her deranged mother. 'Arnold has always been really great to me' (67) is Renata's view, and as J realises, viewing with a shock the new moral cat's cradle constructed by Renata's fresh revelations, her ex-husband has shown more foresight and disinterest concerning somebody to whom he has no obligation than he has shown to herself. The scorned-woman's rage she previously exhibited is reignited. Yet J also realises that since 'Renata was now no one's' (70), J can elect to take her in, 'and with a little luck our future together won't turn out to be all that much worse than futures usually have to be' (71).

This decision resolves matters in J's view – 'I no longer feel plagued by any options' (ibid.) – but the change of heart has come in response to Renata's own conclusion to leave the apartment. Throughout her revelations, Renata has spoken with a clarity, absence of emotion and inclination to see things in the best available light, a manner that shows the child's inner life to be very different from her unprepossessing external appearance and the affect which J, in a characteristic expression of hostility, has compared to that of a 'lobotomised misfit' (18). And the manner is also a vivid contrast to J's. Renata's decision to leave the apartment is a further expression of her unambiguous and uncritical spirit. There being no grounds for her being wanted, and because 'I felt I ought to be honest with you' (70), she believes she should leave.

And leave she does, vanishing into the city, never to be found. J now has images of the child's dreadful fate with which to torment herself. These images of dereliction and death, and the emotional voltage they generate, are in unnerving contrast to the indifference of the cop who comes to help with inquiries. What catches his attention is J's spectacular apartment. To him, Renata's fate is commonplace.

Earlier, J has reflected that 'it is unhealthy the way I spend so much time alone shut up in my beautiful apartment' (10). But the world outside is no healthier – as the cop reminds J, 'this whole city is insane' (77). And no matter where Renata is, she seems bound to be in harm's way, her history a series of alternating roles as either victim or scapegoat. Being a child, she knows in herself nothing more than simplicity. It is her lack of ambivalence, her incapacity to impute ulterior motives, her going her own foolhardy way, and her ultimate rejection of the pretence of family life offered by J that shows her in a light which the adults in their cunning and *amour propre* deny themselves. And yet the adults survive. But in view of the last line of J's final letter – 'Will only write again if I have good news' (96) – the conditions of survival hardly seem enviable.

In a way, *The Stepdaughter* can be read as a fairytale gone wrong. Indeed, J sees that her attitude towards Renata 'is much too horribly like the evil stepmother of Snow White' (13). But she typically does not take any responsibility for this view, any more than she does for her perception of Renata as 'this Humpty Dumpty of a girl' (21). And in another way, the novella's imprisonments, cruelties and letters signed with 'Yours in a state of restless anxiety' (84) and similar valedictions bring to mind some of the principal features of the gothic, all the more so since that genre's typical plotline deals with perversions of family romance. In that sense, the apartment may be seen as being in the nature of a Big House, a physical structure whose outward solidity and grand appearance harbours a lack of stability and a grappling with aftermath on the part of those who dwell within. And in keeping with the Big House genre's animating idea, *The Stepdaughter* certainly does focus on an impossible situation.

But regardless of Blackwood's play with genre, her novella depicts a broken world, in which powerlessness and marginalisation are the order of the day. Those who might be expected to be attached to each other either by ties of nature or the ethics of nurture prevent themselves from doing so. J's emotional incompetence as mother to Sally Anne replicates her reluctance to care for Renata. She and her stepdaughter, rather than finding common cause in their abandonment, are at odds because of differences in their subjective reactions to it. Arnold is essentially a fixer, which is evidently all that can be expected of 'a very clever lawyer' (31). It may be his withdrawal which has created the novella's inner world – the apartment as well as its most uncomfortable mental furniture. But it is the two women's conflicting subjectivities – passive in Renata's case, overactive in J's – that make that world a recognisable human landscape, unreliable, disunited, fallible and fallen. The problem is not merely the gap between self and other, but the intimacy with which that gap is known. In the naked emotional textures with which it represents the gap and the knowledge, *The Stepdaughter* is the verbal equivalent of a painting by Lucian Freud.

Supplementary Reading

Caroline Blackwood, *For All That I Found There* (London: Duckworth, 1973)
Robert Jones, 'The Illusion of Refuge', *Commonweal*, vol. CXIII (9 May 1986), pp. 279–82
Nancy Schoenberger, *Dangerous Muse: The Life of Lady Caroline Blackwood* (New York: Doubleday, 2001)

Also Published in 1976

John Banville, *Doctor Copernicus*; Brian Moore, *The Doctor's Wife*; William Trevor, *The Children of Dynmouth*

1977
Benedict Kiely, *Proxopera*

Benedict Kiely's first book, Counties of Contention *(1945), was a non-fiction study of partition. A long and prolific career (1919–2007) saw him produce nine novels, including* Honey Seems Bitter *(1949),* In a Harbour Green *(1950), and* The Cards of the Gambler *(1953), as well as a substantial body of work in a variety of other genres, most notably the short story. A good deal of his output presents his native Omagh, County Tyrone and the surrounding countryside as a repository of memory, romance, curious learning and popular song, a realm not untainted by social and historical realities, but by no means defined by them. The Troubles appear in his work as a threat to that vision, and at the time of* Proxopera's *publication they were at their most intense, largely owing to an increase in the targeting of civilians. The proxy bomb – also the subject of Brian Moore's* Lies of Silence *(1990) – was one method of targeting.*

This novella opens with an act of trespass. The Binchey family – ex-schoolmaster protagonist, his son Robert and Robert's wife and children – return home from a holiday in Donegal to find the protagonist's house taken over by three masked terrorists. Their plan is to hold the younger members of the family hostage as a means of coercing Binchey Senior to drive a bomb-laden car into the nearby town, where it will destroy either the courthouse, post office or the home of Judge Flynn, a pillar of the community. This attack is a 'reprisal' (348) for the murder of a local pub-owner, whose long-dead body has been recently discovered in an adjacent lake.

The house, the lake, the town, the victims – everything in the scenario is local and intimate. Binchey Senior even recognises two of the terrorists as neighbours from physical characteristics they have inherited. It is the primacy of the local which trespass violates, not only in the commandeering of Binchey's home but also in the case of the body in the lake ('That lake would never be the same again' (335)), the acts that led to the body's immersion, and the countless other acts whereby the Troubles have usurped the integrity of person and place, as well as the integrity of the relationship between them. The definitive instance of such acts is the proxy bomb, which compels the innocent private citizen to be an accomplice to trespass and destruction. Appropriation of the home is a metonym for the effects of the wider plot.

Not only does the bomb have the potential to add 'the town he was reared in' (376) to 'the world [that] is in wreckage' (378), it also has the power to shatter the protagonist's mental landscape of association, memory and tradition. The bomb will turn upside down the locale in which Binchey made his life, married, sired, taught and played, rendering null and void such activities and the spirit of such activities as they live in memory. A Latinist with a taste for Catullus, Binchey is a sensualist, deriving his marked relish for living both from the natural world around him and from the open-minded but not uncritical outlook fostered by his profession. Latin led him to the woman who would become his beloved wife, and the humanistic backdrop of their relationship is of far more consequence to Binchey than the fact that his wife is a Protestant. His desiring nature led him to his beloved white house – 'my living dream' (388), a domicile obviously in no need of change – previously the property of a Presbyterian family. All his inclinations tend towards honouring, commemorating, upholding, preserving, so that in effect his status as *un homme moyen sensuel* acts as an ideological rebuke to the evil that men do, as embodied by the three strangers in his house.

The danger that the trio represent, real enough in physical terms, is consolidated by their ignorance. Both local terrorists are ineducable former students of Binchey's, and he remembers the father of one of them toting around *Mein Kampf* as an expression of his unimpeachable anti-Britishness. 'Oil' (359), says one, is the rationale for the Troubles, while the leader claims, 'That's the way we'll bugger the Brits. Technology' (362). He is referring to the proxy bomb, which in this case is concealed inside a milk churn, a piece of modern grotesquerie illustrating yet again how the world of pastoral associations and natural nourishment is being turned upside down. Nothing is any longer sacred in the terrorists' eyes, while to Binchey pretty much everything is: 'These morons have blighted the landscape, corrupted custom, blackened memory, drawn nothing from history but hatred and poison' (369). And among the innumerable perversions which their cause is said to justify is that of Irish republicanism itself, whose self-sacrificing, voluntarist ethos is explicitly contradicted by the principle and practice of the proxy bomb. Their masks enhance the general sense of the terrorists' deformed identity and unfitting presence. Where they belong is 'cowboy country' (342), an unruly realm far from the peace and plenty of Binchey's locality (coincidentally, Robert Binchey is a farmer).

Represented in these terms, the three come across as stereotypical bad guys, their demeanour as out of place as their fight against 'an empire gone forever into the shadows' (375). They are devoid of the intimacy which connects Binchey to home and homeland, as is underlined by the leader being from Cork, at the opposite end of Ireland – although that part of the country's traditional renown as the rebel county also seems to be derided here. Representing terrorists as monsters, however, simplifies the dramatic scheme of *Proxopera*, risking a reduction of the issues to a starkly simple conflict between good and evil, innocence and malevolence, preservation and destruction. A similar polarity exists between the remoteness of what the terrorists stand for and Binchey's memory of the town as 'a lost lyrical innocent place' (361), where his own Catholic family worked in amity with other Protestant businesses, where soldiers of the English garrison mingled without much trouble with the locals, and where the pomp and circumstance of Orangeism seemed largely a matter of ritualistic novelty.

That mixed state of communal affairs stands in opposition to the singularity of the terrorists' credo and activism. The contingencies of the everyday contrast with ideological rigidity. On his bomber's mission, 'his mind running crazily on irrelevancies' (374), Binchey personifies the qualities of the contingent. His stream of consciousness conveys not only a sense of multiplicity and abundance, but also an amenability to creativity and interconnection. As a creature of consciousness, Binchey not only upholds certain unremarkable, though honourable, conventions of right thinking, he also delineates a sense of life unimpaired by sectarian narrowness. From every point of view, it is impossible for him to be a bomber. If he suffers from heart trouble, his heart nevertheless is in the right place. And if he does not emerge unscathed from his ordeal, the sense of values that he represents – loyalty, mindfulness and a Virgilian piety – is preserved intact and untarnished, as though to burnish an alternative ideal of *res publica*.

Supplementary Reading

Benedict Kiely, *Counties of Contention: A Study of the Origins and Implications of the Partition of Ireland* (Cork: Mercier Press, 1945 (2nd ed., 2004))

Thomas Flanagan, 'Introduction', *The State of Ireland* (Harmondsworth: Penguin, 1982), pp. 3–15

Michael Parker, *Northern Irish Literature 1975–2006* (Basingstoke: Palgrave Macmillan, 2007), Volume 2: *The Imprint of History*, pp. 9–16

Gerald Dawe, '"My Town": *Proxopera* and the Politics of Remembrance', *Irish University Review*, vol. 38, no. 1 (Spring/Summer, 2008), pp. 89–97

Also Published in 1977

Aidan Higgins, *Scenes from a Receding Past*; Jennifer Johnston, *Shadows on Our Skin*; Edna O'Brien, *Johnny, I Hardly Knew You* (US title, *I Hardly Knew You* (1978)); James Plunkett, *Farewell Companions*; Ronan Sheehan, *Tennis Players*; Francis Stuart, *A Hole in the Head*

1978
Patrick McGinley, *Bogmail*

In the Ireland of many of the eight novels Patrick McGinley (b. 1937) published between 1978 and 1994, things are not what they seem. Crime stalks the fields of the author's native County Donegal, where many of his works are set, most notably The Trick of the Ga Bolga *(1984), and alternative readings of such familiar themes as Anglo-Irish relations – in* Fox Prints *(1983) – and the life of siblings – in* Foggage *(1984) – are the subversive norm of McGinley's oeuvre. Esoteric vocabularies, bravura passages on matters of scientific knowledge and artistic appreciation, together with a playful treatment of point of view, are among the various other recurring features in a quirky and diverting body of work. McGinley has also published an autobiography.*

The subtitle of *Bogmail* is 'A Novel with Murder', and it begins and ends with unexpected, though not unplanned, deaths. From the outset, it is clear that the protagonist, Tim Roarty – an impotent, alcoholic publican, who is also a spoiled priest and a lover of Schumann (a number of passages on this composer's work stand out) – intends to do away with his barman, Dermot Eales. A perfect weapon in the form of poisonous mushrooms has been selected, but in a reversal typical of the novel's sense of inconclusiveness, this approach fails and, instead, Eales is accidentally dispatched by a blow to the head from a volume of Roarty's prize possession, the 1911 edition of the *Encyclopaedia Britannica*. Death by knowledge: readers may hear in that an echo of Flann O'Brien's *The Third Policeman*. The presence of an officer of the law, McGing, amplifies the echo. He does not have a clue, which enables *Bogmail* to satirise the police procedural and the notions of cause and effect on which that genre relies.

With as little trouble as he had in killing Eales, Roarty buries his body in a nearby bog, but it is with the completion of the apparently perfect crime that Roarty's troubles begin. The nature of these troubles are signalled in the novel's title. Roarty begins receiving telling messages from a blackmailer who signs himself 'Bogmail', messages which increase in the daring of the sender's demands. Roarty's existence is reduced to attempts to remain immune from the blackmailer's threats, resulting in his increasing obsessiveness and paranoia, a victim of self-generated change. Murder, not surprisingly, proves a burden rather than a release, a conclusion underlined by the resemblance between Eales's death and the novel's second murder. Roarty's realisation that 'in destroying Eales he had destroyed himself' (168) is difficult to dispute. The idea of passing a final, irretractable judgment, of solving matters at a stroke, particularly by the single stroke of a violent act, is shown to be a reductive fallacy. This conclusion, and Roarty's realisation, may be thought to have particular relevance to the violence of 1970s' Ireland. But *Bogmail*, despite a pleasurable and attentive delineation of all aspects of the Donegal setting, has more than local ambitions and its intentions seem more in keeping with philosophical gamesmanship than with providing moral or ideological lessons, which themselves risk being reductive.

The nature of these ambitions is represented by the novel's other main character, Kenneth Potter, an English engineer who has come to the area to prospect for barytes. He becomes a regular at Roarty's pub, and is also conducting an affair with Nora Hession, housekeeper to a local priest, Canon Loftus, whose arrogance Potter desires to deflate. To that end, he organises a committee to protest against the canon's new church and the replacement of the old church's wooden altar, which dates from 1847. The canon retaliates, resulting in Potter's dismissal by his employer, Pluto Explorations. Unlike Roarty, Potter seems immune to plot, and his genial outgoing presence is an obvious contrast to the publican's. Here again, however, McGinley intends the superficial differences between the two to alert the reader to a greater range of contrast. Potter, the miner, is an empiricist. His impregnation of Nora Hession expresses one aspect of his naturalness, while his country rambles show his sympathy and interest in the natural world around him. In conversation with Roarty, Potter is a mine, as it were, of curious and intriguing lore. His seemingly infinite variety, in short, is the very opposite of Roarty's obsessive personality, so that it makes thematic sense for the publican to suspect that the Englishman is Bogmail, even though the suspicion is implausible from a temperamental point of view. And, as events in the form of a sub-plot concerning the age-old rural vice of coveting land eventually reveal, Roarty's suspicions are misplaced.

The world of *Bogmail* represents a dialectic between a wide range of opposites: the singular and the various, the stranger and the native, the life-taker and the nature-lover, the prospector for whom Pluto represents a merely earth-filled and potentially rewarding underworld, and a spoiled priest who unwittingly plumbs the darkness of his own mind. Although the novel is undoubtedly a plausible and persuasive story of violence and fixation in remote rural Ireland, it is also a peg upon which is hung, with equal plausibility and persuasiveness, thoughts pertaining to identity, time, reason and death. Just as Roarty and Potter are coexisting contrasts, so are the novel's physical and metaphysical levels. And these levels, just like the characters, inhere in one another while simultaneously retaining their separate and contrary realities. Similarly, *Bogmail* seems to invite generic classification as a crime story while in the event going out of its way to resist it: as Potter remarks, such stories 'lacked the imponderable ingredient that makes fiction truer than fact' (219). Indeed, the novel resists all types of rigidity, even to the point of both having a plot and for long periods effectively talking itself out of having one – shades of Sterne and shaggy dogs.

The native aims for mastery, and draws on his forensic skills and analytical intelligence (fortified by deep readings in his encyclopaedia) to attain it. The outsider seems glad to accept whatever is available, whether Nora or the countryside. Neither dominates. Potter, embodiment of indeterminacy that he is, becomes more uncertain in ending up unemployed, in love and with nothing much to do but to kill time. Roarty, on the other hand, comes to a more definitive end as a cancer victim. The exponent of the terminal concludes that his fatal disease is a metaphor for his own corruption, seeing his illness as having 'eaten away the fruit until he was left with the poisonous core' (247). While this is a judgment Roarty passes on himself, it is clear that the narrowness and malevolence he represents is being rejected in favour of a more open disposition. And though *Bogmail* is a more rewarding read for the method and manner of its intellectual schema, its treatment of openness and repression has additional interest in the larger context of the contemporary Irish novel. Besides, idiosyncratic though *Bogmail* may be, there is nothing to object to in a novel of ideas by an Irish writer, rare though this is.

Supplementary Reading

Rüdiger Imhof, 'Patrick McGinley', in Rüdiger Imhof (ed.), *Contemporary Irish Novelists* (Tübingen: Narr, 1990), pp. 193–206

Thomas F. Shea, 'More Matter with More Art: Typescript Emendations in Patrick McGinley's *Bogmail*', *Canadian Journal of Irish Studies*, vol. 23, no. 2 (December 1997), pp. 23–37

John Goodby and Jo Furber. '"A Shocking Libel on the People of Donegal"? The Novels of Patrick McGinley', in Elmer Kennedy-Andrews (ed.), *The Irish Novel since the 1960s: A Collection of Critical Essays* (Gerrards Cross: Colin Smythe, 2006), pp. 189–214

Patrick McGinley, *That Unearthly Valley* (Dublin: New Island Books, 2011)

Also Published in 1978

Bruce Arnold, *A Singer at the Wedding*; Ian Cochrane, *Ladybird in a Loony Bin*; Eilís Dillon, *Blood Relations*; Mary Manning, *The Last Chronicle of Ballyfungus*; Alf MacLochlainn, *Out of Focus*; Breandán Ó hEithir, *Lead Us Into Temptation*

1979
John McGahern, *The Pornographer*

The author of six very influential novels, McGahern (1934–2006) was born near Ballinamore, County Leitrim, an area of the country to which his work retains a crucial fidelity. His output is noted for its candidly autobiographical basis, beginning with The Barracks *(1963), and including the controversial* The Dark *(1965). Other novels are* The Leavetaking *(1975; revised edition, 1984) and his most celebrated work,* Amongst Women *(1990). A final novel,* That They May Face the Rising Sun *(US title,* Beside the Lake*) appeared in 2002. A noted short-story writer, McGahern also produced an important* Memoir *(2005; US title,* All Will Be Well*). Generally regarded as the most significant Irish novelist of his generation, McGahern's impact on Irish writing and on Irish readers is similar to, if not greater than, Patrick Kavanagh's on modern Irish poetry.*

There are two sides to *The Pornographer*. One deals with an affair the thirty-year-old eponymous but otherwise unnamed narrator has with Josephine, who is some years his senior and whom he eventually impregnates. The other has to do with his Aunt Mary, hospitalised in Dublin with terminal cancer, whom he treats with a concern and tenderness not evident in his relationship with Josephine.

The affair reaches a crisis when it becomes clear that the narrator refuses to react conventionally to the prospect of becoming a father. Josephine has been his sexual partner; but as he tells her, with typical forthrightness, after their first night together, 'Love has nothing to do with it' (42). And he also rejects with remarkable consistency not only Josephine's anticipation of home and family but her assumption that all will be well because they both are 'good people' (106). In such formulaic roles and outcomes, the narrator can see only a prefabricated existence, devoid of the sense of in-dwelling and genuine rootedness whose lack in his way of life he keenly feels. To establish a home with Josephine and to identify with the settlement and security such a structure connotes would be to cede to sexual activity a decisive influence quite at odds with its inherently contingent and instinctual character. Neither blind biological chance nor the transitory pleasure of love-making are, in the narrator's eyes, a sufficient foundation to authenticate a full sense of self. Merely repeating the sensual moment conceives relationships that are ultimately no more than skin deep.

And power to abort the biological outcome – which, in keeping with the novel's generally unsparing interrogation of choice and change is an option temporarily entertained by the parents-to-be – is a dead end.

Eros is no mentor for the narrator, then. But from Thanatos he has much to learn. And it is in his attachment to his dying aunt that he finds a path towards the kind of life he wishes to live. The 'narrow and strong lives' (10) of Aunt Mary and her brother embody a sense of material adequacy, a feeling of belonging, an unself-consciousness and air of pragmatic command. They seem at home in the world. The fact that the narrator's aunt and uncle reared him after the early deaths of his parents obviously adds to his attraction to the self-reliant, yeoman-like quality of their way of life. It is not surprising to find that he must 'go inland' (203), not so much to take up down-to-earth ways as to imbibe their spirit in the hope of finding in them a meaning for himself.

This decision to return – to make a pilgrimage, in a sense – is obviously an important plot development, but it also contains some significant thematic and cultural resonances. The most prominent of these is the value attributed to rural life. McGahern's *oeuvre* contains a good deal of evidence for his very mixed feelings about the city, and rejection of the city is central to the narrator's attaining a fuller sense of himself. Dublin is the place where he writes pornography, and where his facile editor, Maloney, performs the provocative though rather predictable role of city wit. Maloney is a character, in the local sense of the term, and in his company the narrator can again be seen resisting both a performance and its connotations of the denatured and inauthentic. And when Josephine goes to London to have her baby, the narrator finds himself even more out of tune with life there, and, as though to prove it, is eventually beaten up by Josephine's landlord, an Irish immigrant. Rural life, on the contrary, is more natural in every sense of the word, possesses a more regular tempo, is free of the urban scene's novelties and distractions and less subject to erratic change. The narrator meets Josephine, and her successor, at dances at the Metropole, which is not only a well-known Dublin venue from years gone by but a symbol of the chance encounter, the artificial atmosphere and the syncopated rhythms of the city. In contrast to such mannered falseness is the dignity with which Aunt Mary bears her illness, her essential nature unchanged by either her condition or the hospital's regime. And the narrator honours his uncle with the testimonial 'In him all was one' (15) – a tribute which, in part, reflects McGahern's interest in a Tolstoyan ethos of the organic.

The novel does not use pornography in a metaphorical sense, nor is it a generic term to cover all that is not racy of the soil. Samples provided of the narrator's depiction of his insatiable couple, Colonel Grimshaw and Mavis Carmichael, confirm not only the mechanical character of the writing but the tedium and predictability of the callisthenics on show. His admission that the stuff is 'heartless and it's mindless and it's a lie' (109) is all too amply confirmed. Sterility and artificiality suggest themselves as glosses on this admission. But it is not his writing that challenges the narrator's moral sense; it is Aunt Mary's death. To a sceptic of his calibre, there is something pornographic in the heartlessness and mindlessness of her passing. To find faith in the face of his aunt's enactment of the body's fate is no small undertaking. The narrator recognises his own instinct to affirm, but how to harness that so it becomes a source of meaningful being and valuable action remains problematic. As a friend of his remarks, 'If you can tell where instinct ends and consciousness begins you'll make all our fortunes' (113).

Consciousness begins in the possibility of change and the location in the rural environment of how tradition dovetails with personal history. With its attributes of intentionality, self-possession and determination, consciousness is what the narrator comes to embody. His individuality is validated by his arrival at a point where self and world have a chance of being one. To show that his inland discovery is neither egotistical nor solipsistic, the narrator is aided in his quest by one of Aunt Mary's nurses, who not only replaces Josephine as a physical partner but exemplifies, by the manner in which she inhabits 'her only life' (209), the virtues of energy, engagement and service. This girl is from the country, and her signature in the narrator's mind is 'healthy' (ibid.). Her profession indexes moral well-being for him (by contrast, Josephine is a bank official). Moreover, it is from the nurse that he learns a critical lesson about paying attention, and comes to see his not having done so to be a cardinal offence against his own better nature: 'I had not attended properly. I had found the energy to choose too painful' (251). By choosing, he changes. And the change is a change of heart, leading to a renewal of spirit, a capacity to praise, and a strength to face down 'the larger anxiety of the darkness' (238), all the more necessary and impressive when self-awareness compels that darkness's constant presence.

The possibility of such spiritual reintegration is also borne out by Aunt Mary's funeral, whose ritualistic and communal elements override in significance its religious dimension. In examining how 'The superstitious, the poetic, the religious are all made safe within the social, given a tangible form' (238), McGahern retrieves terms like 'soul' and 'spirit' from their familiar, jaded, Catholic usage, and in doing so points to an Ireland becoming increasingly post-Catholic. And although in its tense, rather tendentious style, in the depths of its narrator's existential emptiness, and the somewhat schematic quality of the narrator's conflict, *The Pornographer* is probably McGahern's least popular novel, it is not only an important work in his development. It also confronts with an intensity not often matched in the contemporary Irish novel difficult questions of being and becoming, as well as asserting that an enlightened citizenry is one that finds ways of taking those questions with the utmost seriousness.

Supplementary Reading

Denis Sampson, *Outstaring Nature's Eye: The Fiction of John McGahern* (Washington DC: Catholic University of America Press, 1993), pp. 137–61

Éamon Maher, *John McGahern: From the Local to the Universal* (Dublin: Liffey Press, 2003)

Stanley van der Ziel (ed.), *John McGahern. Love of the World: Essays* (London: Faber, 2009)

Denis Sampson, *Young John McGahern* (Oxford: Oxford University Press, 2012)

Also Published in 1979

John Broderick, *London Irish*; Anthony Cronin, *Identity Papers*; Jennifer Johnston, *The Old Jest*; Brian Moore, *The Mangan Inheritance*; Seán O'Faoláin, *And Again?*

1980

Julia O'Faoláin, *No Country for Young Men*

Julia O'Faoláin (b. 1932), daughter of the writers Seán and Eileen O'Faoláin, was born in London. Her career has produced novels of two different kinds. There are her historical works such as Woman in the Wall *(1975), dealing with medieval women and sainthood;* The Judas Cloth *(1992), set in the Rome of Pius IX; and* Adam Gould *(2009), whose subject in part is psychology's early days. In contrast are novels with present-day settings focusing on women's domestic and sexual experiences –* Godded and Codded *(1970; US title* Three Lovers

(1971)); The Obedient Wife (1982) and The Irish Signorina (1984). O'Faoláin has also written several collections of short stories which, like her novels, cast a stylishly satirical eye on her characters' illusions and deceptions. Her non-fiction includes an important volume of documents relating to women's history, co-edited with her husband, Lauro Martines.

In general, Julia O'Faoláin's novels have not been particularly wedded to Irish national themes or interests. On the contrary, she may be one of her generation's most cosmopolitan writers. Her work exhibits the flair and sophistication cosmopolitanism connotes, as well as a fascination with the power and pretensions of the European *haute bourgeoisie*. Judging by *No Country for Young Men*, these qualities alone seem insufficient to deal with the matter of Ireland, and to them is added an elaborate narrative that draws both on the foundation of the state and on its present-day legacy. The two-pronged approach has the effect of treating a storyline relying on historical information in an artistic spirit that borders on the *buffo*. The storyline shows O'Faoláin's close acquaintance with Ireland past and present, while her aesthetic approach – style, tone, point of view – suggests a desire or need that her characters and their largely repellent antics and outlooks are kept at a distance. The general intent – as is suggested by the novel's title substituting 'young' for 'old' in the well-known opening line from Yeats's 'Sailing to Byzantium' – is subversive. And in a plot that proliferates diffusely, subversion is a key element, together with betrayal, concealment and unmasking.

As a result, when all has been said and done, it is not easy to know if this is a country for men of any age, young, old or middling. None of the male characters emerges from the goings on with much honour. But then they didn't have very much to begin with. Instead, what they have is power. There is the political power exerted by Owen Roe O'Malley, who uses his government position to undermine the government. He also happens to be fond of riding horses – one resonant instance of the novel's presentation of modern Dublin as the haunt of the *parvenu* and 'the green-room of Europe' (66). And the outlook of the O'Tooles, an American-based pair of nationalists, expresses the murderous power of ideological purity. In a story that can seem to be excessively internecine – though this too is consistent with the author's view of the asphyxiating smallness of the Irish scene – the power of family connections also drives the schemes of manipulation and deception which distinguish the characters' treatment of all around them, especially their nearest and dearest.

The manner in which these manifestations of power have their way is focused in the adventures of James Duffy. A native of California, he has been sent to Ireland by the rabidly republican O'Tooles to make a pro-IRA documentary for Banned Aid, an American fundraising organisation. Duffy is in many respects a painful case, and has taken the O'Toole assignment in the naive hope that the old country will prove a site of rehabilitation where he can restore his flagging professional fortunes, failing marriage and self-respect. While James himself says 'This country is between worlds' (233), O'Faoláin's portrait of the Irish-American as an innocent abroad in the land of his fathers is a representative instance of the kinds of ironic reversal on which the narrative thrives. But although O'Faoláin is clearly having fun, she is not entirely indulging in diverting narrative acrobatics for their own sake. So, while Duffy is a plaything – a patsy – he's nothing like the repellent and amoral O'Malley family retainer named Patsy, a creature who is no joke, as Duffy discovers to his cost. This discovery comes when, in the course of researching his documentary, Duffy becomes the unwitting means of unveiling a long-repressed family secret. The family attained its current prominence in public life on the strength of its own past republican credentials. Suddenly, a certain notorious detail from that past poses the distinct danger of upsetting all that the family seems to represent.

The detail concerns the fate of a young American, Sparky Driscoll, who had been deputised by Irish-American interests to monitor the course of military and political events in the Ireland of 1922, with particular attention to the role of the O'Malley family. Driscoll's mission is a prototype of Duffy's. And the idea of history repeating itself is reinforced as the narrative switches back and forth between modern Ireland and the country of a previous generation. If events seem to be repeated as farce the second time around, it does not mean that their outcome is now likely to prove less lethal, nor has their life-denying power been diminished. How Sparky ended up is a preview of what happens to Duffy. In neither case, however, is their fate the result of a rift in Irish-American relations, if relations is the word to describe exchanges between two peoples separated by a common ideology. Instead, they both fall victim to a power more deep-seated and irresistible than any political or ideological weapon – the power of passion.

By adding a narrative of sexual politics to those of nationalist ambition and political double-dealing, O'Faoláin supplies her culminating subversive touch. This extra narrative layer is at the heart of the story not only because the O'Malley family secret concerns sexuality and passion. In addition, by introducing it, an unfamiliar, even scandalous, agency is given to women as makers (and potentially unmakers) of the ostensibly unwavering principles and steadfast flag-saluting by which the family's fortunes have been secured. This agency and the alternative family history deriving from it can create an impact sufficient to undermine prevailing hierarchies. Both in 1922 and fifty years later, suppression of the woman's side of things is of the utmost importance. Let us by all means reflect that this indeed is no country for young men, as we glumly observe Owen Roe recruit his fourteen-year-old nephew, Cormac, to the cause of contemporary militant republicanism. But the question of what kind of country it is for young women does not arise. And the portrait of Cormac's mother, Gráinne, shows the country to be problematic for women of any age.

Michael O'Malley, an alcoholic shadow occupying a sinecure, is Cormac's father. He is clearly unable to be the husband Gráinne needs, and the result of her dissatisfaction with her family circle as well as with herself is to have an affair with James Duffy. In their illicit loving, this couple replicates the relationship between Kathleen O'Malley (née Clancy) and Sparky Driscoll. In the eyes of her sister, Judith, Kathleen's romantic adventure was morally offensive and politically threatening. Sparky was thought to be as untrustworthy in the one concern as in the other, and Judith violently dispatches the American. Judith's reward for her supposedly honour-preserving act was to be silenced and neutered. Placed in a convent, she is removed from public access and also has her womanhood – or at least her sexuality – made redundant. The family makes it known that Sparky was killed by the British: another martyr for old Ireland. Gráinne is no Kathleen. She is far more daring and resourceful, far more in touch with her emotional nature and with her desire to change her currently sterile situation. But none of these qualities matters. In another ironic reversal, Gráinne's story comes to effectively the same conclusion as Judith's. She, too, is subjected to a combination of political self-interest and sexual repression.

Sexuality's empowerment of the individual, its bearing on such matters as emotional maturity and the need for intimacy, as well as its relevance to mental health – which, with regard to Judith's aversion to it, is apropos – is as inadmissible a dimension of being in the world of modern Ireland as it was fifty years earlier. Nothing has changed; as

Gráinne tells James, 'In other countries people sometimes come to grips with something new. Here the old bogey returns' (208). The patterns of response have been established, and woman – always a generic entity in the minds of the novel's Irish males – has to respond in the approved manner. The sense that there is something archetypal about the place of women is suggested by the echoes in the affair of O'Faoláin's modern lovers of the legend of Diarmaid and Gráinne, another powerful illustration of sexual self-determination oppressed by political considerations. And the archetypal note resonates with a certain mocking irony in the female characters' names – Kathleen and Gráinne being among the soubriquets of the feminised nation (and the latter's full name is Gránuaile). Even Judith's name may be an ironic invocation of her biblical namesake, who slew Holofernes in the name of liberation.

'Myths unify' (320), Larry O'Toole tells James Duffy. But, if the history of the O'Malley family is anything to go by, unity is imprisoning and destructive, a claustrophobic romance of sameness. The method, manner and themes of No Country for Young Men individually and collectively are committed to subverting complacent and preordained forms of unity. Gráinne's husband Michael tells her that 'Our grandparents were chameleons on tartan . . . . You and I, the chameleon grandchildren, didn't know how to react and keep our individuality' (327). There are times when No Country for Young Men seems determined to have the last word on the sorry state of late twentieth-century Ireland and its people, with results that sometimes make O'Faoláin's impatient and derisive critique forced and uneven. As a revised reading of the young Judith's vision of the nascent republic as 'a country run by young men' (213), however, this novel, in intent and execution, exemplifies the kind of modernising cultural gesture its characters shirk.

Supplementary Reading

Seán O'Faoláin, 'No Country for Old Men', in I Remember! I Remember! (Boston: Little, Brown, 1961), pp. 213–40

Ann Owens Weekes, 'Diarmuid and Gráinne Again: Julia O'Faoláin's No Country for Old Men [sic]', Éire-Ireland, vol. 21, no. 1 (Spring 1986), pp. 89–102

Rüdiger Imhof, 'Julia O'Faoláin', in Rüdiger Imhof (ed.), Contemporary Irish Novelists (Tübingen: Narr, 1990), pp. 159–73

Robert F. Garrett, Trauma and History in the Irish Novel: The Return of the Dead (New York: Palgrave Macmillan, 2011), pp. 37–49

Also Published in 1980

Mary Beckett, *A Belfast Woman*; Samuel Beckett, *Company*; Desmond Hogan, *The Leaves on Grey*; Neil Jordan, *The Past*; Bernard MacLaverty, *Lamb*; William Trevor, *Other People's Worlds*

1981

John Banville, *Kepler*

Banville (b. 1945) is a native of Wexford town and is the author of a book of short stories, a number of plays and fourteen novels. Early works are Nightspawn *(1971), set in Greece on the eve of the 1967 Colonels' coup, and* Birchwood *(1973), a take on the Big House novel. His noted science tetralogy – including* Doctor Copernicus *(1976),* The Newton Letter: An Interlude *(1982) and* Mefisto *(1986) – was followed by an art trilogy consisting of* The Book of Evidence *(1989),* Ghosts *(1993) and* Athena *(1995). Other works include* The Untouchable *(1997),* Eclipse *(2000),* Shroud *(2002),* The Sea *(2005) and* The Infinities *(2009). All these works are distinguished by their stylistic accomplishments, the effect of which is less to ornament than to counteract the characters' general sense of superfluity and philosophical disquiet. These features also hold good of the crime novels Banville has published under the pseudonym of Benjamin Black –* Christine Falls *(2006),* The Silver Swan *(2007),* The Lemur *(2008),* Elegy for April *(2010) and* A Death in Summer *(2011).*

The Holy Roman Empire is entering its last days. The build-up to the Thirty Years War is well advanced. Religious sectarianism is rapidly becoming more pronounced and more vindictive. Employment prospects for Johannes Kepler, mathematician and astronomer, are not promising, unless he is willing to confine his work to casting the horoscopes of his world's star-crossed leaders. His marriage is a misalliance, his health is not good, and too much of his time has to be spent wandering from Graz to Linz and from Prague to Regensburg, through the riven heart of *mitteleuropa*. And yet, none of this deters him from producing his ground-breaking studies in cosmology, among which are three laws laying out a new theory of the coherence of the cosmos. It is appropriate that the reader first encounters Kepler as he emerges from a dream, given the significance of vision, in various senses, in his work. His coming to his senses coincides with his arrival at the household of Tycho Brahe, the greatest astronomer of the day and court mathematician to the Emperor. The household is in a state of disorder that is characteristic of nearly all of Kepler's domestic and working conditions. And his experiences here in the castle of Benatek are typical of his difficulties in opting for the only source of employment open to him, which is that of court functionary. When he succeeds Tycho Brahe as court mathematician, he is treated no differently by the Emperor Rudolph than he was at Tycho's castle, and his reaction to such treatment is the same. He can do no other, it seems, than think for himself. This stance is evident in his continuing adherence to Protestantism, even though it is socially stigmatising and although he holds no brief for it or for any other Christian dispensation.

The greatest testament to his independence of mind is obviously his scientific thought, if thought is the best term for the manner in which Kepler grasps the first glimpses of his theoretical breakthroughs. A better term might be revelation. The most banal and unexpected occasions – a night's carousing, in one memorable instance – can be accompanied by moments of insight, epiphany and inspiration. Kepler thinks of them as angelic annunciations, a view whose implications are sympathetically broached by the novel's epigraph – 'Preise dem Engel die Welt . . .' ('Praise the world to the angel', from Rilke's ninth Duino Elegy). The point, however, is not just the way Kepler describes these imaginative brainstorms to himself; it is the fact that he goes on to take responsibility for having experienced them. Feeling the touch of an angel's wing has an obvious element of the metaphorical and fictitious about it. But Kepler is determined to subject what he has intuitively perceived to the rigours of proof, as though driven to demonstrate that he is a worthy recipient of his inspiration. And he has the ideal idiom of proof to hand in mathematics. By means of that science's imperturbable objectivity, Kepler imparts consistency and integrity to what his imagination has envisioned. He concludes that the universe exemplifies order and harmony. It might be noted that these qualities are also fundamental to conceptions of beauty and truth, making it appropriate that Kepler's creation is called 'a perfected work of art' (180).

To honour that art, *Kepler* is divided into five parts, each named after one of the astronomer's major publications. As the novel goes on, however, the world in which those treatises were written becomes an increasingly obtrusive presence. The more comprehensive Kepler's conception of the cosmos becomes, and the more refined his claims for its ultimately musical concord, the more inevitably the empire lurches towards disintegration. By speaking his mind, he incurs isolation. He must defend his findings from attacks by former colleagues and teachers as well as hold his own in the face of Galileo's discoveries and the Italian's less than collegial disposition. The politics of notoriety are as fraught as any other kind, and the correspondence by which the story of Kepler's reputation and the challenge to maintain it is told is explicitly lacking in the order and elegance which the astronomer brought to the largely inhospitable scientific community. And, as ever, such is Kepler's dependence on patronage that he also finds it impossible to keep clear of military and political developments. He even accepts the position of astrological adviser to Wallenstein, commander of the imperial forces, which obliges him to inhabit a *milieu* whose uncertainties and erratic movements are also at odds with his pursuit of cosmic harmony.

On the personal front, his wife and children die. And though he remarries happily, estrangement from his beloved stepdaughter, Regina, is a source of further pain. Seeing to his mother's defence against charges of witchcraft, extracting overdue salary from the imperial exchequer, finding printers and paper so as to have his books published – the misfortunes and distractions mount up. Kepler proves equal to them all. The effect of these human travails is to accentuate the capacities for persistence, tenacity, fidelity and engagement which Kepler has already exemplified in pursuit of his vision. As what he endures takes its toll, it also increases his stature. The novel ends on a resonant note of indomitability, ratified by Kepler's own self-awareness. This acknowledgment of will and focus, twin driving forces of a nature that he admits to being passionate, is less a tribute to Kepler's intellectual attainments – much less his training or cultural formation – than to his personal uniqueness. Interestingly, he has found an image of his individuality in Dürer's engraving 'Knight with Death and the Devil', describing it as possessing 'a stoic grandeur & fortitude from which I derive much solace; for this is how one must live, facing into the future, indifferent to terrors and yet undeceived by foolish hopes' (131). Not the least significant of Kepler's legacies is his own consciousness, the vehicle of his knight errantry among the stars, which is all the more winning for the quixotic tinge discernible in its repeated trials, errors and misperceptions. As well as being reminders of human fallibility, however, these failings may also be seen as essential ingredients of those imaginative fictions which proved to be Kepler's pathways to the truth.

In view of his accomplishments, it is a little strange to find Kepler thinking of himself as 'a simple, private man' (147). But this description seems to be consistent with the various counter-positions on which the novel rests. The music of the spheres mutes war's cacophony. If there have to be revolutions, let them be the kind that enhance our understanding of coherence instead of threatening it. If history is a nightmare, as this novel's account of it attests, the dream of an alternative realm is a rebuke to brute force. The possibility of illumination and enlightenment is an act of imaginative faith on Kepler's part, and his endeavours constitute a portrait of the artistic spirit he possesses. Privacy denotes withdrawal from the sphere of action and affairs which the affirmation of other options and different perspectives requires. Driven and put upon as he appears, Kepler may seem to be a man without choices. But every astronomical calculation he wrote down is in effect a choice. And it is also a statement of intent to abide by whatever changes so choosing entails. This degree of intent, this investment of self in the making of meaning, has a moving, exemplary force. And while *Kepler* was being written, the thirty-year sectarian war in Northern Ireland was taking its course – a nightmare which imaginative faith and seeing things in a new light undoubtedly have a role in dispelling.

Supplementary Reading

Arthur Koestler, *The Sleepwalkers: A History of Man's Changing Vision of the Universe* (London: Hutchinson, 1959), pp. 227–427
Liam Heaney, 'Science in Literature: John Banville's Extended Narrative', *Studies*, vol. 85, no. 340 (Winter 1996), pp. 362–9
Derek Hand, *John Banville: Exploring Fictions* (Dublin: Liffey Press, 2002), pp. 94–114
John Kenny, *John Banville* (Dublin: Irish Academic Press, 2009)

Also Published in 1981

Bruce Arnold, *The Muted Swan*; Jennifer Johnston, *The Christmas Tree*; Molly Keane, *Good Behaviour*; Maurice Leitch, *Silver's City*; Brian Moore, *The Temptation of Eileen Hughes*

1982
Dorothy Nelson, *In Night's City*

A native of Bray, County Wicklow, Nelson (b. 1948) is the author of two novels. The second, Tar and Feathers *(1987) is something of a sequel to* In Night's City, *and has a wider social context.*

There is a point in the childhood of Sara Kavanagh, the protagonist of *In Night's City*, where she says, 'What I really wanted was to pretend I wasn't real' (30). But, though we are taken into the deep recesses of Sara's consciousness, and even though the novel's last words are delivered by her *alter ego*, Maggie, there is no use pretending. Sara cannot escape her family. And her failure is not a matter of incapacity or lack of resources. It inheres in the nature of the family itself, and like all the other family members, Sara cannot detach herself from its core of sexuality and violence. She is not exactly – or consistently – complicit in the release of these elemental forces. But she makes no claim to innocence. The novel seems as little interested in moral judgment as it is in prurience. It is the experience that is the point. Sara's story is told from inside the structure she inhabits (the action is for the most part housebound), and part of the originality of *In Night's City* is the manner in which it draws on the modernist device of being, rather than being about, its subject.

The story, highlighting selected moments between 1958 and 1970, is episodic and fragmentary. The death of the father is a framework enclosing earlier phases of the family's history, with a particular focus on crucial periods in Sara's development. Joe Kavanagh, the father, was an abusive womaniser, though he also had a good name in the anonymous seaside town in which the novel is set for being the moving spirit of the local carnival. His family – Sara's three brothers, Joseph, Willy and Ben, and their mother Esther – have been brought back together by the death. But the fractious and antagonistic manner in which they treat each other has remained unchanged. Their exchanges are counterpointed in Sara's mind with vivid recollections of intimacy featuring her father. These oscillate from interludes of sexual abuse to images of his peculiar allure, while momentary memories of the carnival's excitement are followed by a fuller remembrance of his derision and violence when she tells him, 'I'm not going to end up in a council house' (12). Although there has been much amiss in the dead man's relations with his wife and sons, it is clear that his relationship with Sara, through the twin power of seduction and rejection, highlights family dynamics at their most critical and most intense. Joe Kavanagh has made all his dependants fearful of his detested power, but it is Sara – as woman and daughter – who encounters its physically rawest and emotionally most complicated effects.

She occupies a distinctive place between her brothers and her mother. Graphic scenes of the beatings Willy and Ben receive leave no doubt as to the boys' defencelessness against their father's physical abuse. But the boys are not subject to his sexual predation. In Esther's case, both sexual and physical abuse are present, but she cannot prevent her husband's exploitation of Sara's vulnerability and confusion. Esther has hardened herself to the tenor of family life, has arbitrarily selected Ben as the apple of her eye, and even takes Joe's part when she believes Sara deserves to be thrashed. Perhaps as a means of defending herself, but also because she has become inured to patriarchy's furious and mindless vindictiveness, Esther does little to counteract Joe's domination besides hate it. Her main ostensible contribution to family well-being is her compulsive effort to keep the house clean, as though doing so will compensate for its moral squalor. Her emotional carapace, which in Sara's eyes contrasts starkly with her increasing physical flabbiness, is shown not only in her rigidity towards her daughter but towards her own past. She has no time for her widowed mother, and her emotionally charged remembrance of her dead sister, Betty, is overshadowed by the proximity of Betty's death to the birth of Esther's first child, Joseph. Her having become pregnant was the reason she married – a more conventional form of sexual entrapment than that to which Sara is subjected; but entrapment nevertheless. An embodiment of a consciousness without a conscience, insomniac Esther is a portrait of 'how life imprisons you' (65). Her nocturnal consciousness reflecting on her past, her late husband and her own disposition is as dissonant a counterpoint to Molly Bloom's soliloquy as one is likely to read.

Seeking respite from her home environment, Sara takes to visiting her grandmother. Tea and biscuits are produced, but not very much sympathy. Sara's matrilineal line, from which she might learn to be her own woman, is well and truly broken. Her attempts as an adolescent to assert a feminine identity for herself – predictable though her clothes and make-up are, and though the opportunities for self-realisation are culturally limited – both parents regard as pretexts for repression. Joe seems intent on denying that his daughter is in the process of becoming an autonomous sexual being, while Esther keeps warning her about the danger of ending up, as she did, with an unwanted pregnancy. These attitudes conceive of Sara as a threat, a deviant, a source of trouble, rather than as a person in her own right. Yet neither Esther nor Joe has any problem in accepting that teenage Sara is now also a wage-earner, a role that ties her all the more strongly to being only what others wish to make of her.

There is, however, another Sara beneath what is being imposed on her. One sign of this self is expressed in various references to what, from early days, Sara 'wrote in my head' (10), which at least suggests the possibility of an individual point of view. In addition, there is the persona of Maggie, whose voice concludes the novel on a note of withdrawal and critique articulated through nightmarish passages of vampirism and dissolution. Typically represented in Sara's thoughts as occupying a space on the wall over her bed, Maggie seems above and beyond Sara's conscious awareness. Maggie freely enters areas of Sara's experience which the young woman herself has yet to come to terms with, acting thereby as a spokeswoman for Sara's current confinement within the family and her unconscious processing of it. Maggie's level of consciousness may be gathered from the fact that it is she who coins the novel's title phrase, although in doing so she seems to be recasting in more poetic and structurally more wide-ranging terms Sara's own sense of 'Big Dark . . . Little Dark' (7). Yet, it is Sara, not Maggie, who has the last word. Unhappily, however, what she says – welcoming the prospect of marriage and children; insisting to herself what she has already insisted to Maggie, 'I don't hate being a woman. I don't. I don't' (99, 114) – is only a vain, futile denial of all that she has known and felt.

Its use of multiple voices and of a form that seems a modification of that used in William Faulkner's *As I Lay Dying* make *In Night's City* a challenging read. But such features also register the difficulty of finding a means to break the silence which existed until quite recently in Irish life regarding family abuse, and the denaturing assumptions that silence concealed about the enmeshing and constricting ways of life under a coercive patriarchy. It might be argued that none of the characters is an individual, and that voice creates an effect of disembodiment. But the story is one of individuality denied and of bodies despoiled – Sara's parents themselves are only physically fully grown, not psychologically. An unsparing and discomforting contribution to women's writing, *In Night's City* is one of those works that offer a glimpse of a culture beginning to acknowledge that it is time to change to more open, and more painful, discourses.

Supplementary Reading

Christine St Peter, 'Petrifying Time: Incest Narratives from Contemporary Ireland', in Liam Harte and Michael Parker (eds), *Contemporary Irish Fiction: Themes, Tropes, Theories* (Basingstoke: Macmillan, 2000), pp. 133–7
Aidan Higgins, 'Fires from Gehenna', *Windy Arbours* (Champaign, Illinois: Dalkey Archive, 2005), pp. 189–91

Also Published in 1982

John Banville, *The Newton Letter*; Sebastian Barry, *Macker's Garden*; John Broderick, *The Trial of Father Dillingham*; Jennifer Johnston, *The Christmas Tree*; Liam Lynch, *Shell, Sea Shell*

1983

Bernard MacLaverty, *Cal*

Author of four novels and several collections of short stories, MacLaverty (b. 1942) explores with a sidelong, sympathetic view and a delicate stylistic touch the complications created by the differences within families and between strangers. His first novel, Lamb *(1980), dealt with the relationship between a juvenile offender and his clerical guardian;* Grace Notes *(1997) portrays a young woman's difficulties in realising her potential as a composer;* The Anatomy School *(2001) is a* Bildungsroman *set in MacLaverty's native Belfast during the beginning of the Troubles.*

Nineteen-year-old Cal McCrystal is on the dole. To the annoyance of his father, Shamie, he lacks the stomach to take the only job available, which is in the abattoir of their provincial Northern Ireland town. Shamie and a Provisional IRA operative, Crilly, are the only Catholics working in the abattoir, and Cal and his father are the only Catholics left in the housing estate where they live. Though he seems anything but ideologically committed, Cal is the driver for the local IRA unit. His disaffection with this role comes to a head after his involvement in the murder of Robert Morton, an unlovely member of the Royal Ulster Constabulary Reserve. Morton's father is also critically wounded in the attack, and the dead man leaves a wife and child. The widow's name is Marcella (*née* D'Agostino), a librarian. Cal falls hopelessly in love with her. After her husband's death, Marcella goes to live with her in-laws. Cal finds pretexts for visiting their rural home. Eventually the Mortons give him work as a labourer. And when, after many threats, Cal and his father are burned out of their house, Cal goes to live in an abandoned cottage on Morton land, though the family learns of this only after soldiers raid the place. When Marcella's father-in-law has to go to Belfast for further medical attention, she and Cal become lovers.

Meanwhile, the local IRA unit has remained active, and a reluctant Cal has no choice but to continue as its driver. The difficulty in distinguishing between the IRA's politically motivated activities and ordinary crime, the subject of much contentious public debate during the Troubles, comes to the fore in the unit's robbery of an off-licence. And the paramilitary tendency to take the law into its own hands – another obviously pressing topic – emerges when Finbar Skeffington, the unit's ideologue and commanding officer, orders Crilly to knee-cap a sixteen-year-old driver involved in a traffic accident in which Skeffington's father has been injured. Perhaps the culminating instance of how local outrages typically blur the lines between social normality and a violent cause is the unit's plan to bomb the library where Marcella works (the charge to be placed in an edition of *Middlemarch*). Learning of this plan, Cal alerts the authorities. Coincidentally, soldiers raid his cottage. Crilly and Skeffington are arrested. It is only a matter of time before Cal is taken into custody, which occurs on Christmas Eve – a coincidence typical of the young man's thwarted and ill-starred destiny.

His relationship with Marcella is the most obvious and substantial of Cal's misfortunes, despite – or because of – the temporary joy it brings. It is tempting to think of the two as a kind of village Romeo and Juliet, though the gaps between them – in age, class and culture – are much greater than those of their illustrious prototypes and require a certain amount of line-blurring of their own. Their attraction to each other is that of two marginal, out-of-place people meeting where individuals are defined in terms of religious and political affiliation rather than the more fundamental human categories of pity and passion. They must help each other remain people, a joint undertaking that requires the dismantling of various borders and security barriers. Clearly there is no avoiding the fact that it is the Troubles that bring

Cal and Marcella together, just as it is the Troubles that determine the impossibility of their remaining together. But the polarities usually associated with Northern Ireland's civil strife are not in themselves the sole sufficient reason for what happens to the lovers. After all, townie Catholic Marcella (she comes from the seaside resort of Portrush, County Antrim) has married a rural Protestant part-time policeman. And Cal, though he exhibits some of the coloration of his tribe in his attempts to learn Irish and his attending a Gaelic football game in what he thinks of as 'the real Ireland' (42) south of the border, will also 'stand for hours on end chatting' (55) with Cyril Dunlop, regarded by Shamie as the locality's arch-Orangeman.

While it hardly denies the impact of the Troubles, *Cal* also suggests that the upheaval they create unmasks an environment of deprivation and a recognition of needs which the fixed norms of the status quo either made bearable or successfully repressed. The Northern Ireland community is changing, even if the change can only make itself known in destruction. Whether the destruction's victims can somehow benefit from their experiences, thereby changing positively, remains an open question. But it is not unthinkable. The thought of suffering's redemptive and even transformative agency is insinuated by various references to Grünewald's overwhelmingly grim Crucifixion – 'the first thing like that which had any effect on me' (121), Marcella says of having seen it. Another version of enriching human change is a capacity for love, which Cal, gormless and inexperienced though he is, possesses naturally. Marcella's embrace of it, and him, is an enrichment of a kind invoked by the arcadian associations of Thomas Hardy's *Under the Greenwood Tree*, a book Cal read at school. The English for Grünewald is greenwood, and both works have in common a foreignness that is no inhibition to the power to move, and a wholeness that is a counterweight to the fractured and incomplete location in which Marcella and Cal find themselves. If artistic creation seems an antidote to, or an escape from, current conditions, it does not in itself bring into being a world where lovers might thrive. But it maintains the idea of such a world being desirable. Meanwhile, there is no need to bomb a library.

Divided within himself, Cal can neither extricate himself from the Troubles nor, as Skeffington recommends, 'Think of the issues, not the people' (26). His callowness and yearning place him to be in that representative zone occupied by many youngsters in contemporary Irish fiction, the state of being in-between, unformed, at risk, inexperienced in the consequences of choosing. Living in the Morton cottage inspires in him 'a sense of a new life' (117), but it also draws him helplessly towards a more intimate appreciation of his two-faced reality. He can hardly help but think of the people, being 'in love with the one woman in the world who was forbidden him' (102). His involvement in Morton's murder not only makes him feel that 'he had a brand stamped in blood in the middle of his forehead which would take him the rest of his life to purge' (99) – an instance of the red imagery that contrasts throughout the novel with the prevailing Northern colour scheme of orange and green. He also realises that his complicity in Marcella's becoming a widow makes trust and openness impossible in his relationship with her. Private shame ultimately coincides with public exposure. The sight of Cal at the time of his arrest, wearing nothing but another man's underwear, is not only pathetic, it also underlines the fact that he is just himself alone. This self he now regards as utterly a victim who, in a final expression of how horribly snarled his situation has become, feels 'grateful' (170) for the punishment he is about to receive, as though choosing it. It is not his prison sentence that Cal anticipates with gratitude but the beating that will precede it – an experience that is the opposite of what he and Marcella briefly shared.

Supplementary Reading

Stephen Watt, 'The Politics of Bernard MacLaverty's *Cal*', *Éire-Ireland*, vol. 28, no. 3 (Fall 1993), pp. 130–46

Joe Cleary, '"Fork-Tongued on the Border Bit": Partition and the Politics of Form in Contemporary Narratives of the Northern Irish Conflict', *South Atlantic Quarterly*, vol. 95, no. 1 (Winter 1996), pp. 227–76

Richard Haslam, '"The Pose Arranged and Lingered Over": Visualizing the "Troubles"', in Liam Harte and Michael Parker (eds), *Contemporary Irish Fiction: Themes, Tropes, Theories* (Basingstoke: Macmillan, 2000), pp. 192–212, esp. pp. 196–205

Michael Parker, *Northern Irish Literature 1975–2006* (Basingstoke: Palgrave Macmillan, 2007), Vol. 2: *The Imprint of History*, pp. 39–46

Also Published in 1983

Bruce Arnold, *Running to Paradise*; Samuel Beckett, *Worstward Ho*; Clare Boylan, *Holy Pictures*; Aidan Higgins, *Bornholm Night-Ferry*; Brian Moore, *Cold Heaven*; William Trevor, *Fools of Fortune*

1984

Desmond Hogan, *A Curious Street*

A leading member of the generation of Irish writers to emerge in the 1970s, Hogan (b. 1951) is the author of five novels, including The Ikon Maker *(1976),* The Leaves on Grey *(1980),* A New Shirt *(1986) and* A Farewell to Prague *(1995). A native of Ballinasloe, County Galway, and a connoisseur of small-town repression, he may be best known for his short stories, of which he has published a number of collections. His work is distinguished by a compressed, highly coloured style and by characters who are outsiders with refined sensibilities. Hogan has also written plays and a collection of non-fiction.*

From a brief newspaper report, Jeremy Hitchins, a British soldier serving in Northern Ireland, learns that Alan Mulvanney has killed himself. Jeremy never actually knew Alan, and the suicide did not take place in Northern Ireland but in the victim's native Athlone, 'the meanest town in Ireland' (182). But the two are significantly connected. For one thing, their emotional histories are linked. Jeremy's mother, Eileen Carmody, had an innocent, sisterly relationship with Alan in her young days. At another level, Jeremy has long felt himself drawn to Alan, finding in his story qualities sadly lacking from the world in which he grows up. Among these qualities are integrity and imagination, and these strike Jeremy as being all the more valuable in view of Alan's suffering both from mental illness and from the lovelessness and isolation to which post-war provincial Ireland condemns his homosexuality.

As well as possessing the qualities in question, Alan has honoured them by writing a novel in which they are the primary motives of action. The novel was written while Alan was a student in Dublin in the 1940s. Entitled *A Cavalier Against Time*, it tells of a young couple who in 1649, the year Cromwell landed in Ireland, travelled the country on a white horse preaching peace and love – a doomed project which left the lovers estranged and in exile. But their failure is not the point. What matters is that the gesture has been made. And the same applies to the novel itself, which is also from a worldly point of view a failure because, once completed, Alan consigns it to his bottom drawer. By declining publication, he has preserved the novel's integrity as a statement of resistance and as a declaration of difference. And he did this at a time when the official mood in Ireland seemed determined to deny resistance and eliminate difference. The same disposition might describe Cromwell's Irish policy, as both *A Cavalier Against Time* and *A Curious Street* make clear – Alan Mulvanney's novel acting as a lens through which the experiences of the characters in *A Curious Street* may be perceived.

Alan's narrative is the prototype of the unavailability of peace and love. That is also the story of Jeremy Hitchins's Ireland, and of his own personal history. The deprivation, heartbreak and victimhood with which *A Curious Street* is suffused are inherited from the dire scenarios of the Mulvanney text. Their recurrence in a modern context is both a critique of, and a homage to, the mystique and singularity of *A Cavalier Against Time*. The real work and the imagined one are both distinct and inseparable, like Narcissus and his reflection. Their closeness is additionally emphasised by the modern characters living in the same towns as their avatars. And *A Curious Street* is set in the general Shannonside area which was a principal crossing-point for those dispossessed Irish being driven by Cromwell's campaign into an impoverished western domicile. It seems inevitable that the ancestors of Cherine, one of Jeremy's friends, 'had been uprooted in Cromwell's time' (37), and indeed many of the characters share a destiny of dislocation and restlessness, foremost among them Eileen Carmody. It is modern youth, however, who to a person are least at home, marked through no fault of their own by a heritage whose distortions have had a disabling effect on their personalities.

The cumulative nature of this inheritance is indicated by the tendency of *A Curious Street* to proceed not by plot development as such but by means of a layered succession of many stories – of parents and other family members, of teachers, of peripheral characters, of battles long ago. Almost without exception, all these testify to the spiritual impoverishment, the sexual abnegation and the hollow independence of modern Ireland. Jeremy is the poster-child of this dire state of affairs. His particular susceptibility to Alan Mulvanney's unhappy story gives him that identity. But as the son of an Irish mother and an English father, Jeremy is also conflicted by birth. It appears that being Anglo-Irish in the most literal sense makes him experience to an exemplary degree the tensions and imbalances typical of the historical relationship between his two countries of origin. The terms of his hyphenated lineage inhibit each other, forbidding wholeness. His hybrid existence fails to gel as a new possibility, but instead remains plagued by an outsider's uncertainty and alienation. His sense of reality is mediated by

the pain of difference, and that, and the fact that he has only his subjectivity of his difference as a resource, also results in his feeling kin to
Mulvanney. Jeremy lacks Mulvanney's talent, and he also does not
possess his self-consciousness of being a beautiful loser. As a result, he
seems a more commonplace and more excruciating embodiment of a
lost soul. A period in England includes admission to a mental hospital,
enlisting in the British Army and a hasty and unsuccessful marriage.

Jeremy may be one of a kind, but he is not alone. His issues also
affect his friends, Eugene McDermott and Cherine Finnerty (the three
seem to comprise a composite picture of Hogan's generation). Eugene
and Cherine also go to England, and they too fail to find themselves
there – in fact, they lose each other. But in contrast to Jeremy, their disaffection and emotional starvation are largely caused by the
shortcomings of post-independence Irish life, characterised by inter-
generational conflict, sexual repression and the pursuit of small-minded
economic advantage. The intimacy of small-town life seems to be based
upon these forms of narrowness, though the limitations in question
represent a thought-out ethos put in place and maintained by church
and state. It seems only to be expected that a struggle should result
between coercive notions of national unity (and the expectation of
sameness those notions seem to endorse) and the diverse character of
actual life. That struggle, however, can be waged only psychologically.
Those who differ from the prevailing ethos will suffer by refusing to
renounce their needs, their desires, their presumed entitlement to their
own natures. They are both innocents and victims.

This double status *A Curious Street* wishes both to privilege and
bewail. Similarly, the novel sings desire only to frustrate it.
Abandonment is depicted with such consistency that it risks being
fetishised. History is painted with a broad brush only for the resulting
picture to be lamented. And in order to enact, rather than merely
describe, its preoccupation with loss and rootlessness, the novel's
syntax and usage are fractured and conventional prose rhythms are
unpredictably accelerated and decelerated, technical devices that
articulate a rhetoric of dismay and disillusion, though they also
produce effects that can be overblown, preposterous and manipula-
tive. However elaborate the narrative, representative the characters or
idiosyncratic the telling, however, *A Curious Street* is undoubtedly a
distressing spectacle of inner deprivation and soul-destroying hurt.
The distress is, in part, the result of the unrelieved sameness and

relentless repetition with which casualties are created, agency is denied and change remains an apparent impossibility. The dissolution and disillusion of a generation, diagnosed and embodied by Alan Mulvanney, create an image of a society indifferently squandering its promise and its hope and its capacity for moral growth. Family is unavailing, friendship is fleeting, ideals are debased, affiliation and belonging are denied, all at the cost of common purpose and common understanding. There is no character for whom crisis is not the norm. During his time in London, Eugene McDermott is told by an anonymous youngster from Belfast, 'It's just yourself, isn't it. All you've got is yourself' (93). The main events of *A Curious Street* – suicide, accidental death, madness – emphasise that self's frailty and the emotional waste and cultural failures which make its vulnerability commonplace, unchanging and unchangeable.

Supplementary Reading

Theo d'Haen, 'Des Hogan and Ireland's Post-Modern Past', in Joris Duytschaever and Geert Lernout (eds), *History and Violence in Anglo-Irish Literature* (Amsterdam: Rodopi, 1988), pp. 79–83

Desmond Hogan, 'Return to Ballinasloe: A Record for November 1990', in Hogan, *The Edge of the City: A Scrapbook 1976–1991* (Dublin: Lilliput Press, 1993), pp. 142–8

Paul Deane, 'The Great Chain of Irish Being Reconsidered: Desmond Hogan's *A Curious Street*', *Notes on Modern Irish Literature*, no. 6 (1994), pp. 39–48

Tony Murray, 'Curious Streets: Diaspora, Displacement and Transgression in Desmond Hogan's London Irish Narratives', *Irish Studies Review*, vol. 14, no. 2 (May 2006), pp. 239–53

Also Published in 1984

Linda Anderson, *To Stay Alive*; Caroline Blackwood, *Corrigan*; Jennifer Johnston, *The Railway Station Man*; Val Mulkerns, *The Summerhouse*

1985

Mary Leland, *The Killeen*

A noted journalist, Leland (b. 1941) has published a number of non-fiction works devoted to her native Cork. She is also the author of a collection of short stories. A second novel, Approaching Priests *(1991), deals with the Irish generation that came of age in the 1970s.*

A note at the beginning of this novel explains the title. It is a transliteration of a word in Irish for 'a church yard set apart for infants', and an additional note mentions a burial place reserved for unbaptised children. In *The Killeen*, the site in question is in the townland of Adrigole, in west Cork, and the resting place is that of two-year-old Thomas Costello, illegitimate son of a local girl, Margaret Coakley, and a left-republican diehard named Earnán Costello. On the run before securing his escape to America – the novel is set in the early 1930s, in the period immediately following Fianna Fáil's first general election victory – Earnán is given refuge in a convent in Cork city, where Margaret has come to work in the kitchen. Their time together is very limited, and the seduction is readily accomplished, leaving the remainder of the brief, charged narrative to detail the larger context into which mother and child are received.

Margaret has taken the position in the convent on the death of her father, partly because one of her teachers thinks it a good opportunity for her but largely to escape her vindictive and abusive mother. The teacher's good opinion of Margaret is confirmed by the regard for her of Sister Thomas Aquinas, a thoughtful nun who finds her not only a promising young woman but, in her origins and forms of socialisation, the bearer of elements of Gaelic tradition, as described in the book she and Margaret read together, Daniel Corkery's *The Hidden Ireland*. To ensure Margaret's continuing well-being, Sister Thomas prevails on Father Costello, the convent chaplain and brother of Earnán, to find a place for her in the household of the widowed Julia Mulcahy, a relative of the priest's. Julia's husband, Maurice, was a comrade of Earnán's, and has recently died on hunger strike as a political prisoner, 'A Republican victim of other Republicans' (40).

Margaret gives birth in Julia's house, and as soon as she does so, Father Costello baptises Thomas, whereupon the child is taken away and placed in a school. This institution is nothing like those orphanages whose history and administration have subsequently become such an unsightly blot on Ireland's moral landscape. On the contrary, the place in question is a haven for the children of political undesirables who have either been jailed or forced to flee the country. Run by a shadowy Doctor Douglas, an Englishwoman keenly interested in the social and political developments in the Germany of the day, the school is vouched for by Bina and Lou Mulcahy, aunts of the martyred Maurice. These two ladies strongly support his brand of thirty-two-county republicanism, although in view of their expectation that fascist Europe will change the Irish political scene, they would probably be as surprised as the reader is to hear Maurice not deny that he is 'a Marxist' (81).

Margaret takes her place in Julia's kitchen, but the story remains upstairs to deal with Julia's background, marriage, complicated sense of home, and devotion to her young son, Pat. Caring for Pat becomes a large part of Margaret's domestic duties, an irony that seems all the sharper when it is made known that Julia, too, was pregnant before she married Maurice. At that time, Julia was on her second sojourn in Paris, a city where her sophistication, taste and sense of independence was more welcome than it was in Cork. Though she has no discernible abilities and no obvious sense of direction, Julia's following her own inclinations is a reproof to the limitations of her native place – and in this, too, her story finds an unexpected echo in Margaret's. The Margaret who 'followed her instincts' (55) is not all that different from Julia, despite dissimilarities in their social standing. The connection between them is further underlined by the position both Julia and Margaret are placed in by Maurice's aunts. In complementary ways, with Bina keeping watch on Julia and Lou never having a good word to say about Margaret, the two older women maintain the framework into which the two younger ones must fit. Julia is meant to spend the rest of her life honouring Maurice as a 'hero and martyr' (40), while clearly Margaret is deemed unfit to say even one word about her place in the scheme of things.

Yet, though Julia and Margaret have obvious points of contact, they are unable to make anything of them. Margaret accepts Julia's advice to marry the builder who likes her, to go to England with him and to forget her abandoned son – even though Julia is both unable and unwilling to forget her own sexual history. And Julia feels easier in her mind about her eventual departure from Cork by deciding that Thomas will do very well as the ideological ward of her aunts that they intended Pat to be. Margaret forestalls the substitution by entrusting Thomas to her brother, Michael, with whom, she believes, the child will be safe in the home place – 'there was some yearning thrust in her towards the land' (93). But Thomas is not safe. His grandmother beats and burns him, and Michael's efforts to protect him are not enough. Thomas sickens and dies. The local priest denies him a Christian burial, an additional gratuitous brutalisation of innocence. Michael loses faith in the land. The killeen may be a type of oubliette from the church's point of view, but the community will always associate

Michael with Margaret's story and Thomas's fate. Michael's life in Ireland is also buried in that godforsaken ground. He goes to America, never to be heard from again.

Although Michael's search for a headstone suitable for Thomas's grave comes across as a civilised gesture, expressing a sense of tradition and of self-motivated secular propriety and observance, it also draws attention to troubling themes that seem more central to the novel. Among these is the emptiness that seems to be at the heart of Irish experience, particularly that of the common people. It is from the history and culture of these inhabitants of rural Ireland that an elaborate imagery of what constitutes the real people and the heart of the country has been woven. But that history and culture, suggested by Margaret's knowledge of Irish and her repertoire of folk songs, avails little in the circumstances. The land itself seems best forsaken. The malevolent mother who presides over it – the archetypal Hag of Beare hails from exactly that part of the country where Adrigole is located – appears to be the farrow-eating sow that Stephen Dedalus said Ireland was. Thomas, deprived of the nurture and sense of belonging that would in time allow him to succeed to his heritage, represents the death of the future, an outcome articulated in a different but no less conclusive way by the emigration of all the novel's young adults.

In Cork city, the judicious Sister Thomas can influence matters only to a degree, and is in any case ailing, as though to suggest that the days are numbered for the balance she maintains between a class-bound perspective and an informed sense of charity. She lives in the same world where Margaret and Earnán trysted – an environment suffused with sensorial stimuli shared by nature and religion alike. The city beyond the walls, as represented by Bina, Lou and Doctor Douglas, for all its emphasis on faith and purity, and for all its apparent interest in Irish unity, is a world of disruption, interference and rigid control. There, too, no less than in the killeen, the young – particularly young women – have their lives denied. The sharply focused, emotionally sophisticated representation of the many levels of that denial is all the more telling for being written at a time when passion, politics and legitimacy were being rethought by Irish women so that they would be in no danger of history repeating itself.

Supplementary Reading

Kristin Morrison, 'Child Murder as Metaphor of Colonial Exploitation in Toni Morrison's *Beloved, The Silence in the Garden,* and *The Killeen*', in Toshi Furomoto et al. (eds), *International Aspects of Irish Literature* (Gerrards Cross: Colin Smythe, 1996), pp. 292–300

James M. Smith, 'Retelling Stories: Exposing Mother Ireland in Kathy Prendergast's *Body Map Series* and Mary Leland's *The Killeen*', in Jennifer Grinnell and Alston Connelly (eds), *Re/Dressing Cathleen: Contemporary Works from Irish Women Artists* (Boston: McMullen Museum of Art, 1997), pp. 42–51

Christine St Peter, *Changing Ireland: Strategies in Contemporary Women's Fiction* (Basingstoke: Palgrave Macmillan, 2000), pp. 75–81

Linden Peach, *The Contemporary Irish Novel: Critical Readings* (Basingstoke: Palgrave Macmillan, 2004), pp. 58–61

Also Published in 1985

Dermot Bolger, *Nightshift*; Carlo Gébler, *The Eleventh Summer*; Benedict Kiely, *Nothing Happens in Carmincross*; Liam Lynch, *Tenebrae*; Patrick McGinley, *The Trick of the Ga Bolga*; Brian Moore, *Black Robe*; Francis Stuart, *Faillandia*

1986

J.M. O'Neill, *Open Cut*

The author of six novels, Limerick-born O'Neill (1921–99) was also a playwright and his theatre company, Sugawn, was an original and important focus for London's Irish emigrant community, among others, in the 1970s. His first three novels – Open Cut, Duffy is Dead (1988) and Canon Bang Bang (1989) – open fresh perspectives on the lives, or half-lives, of the Irish in London. These works are set in such unglamorous areas as Haringey and Barking. O'Neill's experiences as a young banker in west Africa provides the basis for Commissar Connell (1992), and two later novels – Bennett and Company (1998) and the posthumously published Relighan, Undertaker (1999) – are set in Ireland.

From his very comfortable Highgate 'little fortress' (8), Nally is master of all he surveys. He has his greedy fingers in many lucrative pies – trucking, gambling, property – none entirely legal. And he has a network of fixers and enforcers to make sure things go his way without his having to get his hands dirty. In a dog-eat-dog world, he is the top dog, thoroughly urbanised, though arguably not completely Anglicised, having inherited the qualities of a grandfather who, for all his years in London, 'remained the indestructible Celt, clever and perverse' (11).

The enterprising Nally is now planning a bank robbery, and to carry it out has enlisted one of his truckers, Hennessy. (The male characters in *Open Cut* are known by their surnames only, and the much more minor female ones by their forenames, signalling the semi-anonymity in which they pass their lives.) Hennessy, however, has a plan of his own, which is to do the job before Nally gives the green light. From this, an elaborate set of moves and counter-moves arise, in which the hunter and hunted go through a number of changes of identity and where double-crossing is the norm and a certain crazed logic, grounded in silence and cunning, produces not only inevitably unexpected manoeuvres but fissures and leaps in narrative continuity. The players seem ahead of the game, which gives them a family resemblance. Not being of their world, the solitary reader can only try to play catch-up. Hennessy reflects, 'Thieving was easy, it needed anger, hardness, that was all. But the double-deal was something else' (20). In entering into the twilight world of doubleness, a world lit by the grey of early November and whose inhabitants restlessly scan the metropolis's grey pavements, *Open Cut* not only sounds a set of formal variations on the idea of plot. It also rehearses such key aspects in the emigrant experience as isolation and dependence, vulnerability and risk and a thorough familiarity with the deceptive practices required to maintain the appearance of legitimacy.

Nally is able to run Hennessy to ground owing to the unexpected fall-out of a violent attack which he commissions. And with Hennessy out of the picture, Nally is able to proceed to cheat his own partner in crime, the shadowy McLeod. On those twin notes, the novel ends. Manipulation, lies, a coldly calculating amorality are the principles of order that govern the novel's nether world. The unremitting application of these principles creates a closed system, with no deviations or transgressions allowed. By taking his own initiative, Hennessy has obviously offended and therefore must be eliminated. Hennessy knows quite well the risks he is running by transgressing. Others, however, come to grief by virtue of being human – which in this case means lacking the necessary 'hardness' – and the inclusion of their weaknesses becomes a crucial pivot around which the plot concerning Hennessy and Nally turns.

Kirwan is one such character. He works on the same Walworth building site from which Hennessy drives truckloads of spoil, and shares the same Archway rooming house as Hennessy, where he spends his nights with Maisie, a naive, good-natured musician. (Both the building site and the rooming house are Nally concerns.) Kirwan seems destined to become a derelict, but Hennessy takes him under his wing, and though the latter's motivation for the bank robbery is not explicitly stated, its proceeds will hasten the time for 'upped sticks' (18). Maisie's provision of some creature comfort obviously appeals to Kirwan as well, and he takes a notion that they should be married. But despite wedding plans and Hennessy's initial outfoxing of Nally, these possibilities come to nothing. Under the malevolent direction of Feehan, the building site foreman, Hennessy inadvertently kills Kirwan, invisible at the time of the accident in the open-cut trench which gives the novel its title. Only the anonymous city agencies of police and ambulance crew can do anything now for Kirwan, 'A man dead in his own stupidity' (114).

Parallel to Kirwan's story is that of Cleary, a clerk at a repair shop, also owned by Nally and run for him by Bredin. Physically frail, terminally alone, 'helpless and almost a fool' (125), Cleary sees in the antagonism between Nally and Hennessy an opportunity to make himself significant. This foolhardy notion leads him into greater danger than he ever envisaged and, to save his skin, he falsely represents Hennessy to Bredin as an informer, thereby bringing the latter – 'a coarse blunt island of integrity' (160) – into the thick of things. Bredin's involvement becomes decisive after Cleary has been beaten to death by Feehan, on Nally's orders. And it is Bredin, to avenge Cleary, who does Nally's bidding by eliminating Hennessy – a telling instance of Nally's 'set a mick to catch a mick' (55) strategy. Nobody is innocent. Bredin's aspirations to autonomy, Cleary's freelancing, Kirwan's notions of escape have no currency in a world to which they do not belong, where they exist on sufferance.

The novel's culminating events take place against the background of Guy Fawkes' Night (5 November). Obviously the fireworks which are an English tradition on that night fail to illuminate the dark places where Nally's writ runs, and the orthodoxy and childishness of the public display is a distraction from the hard facts of a brutally material culture with which Nally completely identifies. The social reality of firework night's ritual and recreation is a flash in the pan compared to the much harder-hitting realm of mud and blood in which Nally traffics. The gap between the two spheres delineates the emigrants' space; a trench, as it were. Here they have their use as tools and playthings – the same things as they make of each other, without knowing it. Hennessy, initially the exception to the common lot, ends up being typical of it – partly because he tries to change the system in which he is caught up by using its methods. His first effort is the misguided bank robbery, and he fails to beat Nally at his own game. The second attempt to do something different shows Hennessy's human side in his fortuitous involvement with the enigmatic Kiki, his weakness for whom leads him to play into Nally's hands. The ways of Hennessy and his kind are governed by, as the character himself notes, a 'haphazard providence' (99). The operation of such an contradictory agency is strikingly reproduced in the pace and plotting of *Open Cut*. And at other levels that agency's dehumanising potential is realised amidst a bleak poetry of unhymned habitats – Archway, Hoxton, Clissold Park, 'lower Holloway, a grimy congeries annealed in transience and dispassion' (169).

Supplementary Reading

Kevin O'Connor, 'Obituary of J.M. O'Neill', *The Guardian*, 14 June 1999
Liviu Popoviciu, Chris Haywood and Máirtín Mac an Ghaill, 'Migrating Masculinities: The Irish Diaspora in Britain', *Irish Studies Review*, vol. 14, no. 2 (May 2006), pp. 169–87

Also Published in 1986

John Banville, *Mefisto*; Ita Daly, *Ellen*; David Martin, *Dream*; Michael Harding, *Priest*; Val Mulkerns, *Very Like a Whale*; Billy Roche, *Tumbling Down* (revised edition, 2008)

1987
Carlo Gébler, *Work and Play*

Gébler (b. 1954) is the author of eight novels, a collection of short stories and four books of non-fiction, including the memoir Father and I *(2000). He is also a playwright and has published fiction for children and young adults. Born in Dublin and reared in England, one of the recurring themes in his early work is displacement, whether in the west of Ireland –* The Eleventh Summer *(1985) – or on a wider international stage –* August in July *(1986),* Malachy and His Family *(1990) and* Life of a Drum *(1991). He has written two historical novels set in nineteenth-century Ireland,* The Cure *(1994), based on the notorious Bridget Cleary case, and* How to Murder a Man *(1998), dealing with the killing of a land agent. Contemporary Northern Ireland provides the setting for*

A Good Day for a Dog (2008), *while the background for* The Dead Eight (2011) *is Ireland in the 1930s.*

A former law student, now expelled from university for spending his summer term on a London drug binge, Fergus Maguire has returned to Ireland and is recuperating in rural County Wicklow. He is still trying to mend fences with the rest of his family – mother, sister Pippa and highly irate father – who live in Dalkey. On a visit home, Fergus and his father go swimming and Mr Maguire collapses and dies. Fergus finds himself disinherited in favour of Pippa, which induces a state of volatile anger and confusion. Anything seems possible. He returns to London, and though he does not reconnect with the drug scene, his time cannot be said to be profitably spent. In addition to a dead-end job answering viewers' letters on behalf of a television company, he sees a certain amount of a friend from schooldays and former girl-friend, Laura Shellgate, and falls in with her immaturely hedonistic ways. In other words, his days are a combination of equally mindless work and play – 'the way you Britons love to live' (54), as an American friend of Laura's remarks.

Things begin to change as a result of a particularly outrageous night out at the restaurant of a pub called the Sacred Heart. As the police arrive, Fergus swallows a sachet of cocaine, and his ensuing interview at the police station is most uncomfortable, not least because his interviewer has invited Fergus to become an informer. His refusal does not end police interest in him, as subsequent events show. Meanwhile, at work, Fergus becomes an object of attention for the paranoid Mr Wiggins, who has sent a copy of his self-published book – a fantasy of mind-control entitled *The Torture Papers* – to Fergus's office without having received an acknowledgement. The one area of normality, or that is not characterised by excess, that Fergus is in touch with is represented by the Singh family, who live one floor down from his Shepherds Bush apartment. But even here, normality is a relative term, as the Singhs are subjected to racist abuse and attacks. Fergus has also acquired a steady girlfriend, Jennifer, his relationship with whom is as casual as his involvement with life in general. He cer-tainly does not share Mr Singh's view that England is 'a good country' (89) and that Indian history and heritage is 'for the birds' (ibid.). And when Fergus gives the Singhs a history of Ireland as a Christmas present, it is merely a token, not a sign that he thinks they all have a common relationship with England.

Fergus is still too affected by having witnessed his father's death and by the sense of rejection arising from disinheritance to relate with any degree of consistency or objectivity to the world around him. Family feeling boils over when he goes home for Christmas. Pippa behaves with a notable lack of goodwill, and Fergus responds in kind. In contrast, Jennifer's willing body gives him a sense of being insulated. Nevertheless, the world will insist on making its claims on him. An epiphany which occurs during a snow shower (which Joyceans may find derivative) reveals that 'There was a world outside himself . . . and he had to go out to it' (113). In keeping with the novel's understated approach, that realisation in itself does not result in any decisive or immediate change. Nevertheless, Fergus does interrupt making love to Jennifer to go to the aid of the Singhs when racists vandalise their front door. And he is alert enough to get rid of heroin planted by the police in his apartment, though when he complains at the local police station, he gets nowhere – is the law working or playing? Fergus also risks serious injury in his failed attempt to save the lives of Mrs Singh and her two sons during another racist attack on their home. Clearly the thugs responsible are not playing.

The rescue effort is Fergus's plainest acknowledgement to date that he lives in the Singh world as well as in the far different social and economic realm of Jennifer and her circle. But at the cremation of the Singhs, it is himself alone he reproves with 'thoughtlessness' (144), which he suddenly sees 'had been the common quality' (ibid.) throughout his life. Clear at last that, where he and his peer group have been concerned, London has been a privileged sphere where neither work nor play seem to be actions that have consequences, Fergus sees himself and where he is in a new light. The notion of a 'supervising intelligence balancing the actions of bad against good' (149) is now recalled as an idea he had as a child. Instead, 'There was only oneself making sense of what happened' (ibid.), a thought that liberates him from the past and thus reminds him that he is not as devoid of agency and choice as his initial life of drift suggested. In effect, he seems to be on his way to becoming a moral citizen. The country he lives in is less important than his new-found ability to act with pragmatism and react with sensitivity, earning thereby a necessary self-respect.

The law student becomes a law unto himself; the paper world of the lawyer father becomes the morally centred world of the autonomous, non-institutional self; the passive, suburban Dalkeyite ends up a self-aware Londoner; the man who is conscious of his freedom and its responsibilities becomes a rightful heir to secular adequacy. Fergus finds his own inheritance. There are even signs that he is beginning to take his relationship with Jennifer seriously, not least because she has confessed to telling the police everything about the night of the Sacred Heart debacle. Her confession begins to emerge when she, Fergus and their friends play what they call 'the Truth Game' (125) during a country house weekend. After a rift, the new Fergus is able to forgive her. A further aspect of his development is that he is changing into a person, not a West Briton or a turncoat or an Englishman. Inheritance with a national coloration is almost entirely beside the point. When it does come up, intriguingly, it is to show England in a poor light, since it is the Singhs' attackers who most closely identify with the English national story and its mythology. Instead of being a typical Irish emigrant – and indeed helping to revise that stereotype – Fergus is typical of nothing but himself. For this seemingly artless, loosely structured but unmistakably independent-minded novel, that is quite enough.

Supplementary Reading

Robin Rusher, 'Grey Epiphanies', *The Times Literary Supplement*, 7 March 1987

John Kenny, 'Irish Writing and Writers: Some Recent Irish Writing', *Studies*, vol. 87, no. 348 (Winter 1998), pp. 422–30

Carlo Gébler, *Father and I* (London: Little, Brown, 2000)

Michael J. Hayes, 'Carlo Gébler', in Merritt Moseley (ed.), *British and Irish Novelists since 1960* (Detroit: Thomson Gale, 2003), pp. 156–65

Also Published in 1987

Mary Beckett, *Give Them Stones*; Sam Hanna Bell, *Across the Narrow Sea*; Dermot Bolger, *The Woman's Daughter* (2nd, expanded, edition 1991); Ita Daly, *A Singular Attraction*; Roddy Doyle, *The Commitments*; Jennifer Johnston, *Fool's Sanctuary*

1988

William Trevor, *The Silence in the Garden*

Most of William Trevor's fifteen novels are set in England. These include The Old Boys *(1964),* Miss Gomez and the Brethren *(1971),* Other People's Worlds *(1980) and* Death in Summer *(1998). Among his novels with an Irish setting are* Mrs Eckdorf in O'Neill's Hotel *(1969) and* Fools of Fortune (1983). *Trevor (b. 1928) is also a prolific writer of short stories, many of which are set in provincial Ireland, where the author himself spent a peripatetic childhood (he was born in Mitchelstown, County Cork). A development in later novels such as* Felicia's Journey (1994) *and* The Story of Lucy Gault (2002) *is their focus on Anglo as well as Irish settings and characters, which in effect revises the cultural range and relevance of the category Anglo-Irish. Trevor has also written plays and some non-fiction, including* Excursions in the Real World (1993), *a collection of autobiographical essays.*

'The past is never dead. It's not even past.' William Faulkner's dictum seems particularly applicable to William Trevor's Irish novels. In them, the past – and in particular the War of Independence – exerts a complicated influence over the present. The history of that war proves to be a burdensome legacy, not only for the spectre of violence it has bequeathed but for the consciousness of change it has created. The change in question concerns the whole social order, and is revealed in alterations to such fundamental social realities as relations between the classes, the value of property, the fall into marginality of formerly prominent families and the rise to authority of those previously with no standing other than that asserted on the basis of a narrow nationalist ideology. Trevor's interest, presented by closely focusing on individual destinies and communicated in a sober, detached, though not entirely impersonal style, is in delineating the uneasy interactions between the opposing parties which history's bloody turmoil has brought to the fore. His is a moral landscape where, in the superficial quiescence of aftermath, inherited rights and wrongs still haunt the thoughts and actions of families and communities.

Although *The Silence in the Garden* opens in 1971, the main action takes place forty years earlier, and that, in turn, is overshadowed by still earlier events. In 1931, work is begun on a bridge linking the island where the principal characters live to the mainland. The Rollestons own the island estate of Carriglas, where their neighbours, the Pollexfens, also live. So do the Dowleys, members of the lower orders. In the distant past, when the present Rollestons and Pollexfens were youngsters, they tormented Cornelius Dowley, an act that 'damned a household' (186). Cornelius later became a member of the IRA – 'balm for the bitter heart' (ibid.), according to old Mrs Rolleston – and among his numerous exploits was the accidental murder of Linchy, the Rolleston's butler, by a bomb intended for the Rolleston children. Linchy was about to marry the Rolleston servant whom he had impregnated. Cornelius is later shot by the Black and Tans, which ensures for him an afterlife as a local hero (the bridge is to be named in his honour). For their part, the Rolleston and Pollexfen men serve in the First World War, which depletes them and also infuses the peace with an air of stagnation and sterility, indicated by the blighted course of love in their inappropriate marriages and liaisons.

The lives of the female members of these families are no more promising. Villana Rolleston breaks off her engagement to Hugh Pollexfen, marries Finnamore Balt, a desiccated local solicitor twice her age, and spends her days reading romances. Sarah Pollexfen, a governess of the Rolleston's when life at Carriglas was an 'idyll' (20), is also book-bound. But in contrast to Villana, her books are not escapist; instead, she has opted for the role of recording angel, documenting in leather-bound books her recollections and interrogations of what has transpired (italicised in the text). Both Villana's reading and Sarah's writing are forms of silence, neither of them being able to give utterance to the offence that has tainted Carriglas. Villana 'loved it when whatever was wrong became right' (92) in her romances, though it is only the fabricated requirements of the genre that can bring about such rectifications. And Sarah's account books cannot balance the profit and the loss of an economy of bloodshed. She feels that 'I live in a cobweb of other people's lives and do not understand the cobweb's nature' (116). Old Mrs Rolleston does appreciate the full implications of Cornelius's having been terrorised and humiliated, and of how the act is also part of Carriglas's ostensibly decorous grounds. But she keeps quiet about it until she is on her deathbed, the price of her silence being the blackmail she pays to Kathleen Quigley, a former Carriglas servant enamoured of Dowley.

Of the three stranded women, Sarah is the most attentive and conscientious, and even though she is an outsider, her testimony has its value. The provision of a home for her in Carriglas is a fitting tribute both to her loyalty and to the dedicated consistency of her documentation. The house's true heir, however, is Tom, the murdered butler's son. The circumstances of his birth make him illegitimate, but such a designation belongs to the rigid legal frameworks beloved of Finnamore Balt. In all other respects, Tom is the legitimate inheritor, not least because he appears to be a son of the house, through his father, and a son of the people through his mother. He also is drawn to the island's ancient history, tending its early Christian well, although the unChristian mainland community to which the bridge will connect Carriglas treats Tom as a pariah. Shopkeepers and other solid citizens ostracise him and he is put upon by Holy Mullihan, a religious crackpot. But despite these disadvantages, even in adulthood 'his eyes have retained the innocence that was there in the past' (192). This quality enables Tom to act as though the past has no power to oppress him. He has no inclination to participate in the 'punishment of them-selves' (204) which he sees others having undergone, nor is he interested in Finnamore Balt's 'dream, shared with Villana, that between us we may return Carriglas to its former glory' (127). As much caretaker as owner, Tom settles himself modestly in the house with his common-law wife, Patsy, willing simply to abide by time. He tells Villana that 'he wanted nothing more than what he had' (204), a statement she understands as a definition of happiness.

Tom's self-possession and independence, his tolerance and unassertiveness, show him embodying a temporality that appears to be the antithesis of historical time. His human capital has obviously been coloured by events in the past, but it has not been diminished by the '*distortion; I know no better word*' (116) that Sarah senses in the aftermath around her. And Tom resists the vulgar modernisation the evocatively named Esmeralda Coyne, daughter of the mainland, has in mind for Carriglas, as well as her designs on himself. His evident immunity from past and future places Tom in a world of his own, a setting appropriate to his innocence, replete with the reassurances of domesticity and dig-nified by the prospect of continuity. It is as though, for all the change Carriglas has witnessed, some values have remained unchanged, even if they no longer have a currency in the world at large. Another version of the same statement might be that Tom is willing to live and let live – an old-fashioned value, no doubt, but one intended to offset history's depredations. The silence in the garden connotes a repose that may be associated with burial and also with peace, each connotation evoking, and reconciling with, its opposite.

Supplementary Reading

Gregory A. Schirmer, *William Trevor: A Study of His Fiction* (London: Routledge, 1990), pp. 155–63

Max Deen Larsen, 'Saints of the Ascendancy: William Trevor's Big-House Novels', in Otto Rauchbauer (ed.), *Ancestral Voices: The Big House in Anglo-Irish Literature* (Hildesheim: Olms, 1992), pp. 257–77

Kristin Morrison, *William Trevor* (New York: Twayne, 1993), pp. 55–74

Mary Fitzgerald-Hoyt, *William Trevor: Re-Imagining Ireland* (Dublin: Liffey Press, 2003), pp. 111–21

Also Published in 1988

Sebastian Barry, *The Engine of Owl-Light*; Roddy Doyle, *The Commitments*; Molly Keane, *Loving and Giving* (US title, *Queen Lear*); Éilís Ní Dhuibhne, *Blood and Water*; Edna O'Brien, *The High Road*; Glenn Patterson, *Burning Your Own*

1989

Timothy O'Grady, *Motherland*

Chicago-born O'Grady's novels include I Could Read the Sky *(1997), about Irish emigrants in London, and* Light *(2004), a love story. O'Grady (b. 1951) has also published a number of non-fiction works.*

The action of this elaborate historical fantasia begins in Dublin with the obese forty-three-year-old virginal narrator recalling his return to his mother's apartment to make up with her after a temporary falling-out. He finds the apartment to be a 'macabre, devastated jungle' (6), complete with pet monkey and the family turtle, which is on its last legs, in addition to the familiar bric-à-brac which tellingly includes optical instruments. His mother has disappeared. Alarming though her absence is, it is not surprising. She has wandered away many times before, usually ending up in Northern Ireland. Indeed, the lives of mother and son together have always been peripatetic, since throughout his childhood his mother was employed in a succession of provincial big houses. The most significant of these was in County Kilkenny, where her employer, a retired American judge, was something of a father figure to the narrator. (His actual father was a certain Lawrence O'Bannion, though, as the novel's title indicates, patriarchy is beside the point.) When news comes of the judge's death in America, the narrator is able 'to assemble the rest of the death scene myself' (26), one of the earliest instances of his visionary capacity.

As well as the apartment's state of disarray, the narrator also finds a large, handsomely bound volume written in Irish and French which his mother had been attempting to translate. Published in 1892, the work is a history of the Synnott family from 1169 onwards, and reproduces in their own words and languages that family's account of itself. Intrigued by his mother's interest in this opus, the narrator himself

becomes engrossed in it, and manages to decipher enough to learn that
the opening pages are Hervey Synnott's narrative of his journey from
Bristol to Bannow Strand in the retinue of his learned and enlightened
mentor, the Norman lord, Bertrand de Paor. This passage is the first of
the novel's essays in time-travel, and features not only the well-known
historical and political background to the Normans' arrival in Ireland
but de Paor's visionary ideal for the type of community appropriate to
the new-found land of beautiful County Wexford. But hardly has this
community, consisting of equal numbers of natives and Normans, been
established than it is overrun, dispersing its members, their possessions and their mentalities.

By the time the narrator has mastered Hervey's story, he has
encountered a learned mentor of his own. This white-haired old
gentleman not only befriends the narrator but turns out to be the
source of the Synnott family history. His name is Declan Synnott, and
he is the narrator's grandfather – his mother's father. He informs the
narrator that the family history is incomplete and that his ambition is
to recover the missing material, which he will finally be able to do with
the help of his grandson's visionary powers. This aim is a fiction, but it
gives the grandfather a pretext for acting as something like the narrator's Virgil (the novel's epigraph is from *The Divine Comedy*). And so
the pair set off, or rather there are two pairs, since the humans have
their animal familiars, the narrator his monkey, Synnott his poodle,
Atma. Their journey is to some extent a mental one into the past,
though the search for the missing document culminates in a dangerous
encounter with a detachment of soldiers – there are a number of
underplayed hints of substantial police and army presences in the
country at large; and Dublin is portrayed as a mixture of the coercive
and the carnivalesque. The encounter in question culminates in the
narrator's birth-like delivery from a premature burial under mounds of
detonated soil in the same area as de Paor established his community.

The romance genre – of which *Motherland* is an elaborate instance –
requires that quests end successfully, and after many a twist and turn all
the stories are eventually told, including those of the narrator's origins
and his mother's complicated history. After a circuit of Ireland, the novel
ends in an optician's shop outside Derry in a *dénouement* that brings
together the narrator and his hitherto unknown cousin, as well as
emblematically uniting north and south. This act of unification not only
restores the family circle and reintegrates missing pieces of history. It

also relies on the principle of duality which has been a fundamental feature of the narrative throughout. Beginning with Bertrand de Paor's ideal community, it recurs in every conceivable relationship – in physical resemblances, in the present's connection with the past, in the narrator's visionary faculty, in the attachment between mother and son, in the dual quest and the interchangeability of love and knowledge represented within it, in the interdependence between writing and action, in the apparent reliance between documentation and uncertainty implied by Declan Synnott's pursuit of the missing pages. Most fundamentally of all, it is built into the narrator, whose birth with webbing between his fingers means not merely that he is amphibious but that, in the American judge's understanding of that term, he possesses 'a double life' (25). The function and purpose of that doubleness is what his grandfather intends the narrator to grasp.

Essential as the doubleness principle is, it is less a product of the characters' experience than a mode of vision through which experience is perceived. Its origins are located in the works of the pre-Socratic philosopher Pythagoras, in which both de Paor and Synnott are well versed. So, the principle has a venerable and unimpeachable intellectual lineage. And that lineage's historical reality finds form in the unusual discontinuous connectivity that the history of the Synnotts exemplifies. One of Synnott's explanations of the attraction of Pythagoras is that the philosopher 'thought with his whole being. He was a repository of reason and unreason, unlike others who came after him who regarded the two as exclusive' (186). This embodiment of the whole is the aim and object of a dual focus. It functions as the precondition of retrieval, reconciliation and unification, as is indicated by de Paor's ideal of community, by the fact that the narrator's Derry cousin is – somewhat glibly, perhaps – named Bridges, and by the nature of the book of Synnott itself, a single entity composed of materials dating from different times and depicting heterogeneous experiences, all nevertheless gathered together under the one name and in the name of the one blood.

That book's cover, 'ingeniously intricate, wayward and explosive, so that each individual tooled line pursued its own course through astonishing convolutions to its own unpredictable end' (59), is not only a guide to its disparate elements and the possibility of their integration but also to a reading of Motherland, with its various temporal and familial strands. Although the narrator believes himself to be on the understandably human, though arguably quixotic, quest for his mother, he is also – given the dimension introduced by his grandfather – engaged in mapping a 'workable system of relations known as knowledge' (64). As the novel's title implies, the human archetype of mother resides within the communal archetype of land, and vice versa. The story of the former, conceived of in terms of human need, finds solace and perspective in the latter's story. Yet again, an Irish novel uses the familiar, demotic trope of as-I-roved-out as a pretext for engaging with questions of consciousness and knowledge. Admittedly, 'in twoness there is uncertainty' (190). Yet, in twoness also there is visionary potential and imaginative range, two qualities that *Motherland* claims to be indispensable to its diverting foray into the long-contested national categories of blood and soil.

Supplementary Reading

Kenneth Griffith and Timothy E. O'Grady, *Curious Journey: An Oral History of Ireland's Unfinished Revolution* (London: Hutchinson, 1982)

Philip Horne, 'Dark Strangers, Gorgeous Slums', *London Review of Books*, vol. 11, no. 6 (16 March 1989)

Timothy O'Grady, 'Memory, Photography, Ireland', *Irish Studies Review*, vol. 14, no. 2 (May 2006), pp. 255–62

Also Published in 1989

John Banville, *The Book of Evidence*; Samuel Beckett, *Ill Seen, Ill Said*; Evelyn Conlon, *Stars in the Daytime*; J.M. O'Neill, *Canon Bang Bang*; Frank Ronan, *The Men Who Loved Evelyn Cotton*; Robert McLiam Wilson, *Ripley Bogle*

1990

Dermot Bolger, *The Journey Home*

Poet, playwright and publisher, Bolger (b. 1959) has written nine novels. Beginning with Nightshift *(1985) and* The Woman's Daughter *(1987; revised edition, 1991), many of these works deal with tensions in lower-class family life, contextualised by perspectives on social and historical conditions. The north Dublin suburb of Finglas is a recurring setting, and a type of heightened naturalism the predominant artistic approach. Themes of abandon and redemption feature strongly in such works as* Emily's Shoes *(1992) and* A Second Life *(1994); and home recurs as a problematic focus in these novels as well as in* Father's Music *(1997),* Temptation *(2000) and* The Valparaiso Voyage *(2001). In* The Family *on Paradise Pier (2005), the ideological and historical range is broadened to detail the principles and problems of an Anglo-Irish family, of which the Protestant old lady in* The Journey Home *is a member.*

Two youngsters are on the run from the authorities, a state which draws attention to the complicated implications of the novel's title phrase. Francis Hanrahan (Hano) and his girlfriend Cait are the youngsters in question, and how they came to be in flight is interwoven with their present situation, a narrative method that is only one expression of that sense of duality informing many other aspects of the novel – sexuality, class, political power, Ireland and Europe. The novel's urban and west of Ireland settings, and the contrast between these landscapes' evocative past and their neglected present, also contribute to its sense of the tensions between, and within, worlds. Even Hano's native Finglas is split in two by a modern highway. The reality of a broken world and the desire for a whole one – the latter signified by the idea of home – constitute the novel's thematic interplay. Coming to terms with both reality and desire is the challenge Hano and Cait face, though facing it is further complicated by the memory of their friend Shay, catalyst of much of the action and a primary exemplar of home's ambivalent nature.

Hano meets Shay when he is temporarily employed at the Voters' Register's Office (a general election is part of the background to the personal stories). This office is in Kilmainham, a location whose hallowed historical associations are in ironic counterpoint to the office's atmosphere of pettiness and fecklessness. Shay is the workplace's one animated presence, and Hano – inexperienced and self-doubting, one who 'grew up in perpetual exile' (8) – finds him irresistible. It is additionally reassuring that Shay also comes from Finglas – a home boy. Yet, 'The discovery that we were from the same suburb was made not in terms of common links but of differences' (26). The budding friendship, instead of making home more inhabitable for Hano, leads him into the larger Dublin world which Shay appears to have made his own – 'reality at last' (70), Hano believes. In retrospect, however, he is not quite sure if Shay sees the city in the same way – 'even then I think Shay was merely playing at living his life' (ibid.). Indeed, there is a performative element to Shay's behaviour which makes it seem not only part of the repertoire of the drink and high jinks of the traditional Friday boys' nights out, but a recapitulation of the equally traditional Dublin of pubs and talk, a bogus home.

But there is also a further dimension of the city – 'a grey under-world' (31) – peopled by the economically disenfranchised and the socially marginalised. One figure who stands out in this environment is flashy, drug-dealing Justin Plunkett; 'the angel of death' (80), to Hano. Justin is the son of a noted politician, Patrick, who with his brother Pascal, a property developer and money-lender, comprise a powerful presence in the north city suburbs. Pascal employs Hano's parents, and the Plunkett name is everywhere in the neighbourhood where Shay and Hano share an apartment. (It is while living here in what Hano calls 'my Ark' (212) that Shay brings Cait into his life, having rescued her from drug involvement.) Eventually, both Shay and Hano also become Plunkett employees, Hano as Pascal's driver and Shay, on his return from a spell in Holland, as a drug courier for Justin.

As though to dispel doubts as to Pascal's unsavouriness, there is a dramatic episode during which, to collect a debt, he dangles a baby from a high-rise window. And when Shay – still having difficulty in reconciling 'those two sides of his nature, the fear of being trapped perpetually clashing with the sense of belonging somewhere' (81) – wants to break with Justin, he is killed. The novel's elaborate, not directly linear plot – which also touches on such condition-of-Ireland themes as emigration, the legacy of the past, urban blight and the fate of the Anglo-Irish, to mention merely the most prominent – culmi-nates in Hano planning decisive action. But his wish to avenge Shay by killing Pascal backfires, and instead he succumbs to the latter's sexual advances (as Shay did to Patrick Plunkett's in The Hague). Cait, however, has also planned vengeance and, with impeccable timing, turns up at Pascal's home while Hano is there. Hano then kills Pascal and sets fire to his house. Then it is time to set out on their journey westward.

The west is the part of the country that Cait is originally from – Shay dubbed her 'the country girl' (45). But if her heart is still there, her home is not. Pursued by the police, who refused to listen to Hano when he reported Shay's killing, the pair make their way to Sligo, where Hano locates the friendly old lady he met some years before on a solo trip down the country. 'It's time you came home, Francis' (280), the old lady tells him, and 'the idea of some sort of lost home-land he could belong to' (133) has been on his mind, though the thought's vague phrasing casts doubt on the realm's availability. What the old lady exemplifies shows that Hano's idea of home is in need of revision. Herself dispossessed, belittled by history, she has not lost heart. Being reduced to living in a caravan is less important than the world the caravan contains, images of and testimonials to the 'hundred causes' (178) she supports: 'it was as if she had withdrawn from her own land, knowing it was impossible to change the Plunketts who carved it up, and had concentrated on creating her own country within her caravan instead' (ibid.). Undaunted by the past, undiminished by the present, this old lady seems another iteration of the poor old woman, here a tutelary image of tenacity and resistance. Her internal exile privileges the prospect of a world of one's own. Such a world is what Hano envisages for himself and the now pregant Cait, a world evidently synonymous with the novel's final word, 'home' (294).

This sense of home is redolent of refuge and resting place, a place providing the sustenance and renewal associated with birth. It is not a sense that speaks of homeland or motherland. Prized by Shay as 'the most uncool guy in the world' (72), Hano seems to embody the younger generation of the plain people of Ireland, the anonymous ones whose significance is authenticated in the ideal of a republic itself, and in the form of government that supposedly makes that ideal functional. It is these people that the Plunkett brothers – that duality without a difference – betray. The changes with which such figures are associated are exploitative and extortionate, and are carried out with no regard for their victims' reality, as is shown not only by their actions but by the hypocritical rhetoric of Patrick's flag-saluting speeches. With Justin as their heir, their heritage is evidently poisonous, narcotic. Ireland may be the country for that young man, but it is no country for hapless Hano or spirited Shay. Nor does there seem to be much they can do to change that.

Supplementary Reading

Dermot Bolger, 'Introduction', *The Picador Book of Contemporary Irish Fiction* (London: Picador, 1993), pp. vii–xxvi

Conor MacCarthy, 'Ideology and Geography in Dermot Bolger's *The Journey Home*', *Irish University Review*, vol. 27, no. 1 (Spring/Summer 1997), pp. 98–110

Liam Harte, 'A Kind of Scab: Irish Identity in the Writings of Dermot Bolger and Joseph O'Connor', *Irish Studies Review*, vol. 20, no. 3 (Autumn 1997), pp. 17–22

Ray Ryan, *Ireland and Scotland: Literature and Culture, State and Nation, 1966–2000* (Oxford: Clarendon Press, 2002), pp. 141–98

Also Published in 1990

Roddy Doyle, *The Snapper*; Aidan Carl Mathews, *Muesli at Midnight*; John McGahern, *Amongst Women*: Brian Moore, *Lies of Silence*; Francis Stuart, *A Compendium of Lovers*; Colm Tóibín, *The South*

1991

Hugo Hamilton, *The Last Shot*

Of Hamilton's seven novels, four are set in Germany. Both The Last Shot *and* Disguise *(2008) have Second World War themes, while* Surrogate City *(1990) and* The Love Test *(1995) draw on life in contemporary Berlin. Two other novels –* Headbanger *(1996) and* Sad Bastard *(1998) – feature the south County Dublin cases of the odd-ball policeman Pat Coyne. Ireland's new immigrants are the subject of* Hand in the Fire *(2010). A Dubliner, Hamilton (b. 1953) is also the author of a collection of short stories and of two remarkable memoirs,* The Speckled People *(2003) and* The Sailor in the Wardrobe *(2006; US title,* The Harbor Boys*). The first is essential reading on many counts, among them the background it provides to the author's German connections.*

'A war is only over when the last shot has been fired, and who knows where the last shot of the Second World War was fired?' (3) This question, posed early on in this soft-spoken, searching treatment of war's complicated afterlife, reverberates throughout its two interleaved narratives, related but distinct, both set in Germany. The first narrative deals with the experiences of Bertha Sommer and Franz Kern as they make their way back home from Laun, in Bohemia, where they are stationed. Bertha has spent the war as a clerical worker with the Wehrmacht, Franz as a radio operator. The time is May 1945 (Germany surrendered on 7 May). As Soviet and American forces close in, and as local Czech resistance begins to assert itself, Franz offers to include Bertha in a plan to escape. But their participation in the plan misfires, and they eventually travel with the retreating army as far as the German border. There they find bicycles and set off together for their respective homes, Franz's in Nuremberg and Bertha's farther north in Kempen in the Ruhr. Their journey takes them away from major routes and through an unspoiled countryside which looks additionally welcoming in its early summer finery.

This departure from the mainstream of war traffic and from landscapes typical of a defeated nation consolidates the qualities evident in Franz's initial offer of assistance and Bertha's acceptance of it. Their way back would not be possible without a willingness to trust, a sense of mutual dependence and an implicit faith that the values of disinterest and unselfishness were still available. But their companionship amounts to more than simply an exercise in ethics. During a restorative rest by an idyllic lake – 'In the middle of nowhere. In the middle of Germany' (90) – Bertha and Franz find that they also still have their natures. Their bodies are still their own, and they celebrate this discovery with one another. Almost immediately, however, their expression of love is threatened by its antithesis. In Franz's temporary absence, Bertha is set upon by two travellers heading east. Just as she is about to be raped, Franz finds her and shoots her attacker with the service weapon he has illegally retained (he also shoots the would-be rapist's companion). 'For the first time in his life, Franz Kern turned himself into a soldier' (134), and whether or not in doing so he has fired the war's last shot, he and Bertha 'both realised that they had extended the war' (142).

Both the attack and the rescue have intimately marked Bertha with war's violence, and her survival is burdened with complicated feelings of guilt. Although Franz sees his actions as the only ones conceivable under the circumstances, at Bertha's request he throws away his gun. In a manner of speaking, their relationship has now been battle-tested, and their dream of a new life in America together remains intact. In fact, when they reach Nuremberg, Franz is all for going straight on to Hamburg and emigration, it being unlikely that his wife could have survived the devastating aerial bombardment of the city. But Bertha insists that he attempt to locate his wife, and when he succeeds in doing so she realises that Franz has found his home. In a further gesture of loyalty and disinterest, Bertha honours Franz's commitments and continues back to her own family alone. As things turn out, however, she spends most of her subsequent life in Vermont.

The second narrative begins forty years later, and is narrated by an anonymous American student of his time as a postgraduate in 1980s' Germany. 'There is something about Germany that I want' (23), he says, and a visit to Laun confirms what this is, even though the town has been renamed Louny and has in other ways masked the past. And the narrator does not retrace history in the single-minded way of a researcher; indeed, his inquiries 'made me feel a bit like a Nazi-hunter' (124). Besides, he is caught up in complications arising from his relationships with two college friends, Anke and Jürgen. His affair with Anke continues regardless of her marriage to Jürgen and the latter's continuing friendship with the narrator, and despite the fact that the married couple have moved to another city and have a child, Alex, born with Down's syndrome. And it is not the triangular relationship that brings the marriage to a crisis, but Jürgen's personal and professional conviction – he has succeeded to his father's gynaecology practice – that Alex should receive euthanasia. The child's life chances are extremely limited, and in the course of his four-year life he also contracts leukemia.

These complications echo without duplicating the exemplary concerns in the story of Bertha and Franz – loyalty, obligation, choice, the giving and taking of life. Jürgen's reasoned arguments recall Franz's pragmatic justifications for his killings, while Anke's fraught reactions are reminiscent of Bertha's. In both cases there is difficulty in speaking about those reactions, as though those who have them lack experience in coming out with what they feel. And in addition, the two crises coincide with moments of historical liberation, the fall of the Berlin wall and the Soviet empire supplying the latter-day context. As did the fall of the Nazi empire, the events of 1989 also portend freedom. But the quality and benefit of that freedom remains hard to determine. For Jürgen, the crowds arriving by train from the east (another complicated historical echo) are capable of understanding freedom only as 'the choice between mauve and sludge-green blouses' (71). Yet the freedom he exhibits has its problems too, as not only his tolerance of Anke's affair with the narrator but his decision regarding Alex indicate. The appearance of a Laun Down's syndrome child in the first narrative is seen as 'an overt act of revolution in the Reich' (7). Jürgen's sense of his own son being 'like a refugee' (80) associates him with the fallout of both the major historical events in *The Last Shot*, and also gives him the name of a seeker of freedom and the sense of dignity and value that freedom connotes. But Jürgen does not seem quite sure how to work at making such connections. In contrast, Anke – 'She thrived on freedom' (147) – shows a far greater capacity to see Alex as a person rather than as a case. Seeing how she weeps at her son's funeral, the narrator thinks that she 'was crying for everyone' (167).

That comment's sense of relatedness helps to appreciate the narrator's place in the scheme of things. His understated presence is premised on a quest for connection. In a sense, his involvement with Anke and Jürgen is the opposite of the kind of connection he has intended to make, even as it dramatises for him problems of freedom and choice in a contemporary context. Alex's funeral marks the end of that connection. By that time not only has it long been evident that the narrator is the late Bertha Sommer's son but he has found Franz Kern. His mother's diaries have supplied the factual information on which his searching has been based. But the narrator is also making a crucial differentiation between the historical narrative as such and the human tissue embedded in it. Acts and consequences have an equal claim; external circumstances and their internalised impact are both fundamental to a sense of the record. Franz Kern seems to have such thoughts in mind when in discussing the war with the narrator he remarks, 'Maybe it's still not over' (159).

Questions raised by the war are not disposed of by peace. There is no reason why they should be. As the experiences of Anke and Jürgen indicate, peace brings conflicts too. The conclusion of their story on notes of separation, things unspoken and loss suggests a sense of unfinished business and this, too, replicates the end of the Bertha and Franz story. Such conclusions omit the possibility of one based on connection. The narrator is the mediator of both types of ending. Peace can also be restorative. The large version of this possibility is the reunification of Germany which is taking place as the narrator makes contact with Franz Kern. The older man rejoices in that event. But he is also open to the past which the narrator asks him to revisit. He has 'never forgotten' (159) Bertha. And the experience of reconnecting with her also 'feels like talking to a son' (ibid.). The history of intimacy, and the willingness to discuss it, become essential components of the fate of nations.

Supplementary Reading

Hugo Hamilton, 'Introduction', in Francis Stuart, *The Pillar of Cloud* (Dublin: New Island Books, 1994), pp. 1–4

Steven Belletto, 'Hugo Hamilton', in Michael R. Molino (ed.), *Twentieth-Century British and Irish Novelists* (Detroit: Gale, 2003), pp. 121–9

Carlo Gébler, 'Irish Spoken Here', *The Times Literary Supplement*, 14 February 2003

Hugo Hamilton, 'Heinrich Böll: A German Folk Hero', *An Sionnach*, vol. 1, no. 2 (Fall 2005), pp. 11–15

Also Published in 1991

Ronan Bennett, *The Second Prison*; Dermot Bolger, *The Woman's Daughter* (2nd, expanded, edition); Roddy Doyle, *The Van*; Thomas McCarthy, *Without Power*; Joseph O'Neill, *This is the Life*; Frank Ronan, *Picnic in Eden*

1992
Patrick McCabe, *The Butcher Boy*

The author of a collection of short stories and of a number of plays, McCabe (b. 1955) is best know for his ten novels. Both Music on Clinton Street *(1986) and* Carn *(1989) establish his fictional world, the former with its emphasis on popular culture, the latter by its border-country setting (McCabe was born in Clones, County Monaghan). More obviously genre-bending later works include* The Dead School *(1995),* Breakfast on Pluto *(1998),* Emerald Germs of Ireland *(2001),* Call Me the Breeze *(2003),* Winterwood *(2006),* The Holy City *(2009) and* The Stray Sod Country *(2010). A baroque imagination is evident in all these works, generally expressed in a diverting combination of gothic excess and excruciating comedy which also reveals a satirical eye for social and cultural tastes and beliefs.*

'The Butcher Boy' is a folk song replete with that genre's familiar themes of love, loss and violence, and one of the most ingenious aspects of this novel is the manner in which it adapts not only these themes to meet its own narrative interests but how the notion of the folk is treated in the process. A recording of the song is one of the prize possessions of manic-depressive Annie Brady, mother of the young narrator, Francie. It plays a prominent part in what might be called the novel's soundtrack, a complicated chorus in Francie's head consisting of popular songs from various traditions as well as snatches of film dialogue, real – as with 'Take 'em to Missouri!' (9), a line of John Wayne's in *Red River*, which recurs throughout – and invented, as with the numerous lapses into cowboy lingo and tough-guy argot. And the novel's musical aspect also embraces Francie's father, Benny, an erstwhile trumpeter of some ability who has forsaken playing in favour of drinking.

This soundtrack is just one of the haunting presences that unpredictably assail Francie's consciousness. In time, the accumulation of presences includes his mother, dead by her own hand, and his father, dead of neglect; Francie's fabrication of their honeymoon in Bundoran; his father's brother, Alo, a London-based emigrant beloved of Mary, who has waited for him at home in the anonymous and largely generic town in which the Bradys reside. The haunting is not confined to Francie. Memories of childhood years spent in an orphanage with Alo continue to beset Benny, and he cannot help himself from bitterly referring to that period at a party welcoming Alo home for Christmas. This deviation from the done thing is one of the novel's many instances of being let down. Most of these affect Francie, and their recurrence make them one of the few consistent features of his experience, even if in themselves they are manifestations of inconsistency. Their impact on the youngster obviously shows his vulnerability and neediness, and while their occurrence within the family circle is the product of Annie and Benny being psychologically frail and emotionally undernourished, the let-down Francie experiences at the hands of public servants and their institutions reflects a failure to nurture, which is more difficult to justify and accept.

But failure on the part of police, clergy and psychiatric health professionals seems to be the inevitable concomitant of a more fundamental social deficiency, the nature of which is exemplified by the character who becomes Francie's *bête noir*, Mrs Nugent. Her years in England have evidently led her to raise her son, Philip, above 'blood brothers' (53) such as Francie and his pal, Joe Purcell. She considers Francie, in particular, to be separate from and unequal to her well-groomed, piano-playing Philip, and her calling his family 'pigs' (4) is one of the first voices from outside the family to haunt Francie. His fixation with Mrs Nugent leads to some piggish behaviour towards her and her values. He attacks Philip, invades and despoils the house-proud Nugent home, and acts out his sense of stigma and shame.

In its unpredictability and improvisation, Francie's retaliation is a show of spirit which plainly contrasts with Mrs Nugent's power of judgment and socially discriminatory outlook. This energy is also a feature of Francie's narrative voice, the instrument, so to speak, that not only makes him distinctive and different but establishes him as central to his own experiences, contrary to the counterproductive effects of those experiences when they take place. His war against the Nugents only leads to his increasing powerlessness. Francie's inability to help himself confines him to his parents' realm of helplessness and dysfunction. And Francie's voice, in its unorthodox syntax, shifting point of view and similar irregularities, articulates the environment of breakdown in which he has his origins, while at the same time being the means by which his narrative presence transmits its undeniable vitality.

In seeking to modify Francie's behaviour, Mrs Nugent merely incites it. In expecting him to conform, she confirms the dispiriting and denaturing narrowness by which he is expected to abide. In humiliating him, she exposes herself as the party with something to lose. But, though Annie says 'We don't want to be like the Nugents' (19), acceptable choices are hard to find. Francie's attempts to conform – both institutionally enforced and voluntarily adopted – turn out to be occasions for further dislocation. Affecting piety during his sojourn in an industrial school – a house with a hundred windows, like the one in which his father and uncle were kept – he falls into the hands of a molesting priest. He learns that Joe, guided by his parents, has abandoned him for Philip Nugent. On his release, Francie is employed by Leddy, the town butcher; his job is to collect trash, as though to confirm that he belongs at the pig level. And visiting Bundoran in the hope of finding some evidence to support his idealisation of his parents' honeymoon, he learns instead that indeed Benny is remembered, but for all the wrong reasons.

Never more alone, Francie tries to retrieve Joe from the boarding school that he and Philip now attend, only for Joe to deny knowing him. It seems that all Francie is left with is Mrs Nugent. He is now reduced to being unable to see past her. She is the author of the 'two bad things' (209) that changed his life: his absence when Annie killed herself and Joe's rejection. She becomes a myth of rectitude and righteousness in his eyes, a rigid barrier to his being seen as anything other than a pig. No doubt he means it when he says, 'I had no intention of chopping up anyone' (166). Given how he has perceived his victim, however, his solution to the problem she poses is cruelly out of proportion. But then the same may be said of the form of potentially soul-destroying social sectarianism Mrs Nugent practises. Francie's behaviour is transgressive and invasive, an exaggerated and aggravated display of border-crossing, part of whose effect is to make the reader wonder about the nature of borders and of the vigilance that keeps them in operation.

Told in retrospect, the action of The Butcher Boy takes place in the early 1960s. Change is in the air. Figures from the popular culture of the day populate Francie's mental landscape, and their alluring novelty connotes a vision of youthful promise at odds with Mrs Nugent's politesse (as well as with Philip's piano book, Emerald Gems of Ireland). And at the same time that Francie is engaged in his own private Nugent apocalypse, a larger calamity seems imminent because of the Cuban missile crisis. This, too, might be thought of as lacking a sense of proportion, while the millenarian nature of the local response to the crisis, with its focus on the Blessed Virgin, is similarly deficient in equilibrium and self-awareness. In such an order of things, Francie's thought that 'All the beautiful things of this world are lies' (212) is understandable. That statement, as well as his recurring references to the snowdrop, his frequent displays of childish simplicity, and his sensory spontaneity are reminders that in his accelerated downfall, something human has been forfeited. But in what is perhaps the novel's most pointed critical shaft, it is only Francie himself who has any awareness of his condition. 'How can your solitary finish?' (230) he asks, when eventually released from solitary confinement in the asylum where he finally ends up. The answer does not take the form of a social convention or an approved method of rehabilitation. On the contrary, it is expressed through memory, play and imaginative energy, inner resources that maintain the distinctiveness that the careless and overbearing world of Irish social convention attempts to deny Francie Brady.

Supplementary Reading

Tom Herron, 'ContamiNation: Patrick McCabe and Colm Tóibín's Pathographies of the Republic', in Liam Harte and Michael Parker (eds), *Contemporary Irish Fiction: Themes, Tropes, Theories* (Basingstoke: Macmillan, 2000), pp. 168–91, esp. pp. 172–8

James M. Smith, 'Remembering Ireland's Architecture of Containment: Telling Stories in *The Butcher Boy* and *States of Fear*', *Éire-Ireland*, vol. 36, nos 3–4 (Fall/Winter 2001), pp. 11–30

Tim Gauthier, 'Identity, Self-Loathing and the Neocolonial Condition in Patrick McCabe's *The Butcher Boy*', *Critique: Studies in Contemporary Fiction*, vol. 44, no. 2 (Winter 2003), pp. 196–211

Linden Peach, *The Contemporary Irish Novel: Critical Readings* (Basingstoke: Palgrave Macmillan, 2004), pp. 177–83

Also Published in 1992

Ronan Bennett, *Overthrown by Strangers*; Clare Boylan, *Home Rule* (published in the US as *11 Edward Street*); Deirdre Madden, *Remembering Light and Stone*; Eugene McCabe, *Death and Nightingales*; Edna O'Brien, *Time and Tide*; Glenn Patterson, *Fat Lad*

1993

Roddy Doyle, *Paddy Clarke Ha Ha Ha*

Born in 1958, Doyle is a native of the north Dublin suburb of Kilbarrack, the prototype of Barrytown. He is author of nine novels, including the Barrytown Trilogy – The Commitments (1987), The Snapper (1990) and The Van (*1991*) *– and a second trilogy with the umbrella title of* The Last Roundup, *containing* A Star Called Henry (*2000*), Oh, Play That Thing (*2004*) *and* The Dead Republic (*2010*). *Other novels are* The Woman Who Walked into Doors (*1996*) *and* Paula Spencer (*2004*). *Doyle has also written a number of plays and two collections of short stories. His family history is recorded in his parents' voices in* Rory & Ita (*2002*).

Barrytown: the early days. The year is 1968 and Dublin's outer fringes are beginning to be developed. Where the Clarke family lives is neither urban nor rural but something of a borderland where the old Donnelly farm meets the new Corporation houses before succumbing to them. And, taking a cue from the nature of a setting that seems to be always changing, growing, acquiring additional dimensions, the story highlights the separate spaces in which events occur and lets the more conventional narrative device of linking events over time take a back seat. This change in narrative approach, with the emphasis on immediacy that its perspective brings, places the reader slap bang in the middle of Paddy Clarke's brave new world.

This is the only world he knows, and he finds it 'brilliant', to use one of his favourite, oft-repeated words. It is impossible to begrudge him the delight he takes in having the run of his territory. The energy, spontaneity and wholeheartedness with which he reacts to his surroundings are winning characteristics in their own right, and as such is a noteworthy departure from more familiar pictures of oppressive Irish childhoods. But attractively artless as Paddy's account of himself seems to be, it has more going for it than just its face value, though that value is by no means trivial. Hearing him out in his own terms ratifies the Huck Finn-like independence of his life on the streets and in the fields. He speaks freely, and the reader has no alternative but to accept that freedom – any thought of an alternative being obviously illogical. In a word, Paddy comes across as being no more than himself, like other kids in some ways, different from them in others – the term self-sufficient comes to mind – just as Barrytown itself is in Dublin yet different from, and free of, the city's old metropolitan core.

Such considerations of person and place also arise from Barrytown's continuing development and growth, not necessarily because these advances occur in tandem with Paddy's progress but, more interestingly, because they introduce the idea of structure. Not that this idea crosses Paddy's mind. School, for him, is simply school, an amalgamation of events, sensations, memories, observations and rituals, not entirely dis-similar from his free time. Predictably enough, he remains pretty much oblivious of and indifferent to its institutional and organisational char-acter, except when it becomes heavy-handed and threatening. Yet, the school stands out in the Barrytown landscape as its one social structure outside the home. When Paddy's father starts hitting the bottle, he does not drink at the pub down the road. There is no such place. The Clarkes do not get in their car and drive to the nearby cinema; indeed, the car does not appear to get them anywhere. Even the church seems remote, and what priests there are seem peripheral. There are no sports or social clubs, no branches of political parties or trade unions, no hob-byists, no dramatic society, nothing in the way of Catholic lay activity, no public transport. These missing bits underline Barrytown's newness and its difference from more established communities. Paddy and his pals do very well without them, but their absence underlines that status of the family as the one form of belonging Barrytown residents possess.

The nuclear family, at that. Like those other noted residents of Barrytown, the Rabbittes, whose way of life is the subject of Doyle's *Barrytown Trilogy*, the Clarkes are on their own. But they are not as numerous as the Rabbittes, and seem more vulnerable and less adjusted to the demands of a new life in a new place. (The Barrytown the Rabbittes live in also has some of the communal resources, and also shows some of the social initiative lacking in *Paddy Clarke*.) All that can be said about the Clarkes is that they are residents and parents. And even residents seems too definite a designation; as Paddy reports, 'They were all pioneers, my da said' (157). They've brought enough with them to Barrytown to furnish a house, but it is not clear yet that that is enough to furnish a life. Have they relocated or are they dislo-cated? A bit of both, clearly. And it is difficult for them to find a balance between what they have chosen to do and the effect it has on them. Paddy's escapes, scrapes and improvisations finds its opposite in his parents' insecurities and uncertainties.

The shift in location corresponds to changes in Dublin's physical and demographic makeup, and represents not only the end of places like *Strumpet City*'s Chandler's Court but the introduction of a new set of relations, based on a core-and-periphery model, between the city and its citizens. These changes take place with the anniversary of the 1916 Rising as their backdrop, a rebellion undertaken in the name of the Irish people. Thus, the difficulty in saying quite who the Clarkes are resonates beyond Barrytown. It may indeed be that they are descendants of James Plunkett's workers and activists. More to the point, though, is the fact that this cannot be said with certainty. A great silence surrounds their origins and identities, a silence observed primarily by the characters themselves. A cultural and historical category such as 'the Irish people' is one for which they do not appear to have much use, or much understanding of. Immersed in their own circumstances, they are beginning again, without memory, without history, without tradition or a perceived need for a usable past. Their physical distance from their native city is emblematic of other forms of distance and withdrawal. Dublin seems present to them only in the form of the Corporation's building plans. And they do not impinge on it, either. There are no old neighbourhoods, no former childhood haunts, virtually no visits to or from extended families. And school does not give the next generation much to go on, providing no more than rote learning of Irish and a kitschy commemoration of Easter 1916.

It is tempting to think of Paddy's pretence of being related to Tom Clarke, one of the executed leaders of the 1916 Rising, as the childish dream of affiliation with that ground-breaking event, but Thomas Clarke is as temporary a father figure as another of Paddy's elect, Fr Damien of Molokai, the leper priest. And 1966 is as notable in local minds for England's World Cup victory as it is for the supposed moral defeat of England fifty years previously. In Barrytown, freedom and independence are less historical buzz-words than they are elements of the ordinary, illustrated by everyday actions, to positive and negative effect. They are expressions of desire and occasions of discipline, elements among others in the daily effort of finding one's feet and holding one's ground. Whether Paddy would be better off with a more cultivated appreciation of days gone by and patriotic sacrifice is beside the point. Apart from there being little evidence of such appreciation being available, the times are not hospitable to previous pieties regarding people and *patria*, as the dispersal of Dublin into enclaves such as Barrytown makes clear. And Paddy, in the way he behaves and in the nature of his narrative, is a child of more fragmented, more liberated and more isolating modern times.

When it comes to father figures, this too is a matter that begins at home, in the here and now of life as lived, like everything else in Barrytown – and, like everything else, also many-sided. Paddy Clarke Senior's growing estrangement from family life in Barrytown may be an expression of his wanting something more interesting and engaging, as suggested by his appetite for television news, his admiration for Israel in the 1967 war, his general impatience with daily routine. Or it may be a sign of weakness, stress, insecurity and isolation. Here again, origins are less to the point than outcomes. Regardless of what has brought about the fissures in the family structure, it is what comes next that counts. Young Paddy has no da, and that is nothing to be laughed at. The novel's title, however, is a reminder that Paddy is unable to ignore the mockery of his peers, brought about by his father's departure. He has no alternative but to stay where he is and deal with it. Which is what he does, despite not only the onslaught of public derision but his first painful experiences of adult imperfection, uncertainty and doubt. Like Barrytown itself, Paddy isn't going anywhere. And like Barrytown, he is entitled to his distinctiveness. Frail and without obvious roots as, in each case, that distinctiveness might be, there is also in it a current of indomitability.

Supplementary Reading

Luke Strongman, 'Toward an Irish Literary Postmodernism: Roddy Doyle's *Paddy Clarke Ha Ha Ha*', *Canadian Journal of Irish Studies*, vol. 23, no. 1 (July 1997), pp. 31–40

Caramine White, *Reading Roddy Doyle* (Syracuse: Syracuse University Press, 2001), pp. 98–115

Dermot McCarthy, *Roddy Doyle: Raining on the Parade* (Dublin: Liffey Press, 2003), pp. 119–54

Mary M. McGlynn, *Narrative of Class in New Irish and Scottish Literature: From Joyce to Kelman, Doyle, Galloway and McNamee* (Basingstoke: Palgrave Macmillan, 2008), pp. 120–30

Also Published in 1993

John Banville, *Ghosts*; Briege Duffaud, *A Wreath for the Dead*; Aidan Higgins, *Lions of the Grünewald*; Tom Lennon, *When Love Comes to Town*; Patrick McGinley, *The Lost Soldier's Song*; Brian Moore, *No Other Life*

1994

Dermot Healy, *A Goat's Song*

A native of Finea, County Westmeath, Healy (b. 1947) is the author of four novels, including Fighting with Shadows *(1986), set in the border country of Leitrim–Fermanagh,* Sudden Times *(1999), dealing with Irish emigrants in London, and* Long Time No See *(2011). In addition,*

he has written a number of plays, several collections of poetry, a volume of
short stories and a memoir, The Bend for Home (1996). *Healy is also the*
founder and moving spirit of the ground-breaking periodical Force 10.

Mainly set in the Erris peninsula on the remote north-western corner of County Mayo, which is where J.M. Synge's *The Playboy of the Western World* takes place, *A Goat's Song* has for its protagonist a character whom his mother describes as 'a bit of a playboy' (267). But that is a very casual description of Jack Ferris. True, he writes plays; and in his appetite for drink, his sensuality, his obsession with the love of his life, Catherine Adams, his days and ways constitute something of a rake's progress. More important than the type, however, is the antitype, and Jack's interest as a character largely derives from the ways in which he has to confront the passions and compulsions that make up his nature. There is no necessary connection between him and Synge's hero, Christy Mahon, but if one were to be teased out, it would concern the hidden history of their hungers. And even then, their destinies play out in quite different ways. The title of *A Goat's Song* says as much. Synge's play is a comedy but, as Jack explains to Catherine, '*Tragos* – goat. *Oide* – song' (227) is the etymology of tragedy, and such indeed seems to be the nature of their relationship, given that they are unable either to live together or to live apart.

The novel has a complicated form, one that seems circular as far as Jack and Catherine together are concerned, but which also follows Jack a little way into what appears to be, at least from a physical point of view, a Catherine-less future. Much of the narrative is a reconstruction of the relationship, together with an imagined biography of Catherine before Jack knew her. He undertakes this imaginative journey as a result of voluntarily committing himself to a mental hospital stay when the very likely prospect of the affair resuming fails to materialise. A tacit closeness exists between them by virtue of Catherine appearing in one of Jack's plays in Dublin, though his pursuit of her there yields very mixed results. The unlikelihood of fresh intimacy in the wake of that Dublin encounter is typical of their unstable love, as is the complicated timing and missed messages that bedevil reconnection. Catherine's failure to turn up in Erris as promised leads to Jack suffering a drink-fuelled breakdown, and though as the story unfolds it becomes clear that he is all too liable to such occurrences, his acknowledgement of the need for professional help is the most serious yet of those episodes of being 'no longer able to control the darkness' (27) which punctuate the life of dire want and naked passion that he and Catherine share. In addition, Jack has been drawn to narrative by taking down the stories of his fellow-patients, finding in this activity vivifying expressions of affirmation and continuity.

Such qualities he also attributes to Catherine's history, as emerges from his account of her background. Like Jack, who is from County Leitrim, Catherine is not a native of Erris. She is from Northern Ireland, the younger of two daughters of Jonathan Adams, a failed Presbyterian preacher who has made a career for himself in the RIC. Two events shake Jonathan's sense of cultural security and righteous living. One is the suicide of a Catholic neighbour, Matti Bonner, whose body Catherine discovers one Sunday morning hanging from a tree located between the Catholic and Presbyterian churches. Matti had been more than somebody who lived next door. He was the best man when Jonathan wed Maisie Ruttle in her native Rathkeale, County Limerick. And he invariably conducted himself in a self-possessed and civil manner – without any consciousness of being a second-class citizen, that is. This demeanour is particularly prized by Jonathan in the light of his own loss of control during a Derry Civil Rights march and the subsequent appearance on television newscasts of his baton-wielding brutality. In ways that he cannot work out, 'The death of Matti Bonner and the mêlée in Duke Street became linked in a fatal manner in the Sergeant's mind' (130).

These events, and the blow they inflict on his belief in the fitness of his way of life, are what bring Jonathan to Erris. Holidaying there, his wife Maisie finds a cottage, and the family makes a slow migration westwards, so that by the time Catherine and her sister are teenagers, the cottage is their primary home. Jonathan has difficulty in making the adjustment to the very personalised, uninstitutional peninsular life; indeed, it is debatable whether he ever does feel at home there. But he does attempt to imagine himself into 'some marvellous reconciliation' (175) between his tradition and the local ones, and between his belief system and the rather different forms of life-enhancement that he finds in his researches into Irish mythology and Erris history. On two successive summers he employs Irish teachers for his two girls. But, as in Jonathan's own case, both teachers' personalities get in the way of good intentions. Observing cultural differences 'satisfied some tortured need' (149) in Jonathan, but he cannot sublimate his sense of his flawed self in the manners and narratives of his adopted life. Change is necessary, no doubt, but the quest for a change in one's own formation appears too formidable to bring about, even if it might be argued that it is the pursuit of doing so that keeps Jonathan going.

On Jonathan's death, Jack, who has been working as a trawlerman, comes into Catherine's life, from which point on the main ingredients of Jonathan's story also recurs in theirs. They also hope for peace of mind, and believe that its attainment lies in their being together. Their journey reverses Jonathan's when Catherine finds acting work in Belfast and Jack goes to live with her there. Conditions on the 'edge of the Empire' (283) have deteriorated since the days of Civil Rights marches, and to Catherine's increasing dismay Jack spends most of his time crossing local borders into politically unsavoury pubs and befriending policemen and members of Protestant paramilitary groups. His efforts to integrate himself with local culture by participating in community theatre falls seriously flat. The resulting tension between them is too great for their sexual interdependence to withstand, and they eventually decide to return to Erris, where Jack goes back to sea. Catherine finds it impossible to settle, her propensity for sexual infidelity reappears, and after a period of increasing turbulence and alienation, it is clear that 'Some thin psychic line between them had snapped' (397).

Whether contact can successfully be re-established remains moot. But then so much of the life of this novel is premised on uncertainty, with highs and lows, attachments and sunderings, and with an overwhelming sense of the provisional and the unpredictable. The possibility of division and breakdown is to be found not only in every facet of life – political, social, artistic, sexual, communal, familial – but its presence in each facet influences its manifestations in others. And yet the religious zealots and ideological apostles whose certainty is the enemy of the temporary and the unforeseeable hardly provide an acceptable alternative. Not surprisingly, Jack 'hated those people for whom change was not only unthinkable, but unlucky' (280).

One reason dogma and righteousness in whatever form are to be resisted is suggested by the lovers' experience, which comprises not only the resolution of differences that their love achieves but their quest for such a condition. 'All knowledge . . . is a journey' (194), according to the salmon that Jonathan encounters in his readings of Irish mythology. Once embarked on it, Jack and Catherine find it as difficult to turn back as to continue, and when in doubt tend to opt for the latter choice. Jack's question, 'Where does it reside – the will to go on?' (384) does not receive a pat answer. If answer there is, however, it seems to be connected with the imagination and with the awareness of desire and need that the imagination's images put us in touch with. (As though to illustrate this point, the novel contains several intriguing brief asides on the value of fiction and of imaginative stories.) Jack and Catherine will never inhabit their own beings in the same way as the natural phenomena of Erris – the air, the sea, the flora and fauna – grace that place. Subject to time going by and to time's historical and existential flux, their disconnection from the rich, sensual, pre-social sphere in which the possibility of making a life together has its best chance is a tragedy. There they might have formed a peninsula of their own, as it were, a configuration that would supersede their islanded individual personalities. Yet in their itinerant ways, expressive as those are of their own fluctuating natures, of the disruptive national situation, and of the dislocated character of modern experience, Jack and Catherine also articulate a complicated and densely textured plea for the undeniable need for fresh beginnings and for that impossible but indispensable habitat uncontaminated by the failures of either heritage or human nature.

Supplementary Reading

Roberta Gefter Wondrich, 'Islands of Ireland: A Tragedy of Separation in Dermot Healy's *A Goat's Song*', *Writing Ulster*, no. 6 (1999), pp. 70–87

Dermot McCarthy, 'Recovering Dionysus: Dermot Healy's *A Goat's Song*', *New Hibernia Review*, vol. 4, no. 4 (Winter 2000), pp. 134–49

Izabela Krystek, 'Looking for the Self: Dermot Healy's *A Goat's Song* as an Irish Tragedy of Indecision', in Liliana Sikorska (ed.), *Ironies of Art/Tragedies of Life* (Frankfurt: Peter Lang, 2005), pp. 177–94

Stephanie Schwerter, 'Transgressing Boundaries: Belfast and the "Romance-across-the-Divide"', *Estudios Irlandeses*, no. 2 (2007), pp. 173–82

Also Published in 1994

Dermot Bolger, *A Second Life*; Emma Donoghue, *Stir Fry*; Deirdre Madden, *Nothing is Black*; Eoin McNamee, *Resurrection Man*; Edna O'Brien, *The House of Splendid Isolation*; William Trevor, *Felicia's Journey*

1995

Emma Donoghue, *Hood*

Many of Emma Donoghue's seven novels deal with relations between women, from the coming-of-age story Stir-Fry (1994), *to the historical novels* Life Mask (2004) *and* The Sealed Letter (2008) *to the modern romance,* Landing (2007). *A third historical novel,* Slammerkin (2000), *deals with women's sexuality in an abusive heterosexual context; and the author breaks new fictional ground with* Room (2010). *A native of Dublin, Donoghue (b. 1969) has also written a number of plays and published several collections of short stories. She is also a noted historian and anthologist of lesbian writing.*

Pen O'Grady is grieving. Her lover of thirteen years, Cara Wall, has been killed in a car crash. Pen's name – the same as that of the female swan – seems to have already inscribed her fate, in the sense that swans are customarily thought of as monogamous. But the novel is not only a swan song; it is also a prescription for growth and change. As well as detailing how the thirty-year-old Pen manages the transitions to such female destinies as widowhood and spinsterhood, more importantly and unexpectedly *Hood* charts her passage into full acceptance of her own sexuality. Of spinsterhood, Pen says, 'I'd prefer it to the flapping gingham motherhood, or (god forbid) the wifehood drowned in off-white lace' (114). In contrast, 'dykehood was definitely a baseball cap' (ibid.), the neologism as well as the headgear suggesting informality and insouciance, a jaunty disregard for the conventions of appearance associated with the other 'hoods' mentioned. In a word, dykehood is gay. If she is to have a life of her own, Pen must think of her sexual identity to be permissible outside her closeted relationship with Cara. Being a gay woman holds good in all cases – social, familial, professional. Pen's recognition of who she is independently of Cara allows *Hood* its mourning theme, while also being something of a valediction forbidding mourning.

Shocked and preoccupied as Pen is, this recognition is slow to dawn on her. Besides, there is nobody else on hand to see to the various tasks connected with Cara's death, the Wall family being no longer in one piece. Fourteen years earlier, Cara's mother, Winona (*née* Winnie Mulhuddart from County Limerick) made a life for herself in America with her other daughter, Kate, and is at present too busy to return home. Cara's father, an unassuming librarian, is not a great one for facing reality – in discussing her family's break-up, Kate says, 'I should have known Dad would never have the guts to emigrate' (111). If the other Wall women had remained in Ireland, Pen might have found it more difficult to sustain her affair with Cara. But with the women's departure, there is room enough in Cara's home – what Pen mockingly, though also self-consciously, refers to as the 'Big House' (108) – for her and Cara to live in a world of their own.

Given that Cara's father is a 'gentle Joseph' (113) type, Pen is under the impression – or chooses to believe – that nobody is any the wiser about the affair, though one of her later moments of awakening is the discovery that Cara's father knew all along what was going on. Moreover, it was to Kate that the teenage Pen first felt herself attracted, developing such a crush that Kate's departure for the States caused Pen to do surprisingly poorly at her exams – another example, perhaps, of not only the problems that remaining closeted create but also of what is arguably this novel's greater concern, which is with the ways in which sexual identity impinges on representations of oneself in other spheres, particularly in public. If, to the young Pen, David Bowie 'was living proof that a perv could win fame and glory' (191), then there should be a place in the world for her, too.

Cara's death does bring Kate back to Ireland. She is now not only what Donoghue refers to as a 'het' (hetero), but also, inevitably, culturally very different. Clearly, Kate has left Ireland behind, and considers her native country one that 'has nothing but a past tense' (102). This view resonates with the novel's suggestions that gay identity may be regarded as socially progressive, transgressing familiar, culturally determined norms of marriage, domesticity and the kinds of sexual roles that have conventionally been thought natural to such traditional structures. When Pen comes out to Kate about herself and Cara, she explains that the relationship 'was all very ordinary' (152). But here again, however, she is slightly missing the point, which is that to Kate there is nothing of note in what Pen has told her. And Kate seems to be on quite friendly terms with Jo Butler, a kind of den mother at Amazon Attic, a gay women's collective. Jo is somebody with whom Pen feels at ease, largely because 'she was fat like me' (63). Pen has no inkling of Cara's on-again, off-again relationship with Jo, who is a veteran of 'twenty-odd years of serial and overlapping relationships' (60). How she has chosen to think of her relationship with Cara has kept Pen's girlish naivete intact. And another consequence of doing so is that she has denied herself the worldliness necessary to complete her sexual identity by giving it a public face.

In some ways, Cara and Pen are an odd couple. Cara is from well-to-do south County Dublin; Pen's origins are working-class. Pen comports herself with the loyalty and dutifulness that make a virtue of monogamy – 'I had known well that I shouldn't nanny Cara or smother her or try to run her life for her, and any year now I was planning to really put this wisdom into practice' (254). The difficulty has, in part, arisen from the fact that 'Life seemed to be more of a battle for Cara than for anyone I knew' (186). And another part of the difficulty has been that though Cara acknowledges Pen's passion (as well as the intense satisfactions of their love-making), she is far from being monogamous and has left the relationship a number of times, even if she has always returned. Obviously Pen's devotion to Cara is an expression of emotional commitment, but the liberties Cara takes have their own reality and are not to be thought of as an expression of diminished emotional capacity. Acknowledging the viability of both forms of sexual behaviour makes for a deeper bond, and a different kind of power nexus within the relationship, than one determined and legitimised by either single form. The dual form is, in effect, a kind of 'hood', to Pen 'a funny word' which 'added to nouns made them into states of being' (113). And when 'hood' also covers explicitly intimate sexual detail, the resulting state aligns two ways of thinking about partnership with two forms of social identity – closeted and out.

This sense of new formations has counterparts in other elective and hybrid structures representative of Dublin's modernity, one instance being Pen's quite uncomplicated embrace of *à la carte* Catholicism – receiving communion comforts her, but she has dropped 'the habit' of confession: 'my story just didn't show up in their [confessors'] terms' (189). Another, more resonant, instance is the wake held for Cara at Amazon Attic, where the traditional role of women as mourners is both preserved and adapted. The spirit of such occasions is maintained, but the rituals have been changed. This semi-public occasion inhibits Pen, and she is not able to identify with it. Jo Butler advises her that her coming out remains incomplete, and that doing so has to begin at home, advice that Pen accepts and whose benefits derive from subsequent exchanges between herself and her mother. It is as if Pen's birth family valuably and reassuringly coexists with the neo-familial matriarchy headed by Jo Butler – another unfamiliar alignment. The story of

Pen and Cara is, for Pen, one of private passion, individual limitation and, to some extent, predictable insecurity and equally predictable devotion. It is also one burdened by death, burial and by the closeted – or unchanging – life. Pen without Cara is not yet a story. But she now embodies a sense of possibility and of the need to choose, and in doing so she embodies a coming of age whose belatedness is offset by its novel expressions of self-determination.

Supplementary Reading

Emma Donoghue, 'Noises from Woodsheds', in Íde O'Carroll and Eoin Collins (eds), *Lesbian and Gay Visions of Ireland towards the 21st Century* (London: Cassell, 1995), pp. 158–70

Antoinette Quinn, 'New Noises from the Woodshed: The Novels of Emma Donoghue', in Liam Harte and Michael Parker (eds), *Contemporary Irish Fiction: Themes, Tropes, Theories* (Basingstoke: Macmillan, 2000), pp. 145–67, esp. pp. 154–65

Kathleen O'Brien, 'Contemporary *Caoineadh*: Talking Straight Through the Dead', *Canadian Journal of Irish Studies*, vol. 32, no. 1 (2006), pp. 56–63

Jennifer M. Jeffers, *The Irish Novel at the End of the Twentieth Century: Gender, Bodies and Power* (New York: Palgrave, 2007), pp. 100–7

Also Published in 1995

John Banville, *Athena*; Anne Enright, *The Wig My Father Wore*; Jennifer Johnston, *The Illusionist*; Lia Mills, *Another Alice*; Glenn Patterson, *Black Night at Big Thunder Mountain*; James Ryan, *Home from England*

1996

Seamus Deane, *Reading in the Dark*

Deane (b. 1941) is one of the leading Irish intellectuals and critics of his generation, as well as a poet of some distinction. His critical publications largely reflect his concerns with literary and cultural history, the most notable being the three-volume Field Day Anthology of Irish Writing *(1991). Set in his native Derry,* Reading in the Dark *meditates on history and inheritance from more intimate perspectives. Deane's only novel, in form and style it reveals, among other things, the touch of the poet.*

'I'd switch off the light, get back in bed, and lie there, the book still open, re-imagining all I had read, the various ways the plot might unravel, the novel opening into endless possibilities in the dark' (20). Such occasions are obviously pleasurable to the nameless young narrator of *Reading in the Dark*. But the way he relates to his bedtime story – the novel in question is *The Shan Van Vocht: The Story of the United Irishmen* by James Murphy, published in 1889 – takes a more problematic daytime form, as he attempts to probe the story of his own family. This story, too, derives from historical events of a strongly nationalist stripe. But the darkness in which the narrator investigates the story is not only that of the past as such; it also haunts the present in the forms of the adults who are in the know and the psychological gloom which seems a function of their knowing. In these complementary layers of darkness, the narrator must carry out his researches and his soundings, in the naive but urgent belief that he is entitled to illumination.

As in the case of *The Shan Van Vocht*, reading in the dark is an act of re-reading, a recognition of openings and opportunities that the received text tacitly makes available without taking responsibility for them. In both instances, the authorised version is being amplified and renegotiated, an activity that can conceivably liberate narrative from its own inevitably reductive teleology. By deciphering all a story's levels and meanings, witting and unwitting, the reader – or as with this novel, the inheritor of the narrative – is choosing to complete the story, rather than occupying the traditional and unquestioning role of passive recipient of the storyteller's ostensible intentions. Reading in the dark, then, can be seen as a form of quest, a romance of knowing and of being sure, a foray beyond permitted discursive boundaries, and a release of possibilities hitherto occluded. It is assumed that everybody connected with the story will benefit from such an adventure. In that sense, *Reading in the Dark* is not only a story but a meditation on the power and function of narrative, so that the work as a whole details both the growth of the narrator's consciousness and the more general significance of the depths, subtleties and intricate resources with which knowing his inherited story will furnish him.

Restitution must be made. The assumption guiding this whole undertaking is that there is a missing element whose discovery will banish unease and establish wholeness. The family story that the narrator here pursues certainly indicates an interdependence between meaning and absence. The local landscape counterpoints the narrative's pervasive sense of the missing. Rural County Donegal – 'where we came from' (50) – has the folkloric 'Field of the Disappeared' in which the narrator imagines he sees his Uncle Eddie, one of the family story's numerous inscrutable presences. That territory too is home of the pre-Christian earthworks, An Grianán, in the hollow interior of which sleep Ireland's mythological warriors, 'waiting there for the person who would make that one wish that would rouse them from their thousand-year sleep to make final war on the English and drive them from our shores forever' (56). This historical fantasy, complete with dark depths, has a bearing on the family story, the genesis of which is the War of Independence. Crossing the border into Donegal puts the narrator in touch with invisible and imaginative configurations of the more intimate and personal story that he wishes to unearth. At home, Derry stories of a more material, visible and historical character provide a framework in which themes and speculations reflected in his own story may be probed.

The Donegal and the Derry material have in common a sense of haunting, and in many respects what the narrator wishes to bring to light is a ghost story. The past is a presence that can neither be fully retrieved nor effectively appeased. Its weight on the minds of the two generations of family members involved is all the more oppressive for their complicity in the formative events. And the complicity extends to a spectrum of other members of the community, from Sergeant Burke of the RUC to Crazy Joe, whose damaged mental state does not invalidate the important information he contributes. But over and above these communal ramifications, and revealing a primal scene of intrigue and countermove, is the fact that the story has its origins in both sides of the narrator's family. His father's brother is the republican activist Uncle Eddie, while his mother dated the police informer McIlhenny, who is directly involved in Eddie's fate. And his mother's father has also played a decisive part in the destructive outcome.

It is the narrator's mother who knows most about the excruciating, convoluted pattern of events. Her knowledge, festering in silence, ultimately has a deleterious effect on her mind, its corrosive operation activated in part by her son's compulsive need to know. The mother seems to become a latter-day *shan van vocht*, emotionally and psychologically reduced by an incapacity to change what knowing has obliged her to undergo. The narrator's response to her plea to 'let the past be the past' is that 'it wasn't the past and she knew it' (42). Yet, the more assiduously he seeks to bring the past to light and to rid all concerned of the feeling that 'there's something amiss with the family' (104), the more he comes between his parents – even as 'knowing what I did separated me from them both' (194). Although he succeeds in his quest, the consequences are hardly therapeutic. Subjecting his people to a re-reading of their story results in his estrangement from family and community, a replication of sorts of the earlier informer's eventual exile. The truth has set him free, but at a troublesome cost. He has changed himself, not the past, and not those whose ghosts he has raised. The pursuit of connections whereby meaning and closure may be assigned has led the narrator to see his family as characters in a narrative of self-inflicted entrapment, of a kind of subjective second-class citizenship which is a private counterpoint to their secondary status as Catholic nationalists. In its imaginative impetus towards finality, his reading ends up in conflict with the darkness which the story's subjects have selected as the best place for them. In a sense, it is not surprising that *Reading in the Dark* ends where it began – on the haunted landing of the narrator's home.

Although the opening and concluding setting is the same, the ending also marks the change that has taken place in the narrator's relationship to home. His story was never going to be that of his parents. The novel's form makes that clear, its sequence of discrete tableaux being effective interruptions in the chain of cause and effect inherent in the events that brought about Uncle Eddie's betrayal and death. The narrator's activity, however dependent on the past it might be, is essentially independent of it. As is demonstrated by its numerous instructional set-pieces featuring authority figures of church and state, his story is a *Bildungsroman*. He has exercised the choice to inquire into his parents' stories, and doing so is an expression of individuality and development, his stubbornness and callowness notwithstanding. Laying the ghosts of the past will not make any less haunting their reality in the minds of the older generation. Elders know too much, the young not enough. In that state of affairs the dialectical relationship between reading and darkness also suggests itself. The penumbra of history prompts the need to know. But the knowledge that emerges is that of the alienating pain of personal loss, social amputation and communal silence. This pain inscribes the past of a family – and arguably also that of a community – unable to decide whether or not it can afford to know itself.

Supplementary Reading

Liam Harte, 'History Lessons: Postcolonialism and Seamus Deane's *Reading in the Dark*', *Irish University Review*, vol. 30, no. 1 (Spring/Summer, 2000), pp. 149–62

Gerry Smyth, *Space and the Irish Cultural Imagination* (Basingstoke: Palgrave, 2001), pp. 130–58

Linden Peach, *The Contemporary Irish Novel: Critical Readings* (Basingstoke: Palgrave Macmillan, 2004), pp. 45–55

Robert F. Garrett, *Trauma and History in the Irish Novel: The Return of the Dead* (Basingstoke: Palgrave Macmillan, 2011), pp. 97–112

Also Published in 1996

Ita Daly, *Unholy Ghosts*; Roddy Doyle, *The Woman Who Walked into Doors*; Deirdre Madden, *One by One in the Darkness*; Edna O'Brien, *Down by the River*; Colm Tóibín, *The Story of the Night*; Robert McLiam Wilson, *Eureka Street*

1997

Anne Haverty, *One Day as a Tiger*

The rich farmland of the north riding of County Tipperary, of which Anne Haverty (b. 1959) is a native, supplies the landscape of her first novel. Its treatment of passion and obsession are revisited in her second, The Far Side of a Kiss (2001), an account of the background to William Hazlitt's Liber Amoris; while a third novel, The Free and Easy (2007) casts a cold eye on boomtime Dublin. Anne Haverty has also published a volume of poems and a biography of Constance Markievicz.

Marty Hawkins has a little lamb. He acquires her after abandoning a promising academic career as a historian at Trinity College, Dublin, breaking up with his girlfriend and returning to Foilmore, the family farm, run by his brother, Pierce. Sheep are Pierce's main farming interest, and to improve his flock he introduces to it sheep that have been genetically modified with human genes. In this way, Marty's sheep, Missy, enters his life.

Missy exhibits uncanny human attributes. Marty is greatly touched by her apparent sensitivity to his moods, and to atmosphere generally. He dotes on her, delighting in feeding and bathing her, and unabashedly admits that 'She was the first living thing I loved, the first for whom my love was artless and compassionate and without egotism' (98). Becoming engrossed with Missy gives Marty a focus and purpose he could no longer find in his studies, although his resistance to 'the revisionist stuff' (30) that had become the historiographical norm seems ironic in view of his pet being what might be described as a revisionist sheep (and the care and attention he lavishes on her appears to be a striking instance of revisionist husbandry). But it is not only the city that Marty rejects, or a way of life that secures a future on the basis of the past. He is also out of sympathy with his native place, not so much with Pierce as with their neighbours who in different ways reveal the destinies to which life on the land can lead.

On the one hand, there is Young Delaney. An uncouth bogman, whose farm resembles 'a set . . . for a nostalgic film about rural wretchedness' (50), this character is regarded by Marty as the embodiment of rural traditions which have become antiquated and are closer to folklore than to a modern economy. On the other hand, the example of the Ffrench family, living in 'a run-down pile of a once-grand mansion' (150), also seems cautionary. The family's custom of taking European wives has improved neither their stock nor their fortunes. In contrast, there seems little danger that the Hawkins holding will either become stuck in the mud or degenerate on account of European unions. The Hawkins destiny will be determined not by land management but by self-management. Marty observes that 'In the country, nothing stays the same' (18), an observation that seems at odds with the conventional view of the cyclical nature of rural life. But neither this insight nor the intellectual resources indicated by the sharp, analytical crispness of his first-person narrative, account for his own role as an agent of change.

Initially, it is only Missy that makes Marty different. Otherwise, he fits back into the familiar place and its familiar ways without any apparent difficulty. He drinks at the local pub, goes out and about on his motorbike, and in general relishes the 'oddly arcadian' (5) feeling of home. His pastoral activities do not appear to him as parodies of Pierce's endeavours, nor does Marty grasp the manifestations of displacement in his behaviour. The pleasure he derives from his Missy idyll blinds him to the regime's excesses. What he considers as the delightful control the so-called relationship provides merely indicates his neediness and lack of balance. His love in a cottage is an illusion, all the more so for Marty's being utterly absorbed in its niceties and rituals. And so it turns out that the liberty he takes in his attachment to Missy proves to be the ground of his ultimate undoing – indeed, not only his but his nearest and dearest, Missy included. As he ruefully reflects, 'Fields breed fatalism' (10).

The fall of the house of Hawkins is the last thing on Marty's mind. Nevertheless, that is what he has put in motion. Pierce has a wife, Etti (*née* Goretti) Hanna, and it is for her that Missy is, in effect, a foil. She begins to visit Marty and Missy, and readily goes along with the anthropomorphic charade, soothing the lamb with an Irish lullaby and the like. If anything, Etti takes things further than Marty is prepared to when she refers to Missy as 'The lamb of God' (109). This reference resounds with the note of sacrifice that now begins to make its presence felt in the plot. Before very long, Missy's well-being is sacrificed in favour of Etti's allure. The version of *amour fou* in which Marty indulges with the sheep is replaced by the passion he conceives for Etti. And throughout these developments, it becomes increasingly evident that Pierce is also a sacrificial victim. Etti frequently alludes to her husband's goodness, and seems to be intimidated by its consistency and naturalness. Yet Pierce's innocence also come across as somewhat sheep-like qualities, and the manner in which he is led on also seems ovine.

A brief reconnection with his former girlfriend and a visit from his friend Fintan present Marty with opportunities to rectify the situation. During Fintan's visit there is a disastrous night out in which the brothers come to blows and Pierce is left hysterically crying. By this time, Missy is pretty much out of the picture, though the pathetic state into which she has fallen has the unnerving effect of showing her at her most human. Marty believes that he has no alternative than to act on his 'perverse' (40) love of Etti, who supplies a pretext for their elopement by suggesting that the ailing Missy should be taken to Brigitte Bardot's animal shelter in the south of France. A meandering journey ensues, ending in a sybaritic stay in Deauville. But Marty and Etti have obviously reached the end of the road, and so has Missy. And Pierce has too. Belated efforts to telephone Foilmore find Fintan answering the phone. Pierce is unavailable. Then Fintan telephones with bad news of Pierce. Meanwhile Missy, whom Marty and Etti have been outfitting as their dog, is put down with a dose of sleeping pills.

The title of *One Day as a Tiger* is a phrase taken from its epigraph, said to be a Tibetan proverb: 'It is better to have lived one day as a tiger than a thousand years as a sheep'. Another iteration substitutes 'lion' for 'tiger', though the choice of the Tibetan version may have been influenced by the resonance in an Irish context of 'tiger'. The novel appeared during the boomtime period of 'the Celtic tiger'. And it also delineates a *milieu* characteristic of that period, where traditional forms of continuity such as the land, domesticity, and the home place no longer necessarily hold their own. The scientific breakthrough that has produced a Missy is paralleled in the social sphere by experimental behavioural incursions, blendings and permutations. Passion and unreason have their unnatural and unchecked say, leading to break-down and loss. Surrendering his allegiance to learning from the past gives Marty his freedom, though it is very much open to question if he knows what to do with it. Tigerish intensity obviously has its predatory side, and while a nation of sheep, however highly evolved, is hardly to be recommended, a land where the untamed believe they may operate with impunity certainly brings its own problems. There are no more than inklings of such matters below the surface of Marty's narrative. But perhaps that too is a sign of those times.

Supplementary Reading

Anne Fogarty, 'Uncanny Families: Neo-Gothic Motifs and the Theme of Social Change in Contemporary Irish Women's Fiction', *Irish University Review*, vol. 30, no. 1 (Spring/Summer 2000), pp. 58–91

Gerry Smyth, 'Shite and Sheep: An Ecocritical Perspective on Two Recent Irish Novels', *Irish University Review*, vol. 30, no. 1 (Spring/Summer 2000), pp. 163–78

Nainsí J. Houston, *How Irish Women Writers Portray Masculinity: Exposing the Presumptions of Patriarchy (Interviews and Novels by Clare Boylan, Maeve Kelly, Mary O'Donnell and Anne Haverty)* (New York: Mellen, 2006), pp. 151–8

Also Published in 1997

John Banville, *The Untouchable*; Ronan Bennett, *The Catastrophist*; Dermot Bolger, *Father's Music*; Mary Dorcey, *Biography of Desire*; Brian Moore, *The Magician's Wife*

1998
Joseph O'Connor, *The Salesman*

A member of the generation of Dublin-born writers who began pub-lishing in the 1980s, and which includes Roddy Doyle and Dermot Bolger, O'Connor (b. 1963) is the author of seven novels and a collection of short stories. He has also written plays and a good deal of non-fiction, including a trilogy of light-hearted observations on the Irish male. His first novel, Cowboys and Indians (1991), dealing with new Irish emi-grants in London, is in the same light vein. Relations between parents and children introduce a somewhat darker tonality in Desperados (1994), set in war-torn Nicaragua, and Inishowen (2000), in which questions of identity are also investigated. His recent work – Star of the Sea (2003), Redemption Falls (2007) and Ghost Light (2010) – has taken a historical turn, the first two being concerned with emigration and the Irish-American experience, the third a treatment of the relationship between the playwright J.M. Synge and the actress Molly Allgood.

It is the scorching summer of 1994. Young Maeve Sweeney is in a coma, and her father, Billy – the salesman of the title – has decided to kill the person who put her there. This individual is Donal Quinn, a drug-dealer, who with three henchmen attempted to rob the petrol station where Maeve worked. Attending the foursome's trial is when Billy makes his avenging decision. But before he can put it into action, Quinn absconds. Billy accidentally discovers him in Bray, County Wicklow, where he is living in disguise and under a false name, and hires a pair of toughs, Nap and Pony Sheehan, to deliver Quinn to him.

All this and its aftermath Billy writes down for Maeve, writing being an act of faith in her recovery. His narrative also includes much of Billy's own history, in particular the history of his marriage to Grace Lawrence, Maeve's mother. Like the revenge story, this material's main features are breakdown and destructive behaviour. The courtship of Catholic Billy from Ringsend and Jewish Grace from Harrington Street – capped by a memorable account of the Beatles' Dublin concert in 1964, which includes street scenes that 'reminded me of an old newspaper photograph my father had once shown me of a famous riot that had happened during the 1913 Dublin trade union lock-out' (31) – initially thrives. But Grace becomes pregnant by somebody other than Billy and disappears to England to have her baby. A chance meeting some years later leads to their getting back together and eventual marriage. Billy unreservedly accepts Grace's child Lizzie, though relations between him and Lizzie seem distant, all the more so when she goes to live in Australia. In any case, accepting himself seems more difficult, and after a series of incidents brought on by his heavy drinking, Billy not only loses his teaching position but is 'a man on the run from love' (22).

His love for Grace remains undimmed – 'she was probably the most emotionally generous and spiritually wise person I have ever met' (113) – but when in a drunken rage he brings up the matter of Lizzie to insulting effect, things fall apart for good. The shock of separation does cure Billy's drinking (only to begin again when Quinn comes into his life), just in time for the sobering experience of trying to raise a teenager. Unable to stand living with her mother, Maeve moves in with Billy in the family home in Dalkey – the name of the house is Glen Bolcain – and acts out in a predictable manner that includes punk fashions and 'Yeats is dead' (183) scrawled on her bedroom ceiling (both Billy and Grace are poetry lovers). Just as Lizzie's marriage and children in Australia reduces distance, however, Maeve too in time grows closer to Billy, both developments illustrating the possibility of recuperation which is among *The Salesman's* prominent concerns. There is even an easing of tension in the stand-off between Billy and Grace. But then, as though to show that recuperation and the sense of natural justice it implies also has its limits, Grace is killed in a car crash.

After a good deal of stalking and waiting, Billy is able to take Quinn into custody at Glen Bolcain, incarcerating him in an aviary in the back garden. The narrative changes temporarily, its more composed confessional tone yielding to diary entries notable for their immediacy and desperation. These entries are made in a diary belonging to Billy's boyhood friend, Father Seánie Ronan, and its clerical format sketches in notions of sacrifice, ritual, thoughts for the day and related sources of perspective and context. All these clearly pertain to the situation at hand, though just as clearly are too general and impersonal to guide Billy through the situation. This depiction of the church's peculiar extraneousness recurs later when Seánie, *en route* to missionary work in Nicaragua, confesses that before entering the priesthood he fathered Lizzie (who in the meantime has returned from Australia with her husband and family). Seánie's knowing silence contrasts painfully with Billy's honest moral perplexity about what doing the right thing with regard to Quinn would be. But after denouncing Seánie and the institutional culture he stands for, Billy forgives him. This exchange between old friends is another expression of the novel's interplay between breaking and mending. But its timing is such that its conclusion in reconciliation comes as no great surprise. By this point, Billy's hostility towards Quinn has petered out, and avenger and victim have arrived at a *modus vivendi* of sorts.

This state of fragile equilibrium has been hard-earned. In Billy's custody, Quinn was subjected to much degradation and pain. Then, rather unexpectedly, Quinn turns the tables and it is Billy's turn to learn what his captive has been through. Deeply enraged as their enmity is, however, neither is able to kill the other. A stalemate ensues, and it is not too long before Quinn is living in Glen Bolcain with Billy and making good on the damage he vengefully inflicted on the house. He also works on the garden, which in the course of events has become something of a symbolic site where natural growth and unnatural restraint have coexisted. As on other occasions, however, complete reconciliation is not possible. Billy draws the line when Quinn expresses a wish to visit Maeve in hospital. And Quinn's past is slowly but surely catching up with him, IRA elements in Bray having designated his drug-dealing presence as undesirable. It is to these enemies, for whom the front man is Pony Sheehan, that Quinn ultimately succumbs. Billy 'felt tears smoulder in my eyes' (384) when he finds Quinn's mutilated corpse in the garden of Glen Bolcain. And perhaps as a substantiation of his earlier statement that 'a salesman has to have hope. It is not a way of life for a pessimist' (22), the novel's final image is of Billy at work restoring his garden with Lizzie's daughter by his side.

Billy's occupation of satellite salesman brings to mind keeping lines of communication open. The importance of doing so is indicated by Billy's writing. Like his dealings with Quinn and his various other choices, Billy's deciding to keep the story alive for Maeve is something nobody else can do for him. It is an expression of his solitude but also of his commitment, and in these respects seems to be a means of acting on a lesson that he has for Maeve: 'if I have learned anything at all – if I have one thing to bequeath to you – it is that every single statement on the subject of human morality that contains the word "we" is a lie' (142). At the same time, satellites are consistent with the star-gazing side of Billy, whose solitary naming of the constellations is a further sign of his isolation and a kind of compensation for it.

This singleness of Billy's may be thought a mark of his modernity. But even though he has little use for 'the Great sodding Famine' (249) or any other event in the collective past, his feeling of being 'modern . . . European' (208) that comes from doing 70 mph on a dual carriageway seems self-mocking. Besides, although he is not conscious of it, his name echoes the title of the celebrated medieval romance *Buile Suibhne*, while the name of his house is the same as that of the valley of the mad in that work. (Other connections include *The Salesman*'s abundant bird imagery, and the fact that Billy's drinking hospitalises him in Carlow, the county where the original Sweeney was rescued from his outcast existence as a demented bird.) Like the stars, ancient Sweeney is also distant but discernible, an objective framework providing a context for subjective travail but not alleviating it. If any alleviation is available, that has to be provided by the subjects themselves. To a greater or lesser extent, efforts to do so will have limited success – Grace is lost, Quinn is killed, Maeve's condition remains the same. Yet, despite such damage, the fact that Billy, however unreasonably, is prepared to take the weight of his own world upon himself also has to count both for its spirit of redress and its tormented struggle to reconcile with change. At the end, he writes that 'all gardens are stories . . . and all gardeners are story-tellers' (390). Not the least notable aspects of Billy's sense of his entitlement to his own story is the strenuousness with which it is initially asserted and the change of heart that strenuousness brings about.

Supplementary Reading

Joseph O'Connor, 'Questioning Our Self-Congratulations', *Studies*, vol. 87, no. 347 (Autumn 1998), pp. 245–51

Linden Peach, *The Contemporary Irish Novel: Critical Readings* (Basingstoke: Palgrave Macmillan, 2004), pp. 54–8

Tim Middleton, 'Joseph O'Connor', in Michael R. Molino (ed.), *Twenty-First-Century British and Irish Novelists* (Detroit: Gale, 2003), pp. 271–8

José Manuel Estévez-Saá, 'An Interview with Joseph O'Connor', *Contemporary Literature*, vol. 46, no. 2 (Summer 2005), pp. 161–75

Also Published in 1998

Sebastian Barry, *The Whereabouts of Eneas McNulty*; Maurice Leitch, *The Smoke King*; Colum McCann, *This Side of Brightness*; Mike McCormack, *Crowe's Requiem*; J.M. O'Neill, *Bennett and Company*; Keith Ridgway, *The Long Falling*

1999

Glenn Patterson, *The International*

A native of Belfast, Patterson is the author of seven novels, including Burning Your Own (1988), Fat Lad (1992), Black Night at Big Thunder Mountain (1995), Number 5 (2003), That Which Was (2004) *and* The Third Party (2007). *Set mainly in Belfast, these works dwell on the ostensibly plain people of that city with a subtle and humane regard for their inimitable individuality and the wide variety of their experiences and perspectives. Patterson (b. 1961) is also the author of a memoir –* Once Upon a Hill (2008) *– and a collection of non-fiction.*

'I wish I could describe for you Belfast as it was then, before it was brought shaking, quaking and laying about it with batons and stones on to the world's small screens' (61), says Danny Hamilton, this novel's gay, eighteen-year-old narrator, a barman at the International Hotel in the heart of the city. He is speaking in 1994, in the wake of the Loyalist ceasefire which effectively brought the major hostilities of the twenty-five previous years of civic unrest to an end. And the time that Danny has in mind is typified by the Saturday in January 1967 in which the action is set. Even then, the *status quo* is showing signs of change. According to Eddie McAteer of the Nationalist Party, 'things were looking up in the North' (31). On the other hand, 'Ian Paisley was basically a joke that became less funny each time you heard it' (88). Plans were in hand for the Belfast Urban Motorway, but that development is more the basis of a derisive acronym than of a sense of social progress – Danny recognises the road's destructive geographical and communal potential. And the previous summer has seen the murder of a barman, Peter Ward (thought to be the first of the sectarian killings that were such an appalling feature of those years when 'Belfast disgraced itself' (311)). Generally speaking, however, in 1967 a win on the football pools remains the likeliest way in which lives would be 'changed utterly' (26). The fire with which the novel opens is merely a fire, not a terrorist exploit. And the city's fame rests more on a figure such as Ted Connolly, a soccer player with a noted career in England behind him (a salute to *The Hollow Ball*, perhaps), than on bullets and bombs. If the name of the hotel has changed from the Union to the International, no symbolic weight has evidently accrued. Life seems much the same as it has always been – 'We were going to be modern tomorrow' (62) – and the novel is in part a knowing and unsentimental toast to local expressions of the civic virtues of geniality and gregariousness. Neither Danny nor anybody else pays particular attention to the fact that the following day the first meeting of the Northern Ireland Civil Rights Association will be held in the International.

What this meeting might entail is the furthest thing from the minds of the novel's politically well-connected trio of Councillor Trevor Noades, entrepeneur Clive White, and a Dublin operator called Fitz. And the careers of the first two will continue to prosper, Troubles or no. On the day in question, Fitz cheats his northern companions, which adds to that particular storyline a satirical subtext regarding North–South relations. But he is later arrested in Galway attempting to sell arms he does not have to the IRA. Clive is Danny's cousin. He has pulled the strings that secured Danny his barman's position when the latter was expelled from school after being found *in flagrante* with a classmate. Danny is no innocent, though this does not mean that he has any time for Clive's wheeling and dealing, despite being connected and indebted to his cousin. And he does not need to overhear the trio's opportunistic scheming to be able to give an account of it, knowing that it is just the familiar story of bribery and corruption in high places. This reconstructed account of the meeting contrasts with Danny's direct reports of the day's other events. And it also establishes his distance from such concerns and the notion of public service they distort, as well as from the vanity, cupidity and posing of the male and his rituals of the deal.

The organisational, institutional, power-seeking realm is not what Danny identifies with. His proper sphere is public in a different sense. The bar's ebb and flow of patrons, the relative degrees of intimacy between staff and public, the lubrication of social intercourse, the civic manner in which service is provided, may not necessarily be taken as expressions of a democratic spirit. The author feels no need to insinuate any such abstraction, which is consistent with his plain, direct, and – playing on the title – intently localised approach. But the bar's ordinary, secular amenities do suggest a kind of regulated, or structured, populism by means of which the life of the human community called the city is evoked and celebrated. At a more elementary level, the bar is a city destination where all sorts and conditions of citizens mix (in addition to being, in January 1967, a place of safety and recreation, as Danny's listing of notorious bar attacks throughout the Troubles reminds us). Danny himself, who as a homosexual and without religion, appears to be in a minority of one, but he seems to belong here. Any such attachment can only be provisional, but for the time being the bar affords an accommodating present and he confidently inhabits it. But he does not presume upon it, so that rather than feeling safely cut off from the public, he is drawn to those members of it who appear out of place. Much of The International deals with Danny's involvement with two such customers, which not only underlines the material's human interest but contrasts it with the type of interest Clive and his cronies represent.

Both Stanley and Ingrid – the outsiders in question – have suffered reverses. Stanley has professional problems, his career as a puppeteer having failed to move forward. Danny is drawn to him sexually, though nothing comes of his attraction, which coincidentally raises questions regarding Danny's emotional future and whether or not conditions will change for the better in that regard. Meanwhile, he is able to protect sad Stanley from the mindless hostility shown him by Jamesie, one of the other barmen, a rampant heterosexual. Ingrid, on the other hand, is distressed for emotional reasons. The man who jilted her is having his wedding reception at the International, and she is acting as something of a ghost at the feast. Danny steers her through some of the day's rough patches and eventually sits her beside Stanley and encourages them to stay until he can join them after closing time. Here, too, is a trio whose public profile of need seems the opposite of the one organised by Clive White. And in its emotional and sexual composition, this trio is also quite different from the threesome that Danny was invited to form with the Vances, an American couple, recent guests at the International. From the £10 that the Vances leave as payment for his attentions, Danny learns that providing room service is not part of his sexual identity – though, winningly enough, he is not so pure that he does not keep the money.

Danny ends his long day in the company of Ingrid and Stanley. But they have no future together. They never meet again, and when Danny subsequently hears of them, they have left the city. A bout of flu makes Danny miss work the next day, when the Civil Rights Association convenes. But in his willingness to lend an undiscriminating hand and an unjudgmental ear – in his willing service – he has already demonstrated the intuitive relatedness upon which a civil rights ethos might be based. That sense of coexistence is all in a pragmatic day's work. In the longer term, it is that sense which enables him to be true to the city. (It is also one of the ideas that enable cities to function.) What Danny has said he wishes he could describe, he embodies instead. It is visible in his deft timing, his self-acceptance, his openness, his good manners. And it is also expressed in the fellow-feeling with which he commemorates Peter Ward, a murder that for many reasons can be seen here as an assault on civility, in addition to being an outrage.

On the January Saturday of *The International*, a shocking international event took place. This was the fire which took the lives of three astronauts aboard Apollo 1. Danny recalls, 'I felt a dreadful pity for the three would-be astronauts; for all of us, maybe, perched forever on the edge of what we can't control or understand' (245). Parlous as that position is, and enhanced dramatically as it is in the modern context of space-flight, that is where Danny Hamilton – ordinary citizen, though not ordinary person – holds his ground.

Supplementary Reading

Aaron Kelly, 'Historical Baggage', Review of *The International*, *Fortnight*, no. 381 (November 1999), pp. 28–9

Glenn Patterson, *Once Upon a Hill: Love in Troubled Times* (London: Bloomsbury, 2008)

Neal Alexander, 'Remembering to Forget: Northern Irish Fiction after the Troubles', in Scott Brewer and Michael Parker (eds), *Irish Literature since 1990: Diverse Voices* (Manchester: Manchester University Press, 2009), pp. 274–5

Marilynn Richtarik and Kevin Chappell, 'An Interview with Glenn Patterson', *Five Points*, vol. 13, no. 2 (2009), pp. 44–56

Also Published in 1999

Philip Casey, *The Water Star*; Roddy Doyle, *A Star Called Henry*; Antonia Logue, *Shadow-Box*; Edna O'Brien, *Wild Decembers*; Ronan Sheehan, *Foley's Asia*; Colm Tóibín, *The Blackwater Lightship*

2000

Mary Morrissy, *The Pretender*

Morrissy (b. 1957) has also published a volume of short stories and one other novel, Mother of Pearl *(1995). That novel, written with the sympathetic and incisive lyricism of all her works, is set in her native Dublin and deals with the complexities of female identity.*

The story told in *The Pretender* at first glance appears to be quite well known, as three films and many books have already dealt with Anastasia, daughter of the last czar of Russia, or rather with the imposture based on that historical figure. Supposedly the only one of the Romanov children to escape the killing floor at Yekaterinburg in 1918, her imposter made herself known in Berlin in 1922. She is now known as Anna Anderson, and interested parties took up her claims to legitimacy, and those claims were maintained until her death in Charlottesville, Virginia, in 1984. Posthumous DNA testing proved that the woman in question was Franziska Schanzkowska and could not have been related to the Russian royal family. Who Franziska was is the subject of *The Pretender*.

Framed by a pair of episodes from her declining years in Virginia, where she has become the wife of history professor Jack Manahan, the novel proceeds like a matryoshka doll. This comparison applies structurally, with each phase of Franziska's biography succeeded by an earlier phase. But it also has a thematic application. Franziska is shown to be a succession of different selves, each one separate from yet contained within its previous embodiment. And as *The Pretender* goes back in time and the protagonist becomes physically smaller, her essential psychological profile seems to enlarge. The doubleness registered thereby finds obvious echoes in a narrative of imposture and reality, and is also figured in various other ways throughout, from the use of egg imagery to Franziska's being a child of her father's second marriage. In assuming the persona of a dead Russian princess, Franziska attains a spurious singularity whose subjective imperative is as comprehensive as its objective fraudulence. From whichever point of view, identity appears to be a manifestation of crisis. Franziska departs from her own history into the unknown realm of impersonal historical events. 'It is what she wants. To escape memory. To become innocent. To enter history' (91). These statements occur at the moment of her attempted suicide.

The novel's main action opens with Franziska being taken to Berlin's Dalldorf mental hospital following her suicide attempt. Here she successfully affects aphasia and is eventually labelled Fräulein Unbekannt, Miss Unknown. The arrival in her ward of Clara Peuthert, a manic-depressive, gradually brings Franziska out of herself. She breaks her silence, though the real – if that is the word – breakthrough comes only when she sees a photograph in an illustrated paper of the Russian royal family in which she finds a resemblance between herself and Princess Anastasia. Attracted to an alternative identity in which elements of her own are heightened and sensationalised, Franziska relinquishes her 'unknown' status and goes through something of a rebirth, which includes being taken up by members of Berlin's social elite. The rest, one might say, is history – though, as the framing scenes in Virginia make clear, the history of Anastasia also culminates in breakdown. Not even a pampered life in credulous and historically innocent America can ultimately save Franziska from herself.

But it is not in her later status as the human equivalent of a crown jewel – or, to invoke one of Franziska's objects of fascination, a Fabergé egg – that *The Pretender* is interested. Its focus is on the factors that went into the making of the persona's false reality. There is a sense in which the impersonation of an Anastasia who has survived historical disaster compensates Franziska for her own inability to overcome what history has done to her. Her suicide attempt is the final act in a series of increasingly desperate efforts to deal with unbearable defeats.

August 1914 sees her arrive in Berlin from an area of the Polish countryside then in the German empire. Initially things go well. She finds
room and board in the Wingerder household, which consists of a
boozy landlady and her two daughters, Doris and Louise. Both girls
work in a munitions factory, where Franziska joins them. Another
lodger arrives, Hans Walter Fröhlich, a Jewish haberdasher. He falls for
Franziska and she becomes pregnant by him. He is called up, then is
killed. Accidentally on purpose, as it seems, Franziska causes an explo-
sion in the munitions factory in which she loses her child. Meanwhile,
the war has made life in Berlin more and more difficult, and Franziska
finds it increasingly hard to cope with it. She allows herself to be mistaken for a street walker by a Russian who pays her with money
received for Romanov jewellery. Disgusted with herself, Franziska
throws the money into the Landwehr canal and throws herself after it.

Her immediate reason for coming to Berlin was a drowning. The
victim was her younger brother Walter, who had usurped Franziska's
status as the apple of their father's eye. Their mother blames her
husband, but Franziska is haunted by the event, not least because of
guilt over her jealousy of Walter. Early twentieth-century life in her
native village of Borowy Las is at one level a typical round of iron-clad
superstitions and unremitting agricultural labour with, for women, the
additional labour of child-bearing. Yet shades of an alternative life are
also present, casually in her father calling Franziska 'Princess' (203) and
somewhat more substantially in her mother's family being members of
what her father describes as 'Poland's curse . . . the minor nobility'
(220). Distressed by being rejected in favour of Walter, Franziska rejects
herself, particularly when it comes to the matter of her emerging sexuality. And she also experiences a sense of displacement by learning that
her father was previously married – 'It made him seem like an imposter'
(232). In addition, her father beats Maria – one of Franziska's half-
sisters – and her boyfriend for alleged sexual activity. Maria is packed
off to become a servant in the home of a distant relation in Poznan,
whereupon she is never heard from again, having evidently entered into
another life. Poland itself is a once and future entity. Considered 'a
dream' (225) during Franziska's childhood, the nation is reborn following the First World War, a development facilitating the sublimation
of old wounds through the experience of a fresh state of unity.

The inverted chronology in which the novel's central episodes are
presented obviates the simplistic reading of Franziska's childhood being

a mere foreshadowing of events to come. Instead, her imposture seems to be the critical mass attained by the burdens she has had to bear. Some of these were the objective forces of family and history that conditioned her. Others were created by her subjective reactions to those forces – her misconstruals, desires and insecurities. The former set of conditions appears to be in the nature of things, though very often hardly seems natural – for instance, the folk ritual intended to enforce the principle that 'Obedience is meant to hurt' (214). And subjectivity, almost by definition, has a mind of its own – deviant, dissident, vigilant, solitary. The interdependence of such forces and reactions may be raised to an extravagant and dramatic level in the case of Franziska Schanzkowska, a level at which she seems to forego all for the sake of being delivered into innocence. Illusion and fabrication are the stuff of life at such a level. Yet the presumption of innocence which can cause somebody to lie to herself about her history makes her a danger to herself and others, however understandable it may be to fabricate a means of fleeing an evidently flawed and menacing modern world.

Supplementary Reading

Annie Callan, 'Interview', *Glimmer Train*, no. 18 (Spring 1996), pp. 89–103
Anne Owens Weekes, 'Mary Morrissy', in Michael R. Molino, *Twenty-First-Century British and Irish Novelists* (Detroit: Gale, 2003), pp. 234–40

Also Published in 2000

John Banville, *Eclipse*; Dermot Bolger, *Temptation*; Anne Enright, *What Are You Like?*; Jennifer Johnston, *The Gingerbread Woman*; Joseph O'Connor, *Inishowen*; William Wall, *Alice Falling*

2001
Eoin McNamee, *The Blue Tango*

The non-fiction novel, pioneered by such luminaries as Truman Capote and Norman Mailer, is the form to which Eoin McNamee's works make a distinctive contribution. Taking a noted event – the so-called Shankill Butchers death squad in Resurrection Man *(1994), the disappearance of Robert Nairac in* The Ultras *(2004), the death of Diana, Princess of Wales, in* 12:23: Paris, 31st August 1997 *(2007), and* Orchid Blue *(2010), on a 1960s Northern Ireland murder – his novels probe in richly metaphorical and often startlingly cinematic prose the evidentiary fine print, labyrinthine motivation and temperamental pathologies revealed by the practice of violence. These qualities were first revealed in two novellas,* The Last of Deeds *and* Love in History *(1989; 2nd revised edition 1992). A native of Kilkeel, County Down, Eoin McNamee (b. 1961) is also the author of the* Owen the Navigator *series of young adult novels and publishes thrillers under the pseudonym John Creed.*

In the early hours of 13 November 1952, the naked body of nineteen-year-old Patricia Curran was found by her brother in the driveway of The Glen, the family home in Whiteabbey, County Antrim, five miles north of Belfast. She had been stabbed thirty-seven times. Patricia's father, Sir Lancelot Curran, was a former member of the Northern Ireland parliament, in which he had held the positions of Minister for Finance and Attorney General. At the time of the murder he was a member of the Northern Ireland judiciary. The crime was supposedly solved when Iain Hay Gordon, a serviceman stationed at a local RAF base, was charged, convicted and sentenced to confinement in a Northern Ireland mental institution, where he spent seven years. In 2000, a Belfast court of appeal overturned Gordon's conviction as unsound, though *The Blue Tango* does not take the story that far, dwelling instead on the multiple contexts – social, familial, personal and forensic – in which Patricia Curran's murder is enmeshed. The girl's actual killer has never been named.

Approached from the many perspectives of all those concerned, the narrative provides something of a prismatic overview of the case. Such a view, with its patience, alertness to incompatible versions of what took place and openness to other conclusions, not only tacitly dissents from the public and private dispositions and methods evident from the record. It also suggests the various degrees of complicity in which the community, and indeed, because of the standing of Judge Curran, the Northern Irish polity, shares. As well as being an expression of certain intimate pathologies, typical of such crimes, the murder can also be read metonymically for the condition of Northern Ireland's ruling class in that quiet, post-war period when its writ seemed to run most smoothly and confidently. Not the least impressive feature of *The Blue Tango* is the semiotic resourcefulness with which the author interprets the moral and social presuppositions of that time and place.

Complicity begins at home. Patricia's righteous brother Desmond, an adherent of Moral Rearmament – a religious fad of the time – is as involved in distorting the evidence as his father, even though he might be thought to have some obligation to the accused, whom he tried to recruit to his religious persuasion. The Glen is a house of unmistakable Gothic character, where Mrs Curran has created an atmosphere in which Patricia – in many ways her brother's antithesis – finds it impossible to thrive. And seven years after the murder, The Glen's new occupants discover what appears to be a large bloodstain under an old carpet in an upstairs bedroom. Though the police are called, the stain remains under the carpet, like so much else in the life of the family and of Whiteabbey. Mrs Curran, whose activities on the day of the murder the narrative examines immediately after the bloodstain discovery, ends up in a mental institution.

For Judge Curran, the essential point about his daughter's murder is that he remains untainted by it, despite his interference with the chain of evidence and other breaches of proper judicial conduct. This point's importance is also kept firmly in mind by Curran's friend, Sir Richard Pim, Chief Constable of Northern Ireland ('a personal friend of Winston Churchill' (127)), who has a keen appreciation of the value of maintaining an image of the judge as a public servant above suspicion. Curran's ability to conceal his heavy gambling and his considerable debts to his Catholic bookie also relies on this image's impermeability. And to avoid possible blunders and indiscretions by the forces of law and order, investigation of the murder is taken out of the hands of the local police and entrusted instead to the noted Chief Inspector Capstick of Scotland Yard. His progress is as inconclusive as the locals', but he is much more willing to incriminate the hapless Iain Hay Gordon, even if doing so requires 'a fake confession, a fiction in the mocking language of death' (vii). Capstick saves the day, adding a layer of suggestive political allegory to the proceedings.

In a sense, there is something predictable about the scenario of denial, evasion and cover-up, and insofar as *The Blue Tango* is a narrative of reaction – in various senses of the term – it concedes as much in its depiction of the superficial manner in which Whiteabbey as a community treats the crime. Interest is largely confined to the murder's sensational and generic aspects, with little sign of it being extended to its troublesome human element. The reporting of the local media has a pre-scripted, prescriptive bias, as though to direct its readership's attention towards shock and horror and away from actual thought. A member of the community such as the lawyer Harry Ferguson, who is aware that there is more to the case than a violated body, is effectively silenced by his judicial superiors. The only ones who can see Patricia

Curran and the status quo in a different light are marginal citizens – Hughes, the judge's bookie, and Wesley Courtney, a gay barber. They are also without complicity. Courtney warns the still closeted Gordon to avoid police attention. But even Gordon is unable to resist the allure he sees in complicity, wishing to be part of the big story even when it leads to his being on trial for his life. Not that he is in danger of execution, his insanity plea and sentence having been determined by Judge Curran and Sir Richard Pim before the trial opens. As to Hughes, his brief acquaintance of Patricia showed her to be a lively, caring, competent young woman.

But there is no social or other structure in which those qualities of Patricia Curran's might be nurtured. She is, as she says, 'a doctor of loneliness' (29). And this leads her to act in ways that her family and Whiteabbey at large consider outrageous for somebody of her age and position. She drinks, she flaunts her sexuality, she is given to self-dramatisation. A student at Queen's University, Belfast at the time of her murder, she has taken a year off and is working as a lorry driver for a local builder's merchant, who sexually molests her. What in other societies might be regarded as wilful and possibly tiresome waywardness and independent high spirits are seen in her native place as an affront to its repressive conventions. Most unnerving of all is the thought that Patricia's evident disregard for these conventions, her flawed and misdirected experiments in individuality, make her, too, complicit in her own end. Her disinclination to sublimate her physical and psychological energies in the buttoned-down *mores* that constitute her birthright unconsciously place her at the mercy of a people from whom she dares to dissociate herself – a people who, considering her fate together over a drink, 'thought she might be better off as a victim of murder' (195).

Supplementary Reading

Neal Alexander, 'Remembering to Forget: Northern Irish Fiction after the Troubles', in Scott Brewer and Michael Parker (eds), *Irish Literature since 1990: Diverse Voices* (Manchester: Manchester University Press, 2009), pp. 276–7

Caroline Magennis, *Sons of Ulster: Masculinities in the Contemporary Northern Irish Novel* (New York: Peter Lang, 2010)

Also Published in 2001

John Banville, *Eclipse*; Bernard MacLaverty, *The Anatomy School*; Joseph O'Connor, *Inishowen*; Jamie O'Neill, *At Swim Two Boys*; James Ryan, *Seeds of Doubt*

2002
Deirdre Madden, *Authenticity*

A native of Toomebridge, County Antrim, Madden (b. 1960) is one of the few women novelists to emerge from Northern Ireland during the Troubles. A number of her novels draw on that traumatic period – Hidden Symptoms *(1986) and* One by One in the Darkness *(1996). But her output also deals with family secrets, in* The Birds of the Innocent Wood *(1988), and a young woman's quest in modern Europe is the subject of* Remembering Light and Stone *(1992). The creative life is the central interest of both* Nothing is Black *(1994) and* Molly Fox's Birthday *(2008). Memorable for their women characters, these novels' deceptively modest style conveys much emotional subtlety.*

To write a novel that upholds a belief in art as a repository of faith, hope and charity is an ambitious and courageous undertaking, but that is what *Authenticity* ultimately amounts to. Deirdre Madden's portrait of the artist Roderic Kennedy is not just a depiction of that painter's processes and accomplishments. In addition, it conveys a rich appreciation – and even a defence – of the value of art as a human activity. At a period when there has been much public debate on the role of the arts, the importance of the arts to cultural and communal well-being, and the contribution of the arts in the creation of a sense of national identity – by being recruited as an acceptable face of the nation for international consumption – the interest and focus of *Authenticity* may seem particularly timely. But the novel takes an explicitly contrary, individualistic tack. For Roderic Kennedy and his fellow artist and lover Julia Fitzpatrick, what matters is the need, not the network; the making, not the product; the spirit that moves, not the market that marks up (though, in that last regard, they are not so pure as to be indifferent to being able to earn their living through their talent). First and foremost, they recognise the need to be answerable to themselves. The rest is not their business.

This sense that what they are within is the important thing is confirmed by their different backgrounds. Roderic, son of a general practitioner in the bland and comfortable south County Dublin suburbs, grows up amidst the not unfamiliar tensions of the nuclear family and siblings. In contrast, Julia is an only child, reared in rural County Wicklow by her widower father, Dan, a mechanic. (Her mother was killed in a road accident when she was six.) These circumstances obviously mark the pair in distinctive ways. Roderic rebels. Julia, in various ways, remains close to home. The differences of their personal histories, however, while ineradicable, also seem complementary. City is counterpointed by country, single-parent family by nuclear family, only child by brother and sisters, white-collar father by blue-collar father – and, as we get to know them better, the sense that they make a match is also developed along such lines as age, sex, artistic interests and attitudes to others. Their backgrounds and circumstances have left their mark, but they do not have the final say in who Roderic and Julia are. Each in his and her own way exemplifies the capacity not only to make and remake themselves but to represent the commitment of such an undertaking in expressive form. The artist can be seen as a noteworthy instance of the self-made person – an image, expressed in work completed, of risk, integrity and open-handedness. Their own gifts donate a gift to the world at large.

Strangers meeting and finding something in one another is one way of describing the private and personal exchange between viewer and picture. And Deirdre Madden may have chosen painting as her artists' mode of expression because it is in this medium that the exchange is typically direct. In *Authenticity*, the exchange frequently takes place in a museum or similar venue, a private transaction gracing a public space, enhancing and adding value to both. But exchanges in general also recur throughout the novel – the unexpected encounter, the moment of attraction, the invisible current of contact, the unconscious gesture, the colloquy of friends. It would be futile to intend or expect such interludes to be definitive. Rather, they are forms of openness, engagement and unpredictability, and as such they exhibit a liberating novelty and sense of renewal. Art preserves a consciousness of these transient transactions, authenticating them. And the value of that expressive enterprise may be considered when regarding the significance of art's hallmarks – passion, sincerity, belief and commitment – to individual lives. Their significance certainly shines through as Roderic and Julia get to know each other. Despite the vicissitudes of their personal histories, their willingness to give and to receive, to criticise and to support, affirms the need for and the creative possibilities of living in each other's intense and revealing light.

The importance of what the lovers embrace is also shown by their connection with two minor characters, William Armstrong, whom Julia befriends, and Roderic's devoted brother, Dennis. Julia first encounters William by chance, and finds him to be in despair. A well-to-do lawyer, he has always wanted to be a painter, and is now paying the spiritual price for not having lived up to that calling. As a result, there is something monochrome about him, and though Julia does manage to inspire him to think it is not too late to affirm his artistic self, his attempts to paint fail. He seems more inclined to take advantage of the attention Julia in her good nature gives him than to come to terms with his inner self. And unless he does make the requisite reckoning, his sense of having devalued himself is bound to persist. As it turns out, William does prove to be a dead loss. In contrast, Dennis Kennedy, a gifted pianist in his youth, has managed to accept that he would never reach the level of a concert recitalist. Instead he becomes a banker. His solitary, apparently virginal, life may seem monkish compared to William's, who has a wife and family as well as falsifying and depleting extra-marital affairs. But in the ways Dennis negotiates family tensions, and in particular his care for Roderic, whom he sees through the roughest times, he embodies an authenticating degree of self-acceptance and responsibility.

William, the artist *manqué*, is least himself with art. Dennis accepts that he is not an artist and is the better for it, and the better able to appreciate what the arts afford. Variations on these outcomes are also evident in the makeup of the novel's two fathers. Doctor Kennedy's love of opera seems to reinforce his temperamental excesses, just as William Armstrong's hollowness is reproduced in his attempts to paint. The under-educated Dan Fitzpatrick resembles Dennis in his solitude, self-sufficiency and emotional generosity. Indeed, Dan, the apparently lowliest of all the characters, may be their superior by being 'simply and utterly and completely himself' (319), which is what the artist strives to become. Life and art are bound up in each other – a truism, no doubt, but, as revisited here, their mutually authenticating interconnections are a means of being able to speak again – and anew – of terms like spirit, vision, transfiguration and transcendence, retrieving these potentialities from the institutional regimes whose sole possession they had appeared to be. To live in the name of those terms is to entertain a sense of the true and the good. In its enactment of that sense, *Authenticity*, in addition to being a portrait of two artists, can be read as an *ars poetica*, the author's own testament to the function and necessity of the secular grace that art transmits.

Supplementary Reading

Aisling Foster, 'Painterly People', *The Times Literary Supplement*, 16 August 2002
Eileen Battersby, 'An Achievement of Intimacy', *The Irish Times*, 2 September 2002
Roberta White, *A Studio of One's Own: Fictional Women Painters and the Art of Fiction* (Madison, New Jersey: Fairleigh Dickinson University Press, 2005), pp. 143–51

Also Published in 2002

John Banville, *Shroud*; Sebastian Barry, *Annie Dunne*; John McGahern, *That They May Face the Rising Sun*; Edna O'Brien, *In the Forest*; Joseph O'Connor, *Star of the Sea*; William Trevor, *The Story of Lucy Gault*

2003

Keith Ridgway, *The Parts*

Ridgway (b. 1965) has published three novels, including The Long Falling *(1998) and* Animals *(2006), as well as the novella* Horses *(1997) and a collection of short stories. Much of this work is set in his native Dublin.*

'Here we are' (3, 457). This is the opening and closing sentence of *The Parts*, and it is not as simple a statement as it looks. Its declarative simplicity inevitably speaks for, though also conceals, the multiform nature of the 'here' and 'we' that the sentence frames. And its temporal immediacy suggests a captured moment – something in the nature of a snapshot – in which the various different elements are in alignment with each other. Disparateness and integration may be two sides of the one rhetorical coin, but if they are related to each other, they are also opposed. And in any event, any presumption of eventual wholeness is so temporary as to be an illusion. The parts are more to the point than their sum – even terms that normally have hyphens are shorn of them here. But if that sum is continually in the process of reorganising itself, it should not be written off. Characters' distance from and connection with each other contribute to and influence the narrative effect. But neither distance nor intimacy is privileged as being more persuasive or more true than the other, and neither has the initiative or is given last word. The opening and closing sentence is a form of punctuation – a pause, not a judgment.

Such a treatment of the material appears to owe something to how fiction represents the experience of modern city life, its temporal ebb and flow, its spatial diversity, its oscillation between the known and the unforeseen. The city is perceived in terms of its parts. And that is how this novel imagines contemporary Dublin: 'Dublin. Plural proper noun. There is a Dublin of the rich of course, and a Dublin of the poor. That's standard stuff' (41). And a witty and incisive list of other coexisting Dublins follows. Kez, the character who visits all the novel's locations – and then some – 'thinks there's thousands' (42). But the point is not merely the technical accomplishment of rendering the city's incompletenesses and continuities. More noteworthy is the different but related ways in which the characters are conscious of themselves as parts – and of the parts they play. Their common but dispersed awareness of their separateness is a basis for some of the parts eventually coming together and, equally important, for some of them failing to. Agency and intention are absent, except in the cases of those who wish to impose their will on others, and they come to a bad end.

One strand of a very elaborate and at times bizarre plot deals with the three inhabitants of a house that is 'an oversized buckle on an oversized belt' (15) in the Dublin mountains. The house's ailing chatelaine is Delly (*née* Fidelma), widow of pharmaceutical magnate Daniel Gilmore. She is being watched over by Kitty Flood, an obese author of romances, currently working on a 'fictionalised, non-fiction' (78) book set in late eighteenth-century Dublin, 'based on city planning and murder' (77) – the opposed forms and subject matter are telling. George Addison-Blake, born into rural Alabama poverty, Daniel Gilmore's adopted son who is now a doctor administering to Delly, is the third member of the household. A second plotline concerns Joe Kavanagh, a radio talk-show host and divorcé, who is 'thrice divided like a little God' (49) confined to 'a Dublin all his own' (ibid.), and the producer of his shows, Barry Quigley, who is gay, though 'unable to think of himself as part of anything – community, society, state, family – without it hurting' (103). All these characters' interest in embodying their roles varies greatly, bedfast Delly and emotionally stuck Barry being the most resistant to doing so, while parasitic Kitty and criminal George are the most proactive. And then there is Kez (*né* Kevin), whose way of life as a rent boy is so far removed from, and at odds with, the structures of the other characters' lives that his activities are recounted in a different typeface. If *The Parts* were a less ambitious, more conventional novel, Kez would be its protagonist. As it is, he becomes the means whereby the worlds of the two plots collide – inasmuch as they can be said to make contact that is generally meaningful. And he achieves this through being more acted upon than acting.

The narrative is laid out in parts, each one separated from the others by an image that operates as a given character's signature – a radio for Joe, a car for George, a house for Delly, and so on. These images are of things. But there are two exceptions, dispelling any thought of consistency in the use of this device. One exception is Barry, whose signature is that of a single man. The second is Kez, who is not represented by anything in the text besides a typeface of his own. A mobile phone is indispensable to plying his trade, and an image of one appears with the other images on the novel's cover. But Kez is not identified with it. He is free from the attachments – and also the doubts, the memories and the entire repertoire of self-scrutiny – which the older characters draw on and repress. Kez's business is in the here-and-now – the 'here we are' – and when he is not working, he visits his mother and chats with a brother who seems to be his pimp. All perfectly unexceptional. In an inversion that typifies the novel's subversive points of view, the character who might be conventionally regarded as the lowest of the low is the one who seems most composed, most alert to the moment, least in need of and least likely to practise George's violence or the emotional manipulations of Kitty and Joe. Kez's unqualified acknowledgement of who he is makes him something of an innocent and gives him freedom of a kind – freedom of choice, at least. He seems to be the figurehead of the unadulterated city. His singularity is underwritten by his acceptance that 'There was . . . nothing singular in the world. In the worlds' (138), and is further borne out by his evidently not having a past, not having anybody to lay claims on him. He is also apparently without the contaminating experience of dependence which makes the other characters seem spare, or discarded, parts – a widow, a divorcé, a house-guest, an orphan (George) and a love-starved gay man. Invited to be a guest on Joe's radio show, Kez is unable to play the assigned part of freak. And to Barry, he represents the possibility of love, which results in Barry playing a decisive role in rescuing Kez from the clutches of evil George.

Before his death, Daniel Gilmore was said to be perfecting a drug that would erase memory. George, a poisonous presence generally who has killed once before early on in the novel, believes that he has discovered the drug, and already has a well-developed sense of its market value 'in Northern Ireland. In Palestine. Balkans' (435). He needs to test it, and selects Kez for his guinea-pig. The ugly American will not succeed, but his scheme is one expression of the novel's scepticism regarding finality and solutions, both of which are associated with excess and indulgence. The glutton Kitty is the physical counterpart to George's hopes of mental profiteering. Her signature image is a knife and fork and her devotion to Delly is her means, she trusts, of inheriting the Gilmore estate. Kitty eventually collapses and expires under her own weight. Joe Kavanagh thinks that the story of a memory drug is 'crackers, nonsense, barmy, the worst kind of third rate cobbled together conspiracy theory that it was possible to imagine' (293). He has a point, but it does not deter him from indulging as a guest on his show Sylvia Porterhouse, the English journalist who introduced the theory. Joe seems to expect Sylvia to indulge the divorcé's *angst* that he foists upon her. But then he afflicts everybody within range with that, including his Nigerian neighbours. Even Delly's longing for death has the self-deceiving, self-indulgent simplicity of excess about it. Like the others, she does not get what she thinks she wants either, though in her case 'Death had somehow missed her' (449) – a failure as instructive as those of Kitty and George. Kez also has a hand in saving Delly from herself, for which – in yet one more unexpected stroke of fortune – he is handsomely rewarded.

Characters who plot to outwit the world, who play the angles and wish to take advantage, end up being outwitted by their plots. Overkill is an antidote to need. Honesty is the prostitute's salient merit. Love, whether in the form of eros or agape, is the last thing on most people's minds. These are among the many interlocking and overlapping lines that structure Dublin's grid of 'hedonistic panic' (286) and 'the hermit heart' (108). Here is a city that seems a headless capital, a stranger to tradition, to civic virtue, to daylight enterprise, and to the thought of home. Lacking visible norms of coherence, it appears to be an unreal place, with nearly all its inhabitants peripheral to their own lives. Joycean paralysis is recycled as atomised hiding and seeking. The urban scene is a tissue of randomly colliding, subjectively enabled parts, and the happenstance of the moment is all. In a word, things are mostly, though by no means definitively, a mess. Mess may begin to spell message, but spelling things out is resisted in *The Parts*, as are all other gestures of finality. Instead of reaching conclusions about what the various plots, the different scenarios, the range of needs and maps of displacement all signify, *The Parts* allows them to have their way. They are all free to declare themselves, and the part the novel itself plays is not to interpret that freedom but to accommodate it. As a result, its most expressive component is its seemingly casual, open-plan architecture (the story begins and effectively ends in Delly's mansion, a place of many disparate levels). Given that paradoxically changeable structure, the citizenry's instabilities seem consistent. The transient reality of their extravagance and need, their presumptions of liberty and their knowledge of loss, the scope of their own limited worlds and the impact of others' worlds on them all contribute to a fluid structure, conveying the sense that where we are is a provisional and uncertain answer to the question that seems in the forefront of most of the characters' minds, even if they are not sure how best to ask it – where are we?

Supplementary Reading

Keith Ridgway, 'Knowing Me, Knowing You' (on Beckett's *Mercier and Camier*), *The Guardian*, 19 July 2003

Michael Pye, 'A Million Kittens in a Sack', *The New York Times Book Review*, 13 June 2004

Michael G. Cronin, '"He's My Country": Liberalism, Nationalism and Sexuality in Contemporary Irish Gay Fiction', *Éire-Ireland*, vol. 39, no. 4 (Fall/Winter, 2004), pp. 250–67

Also Published in 2003

Clare Boylan, *Emma Brown*; Gerard Donovan, *Schopenhauer's Telescope*; Anne Enright, *The Pleasure of Eliza Lynch*; Jamie O'Neill, *Disturbance*; Sean O'Reilly, *Love and Sleep*; David Park, *The Big Snow*

2004

Colm Tóibín, *The Master*

A noted journalist and cultural commentator, as well as a playwright and short-story writer, Tóibín (b. 1955) is the author of six novels. A native of Enniscorthy, County Wexford, which features prominently in The Heather Blazing *(1992),* The Blackwater Lightship *(1999) and* Brooklyn *(2009), his work is equally at home in such foreign settings as Spain in* The South *(1990) and Argentina in* The Story of the Night *(1996). Issues of gay identity are one of Tóibín's recurring fictional concerns, often seen in the context of the intricate intimacies of family life.*

'The intellect of man is forced to choose/Perfection of the life, or of the work'. Yeats's lines seem particularly applicable to the life and work of

Henry James, who in *The Master* resolves their stark polarity by electing to perfect the life in the work. The mastery he attains in the crucial years the novel covers – 1891 to 1899 – is evident in the degree of aesthetic refinement and narrative sophistication he brought to the works of that period. But the inner drama from which these accomplishments issue, and on which *The Master* focuses, concerns significant choices James made regarding his personal history, which he refashioned, and his personal relations, which he maintained in largely a formal social sense.

The first choice James makes is to rededicate himself to his fiction in the aftermath of the disastrous premiere of his play *Guy Domville*. The opening night debacle not only dashes his hopes of the theatre becoming a lucrative sphere of activity, it also enables him to arrive at a more subtle and far-reaching awareness of how best to serve his own creative interests and abilities. One effect of James's response to the challenge of rededication is that his fiction now possesses a greater degree of interiority, manifested in an increasingly nuanced moral sense, a more complex psychological range, and a keener exploration of the pathways of consciousness. Embarrassed by the unavoidably public character of his theatrical failure, he proceeds to turn to creative account failures of a more private kind. Haunted by memories of missing persons and lost loves, he reanimates them as repositories of symbolic value and vehicles of imaginative truth, addressing his work 'as though the processes of imagination themselves were as a ghost' (64).

A case in point is *The Turn of the Screw*. This novella's origins in a dinner-table anecdote are already part of James's scholarly and biographical record. But the story is now also seen to draw on James's childhood, and on the estrangement he and his sister Alice felt when the family undertook its European peregrinations. Such a reading highlights James's own investment in the story, whose shock value is consequently deepened. Similarly, James not only fondly remembers his cousin Minny Temple, but by using her as the prototype for Milly Theale in *The Wings of the Dove*, preserves and honours her radiant spirit. Other instances of the personal dimension of James's late works are also given, though *The Master* carefully avoids the repetition and predictability which would result from exclusively relying on it as a source of narrative development. And the mastery that James attains ultimately says less about the past than about the present in which what has gone before receives its reconfiguring permanence. (Coincidentally, this sense of a revised past, made usable in the interests of a more complete form of preservation than memory alone can provide, has additional relevance in the light of present-day Irish debates regarding the past's cultural function, value and nature.)

For James, the past is not simply the site from which he can extract personages and events with a view to making them amenable to literary representation. On the contrary, his past is an uneasy realm, a site of conflict – with family, with America, and with himself, particularly with regard to his sexuality. And in many ways the conflict has left James at a loss – solitary, an exile, homeless (his 1897 acquisition of Lamb House in the Sussex town of Rye becomes a landmark in the consolidation of his singularity). Yet, were it not for loss – and the *Guy Domville* embarrassment is part of the pattern – there would be no compensating independence and no impetus for the discipline and integrity which distinguish the years in question, when the full plenitude of James's consciousness of himself and others were given artistic form. Facing the past makes more explicit and more comprehensible the necessary critical remove at which he had always stood from the life around him, as in his chastely sharing a bed with Oliver Wendell Holmes, disappointing the dying Minnie Temple's wish that he escort her on a European tour, avoiding service in the American Civil War ('His war had been private, within his family and deep within himself' (111)). And James's sympathetic comprehension of those and other acts of detachment and withdrawal enable him to negotiate the demands of the present, such as an extended bout of grimly comic servant trouble and, more notably, rejecting the companionship of his fellow-novelist and 'his best friend, the person outside his own family who had been closest to him' (186), Constance Fenimore Woolson. This rejection was followed not long afterwards by her suicide, which in *The Master* is perhaps the greatest challenge to his hard-won self-control.

As it is in his fiction, the central characteristic of James's behaviour is its affirmation of choice and an acceptance of the consequences. By electing to be faithful to his own nature, first and foremost, he is not only exercising a right – a right to difference, separateness, privacy, and to inhabiting to the full his house of fiction. In addition, this way of life assumes responsibility for the choosing self, an entity that is so little indebted to social conditioning, inherited obligations and emotional entanglements that it relishes nothing better than imagining what these factors entail for others. This self's signatures are 'a clear ambition and a free imagination' (115). To defend and preserve this person's freedom and clarity, secrecy is required. Too on edge to attend the *Guy Domville* opening, James instead goes to see Oscar Wilde's *An Ideal Husband*, which repels him as much as its author does. Wilde is the James anti-type, as the contrast between their respective sexual identities indicates. James's closeted sexuality is his greatest secret, and is the most obviously costly of the ways in which he holds himself at a distance from others. He is too self-aware to deny his experience of homosexual attraction, and is also haunted by occasions when he might have declared himself. A case in point is his friendship with Hendrik Andersen, a young Danish sculptor he meets in Rome and hosts at Lamb House. Yet, though James has changed, he has also remained the same, and even though, having shared that bed with Holmes, 'He wondered if he would ever again be so intensely alive' (92), he does not act when opportunity presents itself.

This loss, too, is a matter of choice, of self-control, of freedom – an extreme case (one might even say the test case) of the vigilance and commitment required to secure his artistic calling. And with Wilde's fate providing the larger context, James's choice is also a sobering commentary on the social constraints and moral atmosphere in which being gay was then judged. James does not assert his right to his sexuality, and this too perhaps is reflected in the masterpieces of these years, with their typically tense and frequently melodramatic interplay between lover and beloved. The war with himself – the war of self-mastery – is another aspect of James's conflict with the past, and is further testimony of the sacrifice entailed by self-realisation. There is something heroic about James's understanding of what is at stake and also about the integrity of his dedication. Readers will remember that Irish fiction has visited these issues before, in Joyce's *A Portrait of the Artist as a Young Man*, where indeed they attain foundational status. The Henry James of *The Master* is not a young man, nor is he in overt rebellion, sexual or otherwise; nor can his Europe be the same as Joyce's. His is an alternative case, and in its implicit affiliation with James, *The Master* resonates suggestively with other recent Irish reconsiderations of modernity and tradition. At the same time, however, its closely focused prose and the discipline imposed by its reliance on biographical detail defer such revisionist and mythographying interests in favour of paying tribute to the lonely integrity of the individual's impenitent and triumphant creation of a world of his own.

Supplementary Reading

Fred Kaplan, *Henry James: The Imagination of Genius* (New York: Morrow, 1992)

Éibhear Walshe, 'The Vanishing Homoerotic: Colm Tóibín's Gay Fictions', *New Hibernia Review*, vol. 10, no. 4 (2006), pp. 122–36

Stephen Matterson, 'Dreaming about the Dead: *The Master*', in Paul Delaney (ed.), *Reading Colm Tóibín* (Dublin: Liffey Press, 2008), pp. 131–48

Susan Griffin (ed.) and 'Introduction', *All a Novelist Needs: Colm Tóibín on Henry James* (Baltimore: Johns Hopkins University Press, 2010)

Also Published in 2004

Ronan Bennett, *Havoc in its Third Year*; Emma Donoghue, *Life Mask*; Roddy Doyle, *Oh, Play That Thing*; Neil Jordan, *Shade*; Sean O'Reilly, *The Swing of Things*; Glenn Patterson, *That Which Was*

2005

Sebastian Barry, *A Long, Long Way*

One of the leading playwrights of his generation, Barry (b. 1955) is equally well known for his novels. Early works of fiction include Macker's Garden (1982) *and* The Engine of Owl-Light (1987). *The publication of* The Whereabouts of Eneas McNulty (1998) *inaugurated a loosely connected sequence of novels concerning the Dublin-based Dunne and the Sligo-based McNulty families. The fortunes of individual members of these families are recounted in* Annie Dunne (2002) *and* The Secret Scripture (2008), *and typically feature protagonists who prove to be exceptions to the course of events of their time. Set in the early years of the twentieth century, these alternative histories convey arresting revelations in an ornate and sometimes whimsical style. On* Canaan's Side (2011) *continues the Dunne family saga in America.*

Although he seems a long, long way from fully appreciating the fact, Willie Dunne has been marked by history from birth – 'He was called William after the long-dead Orange King, because his father took an interest in such distant matters' (3). And it is not only far-off history that has left an imprint on him. The state of Irish society, and of Irish relations with England, are also unavoidable aspects of his formation and of his pre-First World War world. The Dunnes live in Dublin Castle, their apartment a perk of Willie's father's position as a superintendent of police. Dunne senior describes himself as 'a man that has strove [sic] to keep order in this great city and protect it from miscreants and the evil of traitors and rebels' (247). His rigid adherence to the status quo is such that he finds it difficult to forgive his son for not being tall enough to enlist in the police. The exception that confirms the superintendent's strict rule is his befriending of a trade unionist, Lawlor, injured in a baton attack during the 1913 Lockout, a good deed that leads to Willie falling for Lawlor's daughter, Gretta.

Employed as a builder's labourer, and planning eventually to marry Gretta, Willie nevertheless decides to join up when war breaks out, believing that in this decision 'he had followed his own mind' (13). In this belief he has led himself astray, and pretty much everything else that happens thereafter ensures that he is a long, long way from becoming what he might be. He loses Gretta Lawlor's love through the malicious moralising of a comrade-in-arms. His return home on leave coincides with the outbreak of the Easter Rising, producing among other things an unnerving similarity between the city's main thorough-fare, Sackville Street, and the Flanders trench of the same name in which Willie serves. And Willie finds himself bearing arms against his countrymen, one of whom, the same age as himself, he sees shot: 'he carried the young man's blood to Belgium' (97). Remarking in a letter to his father that 'I wish they had not seen fit to shoot the . . . leaders' (139) of the Rising alienates Willie from that pillar of the establish-ment. The Rising also costs Willie a friend, Jesse Kirwan, who is court-martialled and shot for going on hunger strike to protest the rebels' execution. What Ireland signifies is clearly changing in ways that Willie hardly dares imagine.

At the front, his faith that 'his father's fervent worship of the King would guide him, as the lynchpin that held down the dangerous tent of the world' (22) soon comes under fire. As an unworldly eighteen-year-old, the inner conflict arising from trying to cope with the demands of war is as baffling to him as the tactics and attitudes of his commanding officers. And his outlook is not improved by some of his superiors' bul-lying and racial taunting. He thinks of soldiering as 'bloody manhood at last' (21), but men's travail and the myriad horrifying ways in which the epithet 'bloody' can be applied are understandable sources of moral revulsion to him. Still, even if 'he felt slight enough in the world' (49), he does his bit, and a number of arresting set-pieces show him doing it. A particularly striking episode, which among other things introduces the novel's ghost motif, deals with the foolhardy heroics of a Captain Pasley, who obeys orders to stand his ground while being gassed. Willie understands this obedience to be an extraordinary display of honour

('It was a sacred matter really' (53)). But he also feels it to be above and beyond the bounds of sensible behaviour, a point he makes as well to Jesse Kirwan, who in sticking to his guns also appears to Willie to be throwing his life away.

If others have a claim on Jesse's or on Pasley's life, Willie does not feel bound by it. He might not quite comprehend his own presence, but he cannot regard it in a reductive or depersonalised light. His fellow-feeling for shot 1916 rebels is one expression of his untarnished, un-preconditioned nature. Another is his commiserating visit to Pasley's rural, Protestant parents. Other strange meetings – antidotes to what seems preordained – also take place intermittently, including some socialising between soldiers from the north and south of Ireland and entertainments staged for each other by officers and men (Willie sings 'Ave Maria'; the officers put on Lady Gregory's *The Rising of the Moon* – a somewhat surprising choice, even if little in the war zone is not surprising). Such events are welcome, no doubt, but in their temporariness they are almost a mockingly ironic contrast to prevailing conditions. And an outcome that might 'gather the ravelled ends of Ireland together' (214) seems a long, long way off. This hope of a whole fabric is attributed to Willie Redmond, whose brother John was the politician who encouraged Irishmen to enlist, on the basis that doing so would further Ireland's political prospects. Willie Redmond is killed. What Willie Dunne represents is hardly likely to survive either, not only in the physical sense – being saved and his subsequent convalescence in England are only a reprieve – but also existentially. His desire for wholeness, whether with regard to Gretta, his father, the 1916 dead, or the dead of the First World War, may be a manifestation of his integrity, but it is clearly at odds with the disintegrative modern forces and extraordinarily rapid changes in social values and historical tradition, in the conception of manhood and the value of the human, which the war enforces.

Willie's failure to hold his own is typical of his comrades, and *A Long, Long Way* contains several instances of officers and men who go to pieces from psychological duress and spiritual despair. Loss becomes the dominant feature of Willie's experience. Besides, he never has been able to say exactly what his own is. The assumptions such as service, fidelity and hierarchy into which he was born, and whose cogency he has seen enshrined in the Castle and in the immutable law of the father, no longer seem tenable. He pays his respects to Pasley's remains, but he casts something of a cold eye on the supposedly edifying inscription on the captain's headstone: 'in the empire's service in the cause of righteousness and freedom' (260). His is not to reason why perhaps. In which case, there seems no alternative but to occupy the ultimate subject position – 'He had no country, he was an orphan, he was alone' (289). His is the battleground of the man who has not taken a side, a figure of some novelty in Irish culture.

Willie thinks that if Pasley's behaviour during the gas attack was that of an idiot, 'he was a holy idiot, for certain' (207). Later on, it so happens that one of Willie's comrades is reading Dostoevsky's *The Idiot*, whose protagonist is what Willie thought Pasley to be. But it is to Willie himself, his naively affirming disposition and the suffering it causes him, that the designation properly applies. A line of one of the war's best-known songs gives his story its title. But Willie Dunne is less in tune with martial rhythms than with the bird-song that often catches his ear from above the sound and the fury of bloodied fields.

Supplementary Reading

Keith Jeffery, 'Young Ireland Comes of Age', *The Times Literary Supplement*, 22 April 2005

Ben Howard, 'The Heaving Swell of History', *Sewanee Review*, vol. 114, no. 3 (Summer 2006), pp. lix–lxi

Christina Hunt Mahony, 'Children of the Light amid the "Risky Dancers": Barry's Naïfs and the Poetry of Humanism', in Christina Hunt Mahony (ed.), *Out of History: Essays on the Writings of Sebastian Barry* (Dublin: Carysfort, 2006), pp. 83–98

Roy Foster, '"Something of Us Will Remain": Sebastian Barry and Irish History', in Christina Hunt Mahony (ed.), *Out of History: Essays on the Writings of Sebastian Barry* (Dublin: Carysfort, 2006), pp. 183–97

Also Published in 2005

John Banville, *The Sea*; Dermot Bolger, *The Family on Paradise Pier*; Jennifer Johnston, *Grace and Truth*; Brian Lynch, *The Winner of Sorrow*; Barry McCrae, *The First Verse*; William Wall, *This is the Country*

2006
Gerard Donovan, *Julius Winsome*

Rather than being set in Ireland, Donovan's novels deal with extreme situations in remote European and American locations. His novels include Schopenhauer's Telescope *(2003) and* Doctor Salt *(2005; reissued in a different version as* Sunless *(2007)). A native of Wexford town, Donovan (b. 1959) has also published a number of volumes of poetry and a collection of short stories set in Ireland.*

Except for his dog Hobbes, a bull terrier, fifty-one-year-old Julius Winsome is alone. He lives in the secluded fastness of the border land between Maine and New Brunswick, and when the weather is good earns a living of sorts as a landscaper and mechanic, seemingly antithetical occupations which are a part of the novel's pattern of opposites. Now winter is coming on, and Julius is preparing to spend it with the library of over three thousand volumes which is a substantial part of his father's legacy to him. In addition to his home and a little land, the legacy's other main endowment is how to use firearms, an obvious contrast to the contemplative activity of reading. Both Julius's father and grandfather saw service in the world wars, and his gun is a relic of the First World War, acquired by his grandfather from a British sniper in exchange for his own weapon. As events reveal, this relic is in excellent working order.

The novel opens with the death of Hobbes, shot for no good reason by someone unknown, possibly one of the many locals who hunt in the nearby woods. Julius, unabashed by the cliché about man's best friend, makes no bones about his closeness to the dog, and sets out to avenge Hobbes's death by stalking and murdering hunters with his antique rifle. These actions show Julius to be entirely conversant with sniping technique, and also to have no compunction about taking life or the justice of his vendetta. He posts notices in the nearby town of Fort Kent, promising payment for information. But no information is forthcoming. Instead, disparaging messages about Hobbes's death are written on the postings. Julius reasons that when these messages no longer appear, he will have killed Hobbes's killer. Learning in the wake of his murders that the victims were family men, he feels a momentary pang of regret for their wives and children. But in general he seems as cold and remote as his chosen habitat. The novel may not intend to portray its North Woods setting as a dog-eat-dog world, yet it hardly shies away from such a portrait either.

Despite his library and his delight in reading, Julius appears to have no ethical or philosophical creed or code other than self-interest. The care and dedication he brings to his sniping, the rituals of will and agency that sniping enact, show him to be answerable to nothing beyond a seemingly reflexive sense of his own entitlement to act as judge, jury and executioner. There are occasions while hunting the hostile other, the arbitrarily designated enemy, when Julius's survival depends on an ability to appear indistinguishable from nature. Here his mastery of technique seems to amalgamate the human with the non-human, the former reverting to the latter while the woods and the wild seemingly enable the predator. It is as though the world is sanctioning Julius's self-interest. And self-interest is one of the central tenets of the philosophy of Thomas Hobbes. But the narrative makes clear that neat identifications and apparently simple patterns, permissible in some instances, are to be resisted in others. The dog got his name by chance. And Julius's murderous campaign is undertaken, at least in part, because Hobbes 'was my friend, and I loved him' (213), which complicates the case for self-interest being the sole source of outlook and motive. Indeed, one of the more unsettling aspects of the story that Julius tells – his self-portrait, in effect – is its depiction of a way of life and a point of view which avoid conventional categories of moral value. Having settled at the fringe of the wilderness in order to secure 'A life all of my own choosing' (164), Julius seems to function less with the common good in mind than in tune with the impersonal forces of nature – the novel contains a number of impressive snapshots of snowscapes and of winter weather whose extremes he finds a congenial environment. And if, as he says, 'people will not be controlled, they will not be dissuaded, they are also chained to what is in their minds to do, that too might be called instinct' (ibid.), then Julius Winsome himself is very much an unapologetic case in point.

Yet his saying as much shows that he obviously is not entirely a mere backwoodsman. Hobbes is not simply a pet, either; he also becomes 'a dog made of thought' (148). Julius got Hobbes when he was seeing a good deal of Claire. Consistently with other arbitrary elements of the story, Claire turns up one day out of the blue, having allegedly lost her way in the woods, as though she too is something of a stray, or loner, like Hobbes and Julius. It is on her suggestion that Julius acquires the dog, so that in addition to his inimitable animal presence, the loss of which Julius understandably mourns, Hobbes also bears some emotional weight. He is an emblem not only of a happy time in Julius's life but of the nature of that happiness, with its undemanding companionability, its accepted interdependence, its spontaneous exchange of attentions, its simple domestic system, and the natural – or animal – quality (or, as Julius is disposed to see it, virtue) of sexual intimacy. Like Hobbes, Claire embodies the simplicity and directness, the intuitive and sensory qualities of instinctual life. These qualities are also evident in Julius's conduct of his killing spree, his realisation of absence, as it might be called. With Claire, he obviously experiences the life-enriching forms that are antithetical to killing.

Unlike Julius, however, Claire lacks the single-mindedness to inhabit unchangingly such simple, elemental forms. She leaves, a choice that Julius stoically accepts. Three years after their affair, Julius finds her settled in the conventional security of home and husband in Fort Kent. Her husband is a policeman who also runs a part-time security business. Slowly but surely, with brief, tense, inconclusive encounters between Claire and Julius contributing, it transpires that this lawman, Troy, is the person whom Julius is hunting and the author of the mocking messages. But in addition to this discovery, Julius is also aware that it is only a matter of time before the collective authority of which Troy is the public face – townsmen, hunters, as well as the police – descends on his remote, solitary existence. Yet, in the event, though Julius's superiority in the field gives him the opportunity to conclude his campaign of vengeance, this is not what happens. Having Troy at his mercy does not produce the same effect on Julius as having Hobbes at his mercy did in Troy. Julius cannot shoot his adversary like a dog, for reasons that have a good deal to do with his fidelity to Claire, who in her time with him considered Julius 'a gentle man' (56). Such fidelity does not necessarily redress the situation, but it does underline the limits of self-interest and the evidently undeniable value of the other, however difficult it is to ascertain that value.

Hobbes's shooting gives Julius, 'after a lifetime of relatively nothing' (110), the feeling that his nature has been violated. His actions to relieve the feeling only compound it. Yet these actions also break down his self-sufficient isolation and entangle him with factors beyond his control, revealing that for all his detachment and independence he is also 'a man in parts' (31). He has to allow for the confluence in his nature of chance and choice, love and loss, and to learn the difference between the 'passionate and cold' (177) that his late father has told him a sniper should combine. Try as he will to place himself at a remove from his acts, even to the extent of dealing with them in part by means of a quaint vocabulary garnered under his father's tuition from the works of Shakespeare, he proved more susceptible and more various than he knew. The unobtrusive but ceaseless play of the novel's difficult cross-currents of internal and external worlds, love and death, human and animal, action and repose, to which the narrator's distinctive tone shows him withstanding and surrendering, and making *Julius Winsome* a telling parable on the nature of the human and how its energies continually question us as to how best we might live.

Supplementary Reading

Review by Simon Willis, *The Literary Review* (June 2007), p. 5
Oliver Harris, 'Death of Hobbes', *The Times Literary Supplement*, 8 June 2007

Also Published in 2006

Roddy Doyle, *Paula Spencer*; Claire Kilroy, *Tenderwire*; Patrick McCabe, *Winterwood*; Colum McCann, *Zoli*; Edna O'Brien, *The Light of Evening*; Keith Ridgway, *Animals*

2007

Anne Enright, *The Gathering*

Dublin-born Enright is the author of four novels. Three focus on family themes, and include The Wig My Father Wore *(1995) and* What Are You Like? *(2000), while* The Pleasure of Eliza Lynch *(2002) imaginatively reconstructs the career of a nineteenth-century adventuress – something of a Lola Montez – who became First Lady of Paraguay. Enright (b. 1962) has also published two noted collections of short fiction and a non-fiction work on motherhood.*

'A hosting of the Hegartys. God help us all' (187). That is the gathering that the narrative heads towards. With their faded mother, nine Hegarty siblings, including the narrator, Veronica, come together back home in Dublin – though with no marked expression of togetherness or unity – for the wake and funeral of another family member, Liam, an alcoholic who has drowned himself in England.

Liam's death is not only an occasion for the various rituals intended to impart safe conduct to a passing. It also prompts Veronica's complicated narrative, which weaves together, in a style that combines unsparing directness with felicitous insight, family history, family failings, motherhood, and her thoughts about her own married life with Tom and their two young daughters. Mixing memory and imagination, desire and loss, the non-linear storyline produces a prismatic view of three generations of emotional history. In doing so, it asks wide-ranging and discomforting questions about sexuality, belief, individual frailty and the lives of women. It is not merely the facts of the case that make up the narrative but their inner consequences, and it is in the latter context that facts are disabused of their time-bound, empirical character and converted into presentiments, hauntings, fears, resistances and needs through which the ineffaceable particularity of individual experience is registered. This sense of the half-life of facts, their persistent aftermath and irrecoverable actuality, gives *The Gathering* its acute consciousness of incompleteness and limitation, of the disheartened spirit and the fallible flesh – and of the apparent interchangeability of those two epithets in relation to those two nouns.

The narrative's impetus is announced at the outset: 'I need to bear witness to an uncertain event' (1). And this interplay between feeling and knowing, between personal need and others' behaviour, permeates the novel and all the characters in it. The central occurrence of which Veronica is convinced – even if her recollection of it as a matter of fact is unclear – is that when she, Liam and their sister Kitty were sent to live with their grandmother, Ada, Liam was molested by the oppressive Lamb Nugent, a friend of Ada's husband, Charlie Spillane. Charlie is something of a *luftmensch*, improvident and wayward but, where Ada is concerned, utterly devoted and loving, for which much else can be forgiven him in Veronica's eyes. But while Charlie is away, Lamb Nugent preys on Ada, seeking from her what his own marriage cannot provide, and inclined to avenge himself on the couple. (Much later, Veronica discovers that Nugent has been her grandparents' mean-spirited and vexatious landlord.) Despite, or in addition to, Veronica's belief in what she saw Liam undergo, it is also possible that her sensitivity to the emotional atmosphere of her grandparents' home created an image of such an act as an expression of her deeply held, but uncomprehending, misgivings over being exposed to tensions evidently endemic to adult need.

It is clear that if Veronica is not factually correct about the where and when of what happened to Liam, she does know herself to be in possession of the emotional truth that something did happen to him – 'The only things I am sure of are the things I never saw' (66). This awareness is not necessarily based on knowing from direct observation that Liam, when older, 'was never together' (142). Rather, this emotional truth of hers, informed as it is by an unnerving combination of the primal and the everyday, seems plausible in the light of the inner lives of her nearest and dearest – to use a conventional phrase of the type that Veronica's narrative italicises, drawing attention both to its impersonal, generic, consensual usage and to its utter inutility in conveying the complexities of what is personally at issue. Her parents' marriage is a case in point. Her mother's twelve deliveries, in addition to her miscarriages, convey to Veronica an unavoidable sense of violation. Giving life has taken life, as is clear from her mother's now vacant affect, her lack of presence, her devitalised responses, her missing nature, all of which seem like the early onset of senility – and from a factual standpoint may be – but which also strike home as a depletion of human capital and moral substance, a ruined purchase on being. Here is a mother, Veronica seems to say, with pained impatience, instead of a woman. And Veronica cannot help thinking, or attempting to imagine – the latter activity in effect an attempt at a critique – what her father, a not uneducated man though also a somewhat violent one, conceived his wife's and his own sexuality to be.

Similarly, for all that she is now settled in upmarket, suburban Booterstown – far from Ada's little house in inner-city Broadstone – it seems to Veronica that with regard to her businessman husband, Tom, some things do not change. Tom's sense of her, regardless of its personal nuances and mannerisms, seems to replicate the essential male fallacy of seeing women in sexual terms rather than seeing them as people. Yet, for Veronica, it is not only the fact of Tom's predictably unthinking sexual identity that weighs on her, but also how she can affirm the obvious reality of her own different, more self-aware, sense of sexuality, and of personhood as well. This matter concerns her not only in view of her mother's history but with regard to herself as the mother of daughters. Placed between past and future, Veronica becomes another instance of the stranded modern individual, fully conscious of her isolation and difference but, by virtue of that consciousness, denied an authenticating role in the lives around her. It is difficult to speak with her siblings, her work in seeing to Liam's remains and removal from England goes generally unnoticed, and when Liam's former lover unexpectedly turns up at the wake with their son, Veronica can hardly resist the impulse to mother the child. But in spite of the complicated and variable feelings of distance she experiences, and regardless of how Liam's death and all its attendant requirements exacerbate those feelings, Tom's idea of how best to treat Veronica is to make love to her on the night of the wake.

This act of emotional illiteracy results in a type of closure which is presumably the opposite of the one Tom intended. Yet, when Veronica leaves him, it is only to go as far as Gatwick Airport, where she flew earlier to collect Liam. On this second visit, she becomes a member of a gathering far removed from the traditional one assembled in her brother's name. The airport is permanently crowded with people continually in transit. Veronica belongs with them in that she finds it impossible to say if they, like her, are heading towards their families or away from them. But she also finds it impossible to see herself as no more than a bird of passage. Even with all she knows, she will not allow herself to be carried away or misled. In that, she differentiates herself from Liam. She does have a life, and in acknowledging that fact she does for herself what she has done for Liam and returns home, troubling as that landfall may be. Liam's great talent was 'exposing the lie' (125), and perhaps Veronica's fidelity to Liam signals her capacity to live with what she herself has exposed. At any rate, though it is difficult, 'I look at Liam's coffin and try to believe in love' (229).

That effort, made in the awareness of loss and disconnection, underlines the kinds of questions *The Gathering* asks. Its family focus seems to support Veronica's contention that 'History is only biological' (162). But breeding produces more than children. It also gathers together various disparate people – typically 'human beings in the raw' (188), like the Hegartys – and impresses emotional patterns on them, codes of responsiveness and resistance, cultures of silence and utterance, structures of belonging and rejection. And inasmuch as these patterns receive various types of reinforcement from prevailing social *mores*, they offer a facsimile of cohesion and protection. The challenge to Veronica of how to live with herself, given how others expect her to live with them, is plainly of considerable individual consequence. But it also sheds a revealing light on the integrity and potential of gatherings such as family, generation, class and people. 'It is not that the Hegartys don't know what they want, it is that they don't know *how* to want' (187). As disturbing as this angry admission is for Veronica's emotional well-being, it is equally so in view of the likelihood that it can hardly apply to Veronica's family alone.

Supplementary Reading

Anne Enright, *Making Babies: Stumbling into Motherhood* (London: Cape, 2004)

Heidi Hansson, 'Anne Enright and Postnationalism in the Contemporary Irish Novel', in Scott Brewer and Michael Parker (eds), *Irish Literature since 1990* (Manchester: Manchester University Press, 2009), pp. 216–31

Carol Dell'Amico, 'Anne Enright's *The Gathering*: Trauma, Testimony, Memory', *New Hibernia Review*, vol. 14, no. 3 (2010), pp. 59–74

Liam Harte, 'Mourning Remains Unresolved: Trauma and Survival in Anne Enright's *The Gathering*', *LIT: Literature Interpretation Theory*, vol. 21, no. 3 (July–September 2010), pp. 187–204

Also Published in 2007

Ronan Bennett, *Zugswang*; Eoin McNamee, *12:23: Paris, 31st August 1997*; Éilís Ní Dhuibhne, *Fox, Swallow, Scarecrow*; Glenn Patterson, *The Third Party*

2008

Joseph O'Neill, *Netherland*

O'Neill (b. 1964) was born in Cork , but has spent most of his life outside Ireland, growing up largely in Holland. His novels include This is the Life *(1991) and* The Breezes *(1995). He has also published a number of short stories and a notable memoir,* Blood-Dark Track *(2001).*

The attack on the World Trade Center has obliged Hans van den Broek, his wife Rachel and their small son Jake to move from their loft in fashionable TriBeCa to the Chelsea Hotel, one of New York's most fabled hostelries. Obviously, things could be a lot worse. Husband and wife both retain their very lucrative jobs, Dutch-born Hans as a financial analyst and Rachel – a native of 'undisastrous old England' (126) – as a lawyer. They do not think of their professions as being the two pillars of the world system whose epicentre is New York. Nor does it occur to them that their home countries have been the two formative historical influences on the city of New York. And there is nothing surprising in their not seeing themselves in such terms. Ordinary private citizens do not. And yet those terms, remote and lacking in material substance though they are, do have a resonance and a utility, not so much by being historical facts but by their connotations of origins, home, purpose and continuity. And it is such matters which seem to carry out sneak attacks on Hans and Rachel as they try to go on with their ordinary lives in the aftermath of the 9/11 abomination.

Their efforts are not successful. They find it difficult to provide each other with the required support. Their Manhattan world is no longer what it was, and it is unclear quite where they stand now. Change is locally all around, in the lingering dust, in unfamiliar or suspicious body language, in new forms of vigilance. Yet it seems largely intangible, a matter of atmosphere and texture, unavailable to the kinds of knowledgeable discourse that, for instance, their professions depend upon. Living in the caravanserai-like Chelsea Hotel is in itself an expression of being in transition. But Hans and Rachel have little sense of where they are going or of what they understand by the future. When eventually Rachel leaves with Jake for England, Hans finds that, 'I felt shame because it was me, not terror, she was fleeing' (30). It is clear, however, that the separation of self from world that this statement seems to underwrite is no longer tenable – assuming that it ever was. Rather, it seems a highly subjective testament to the cocooned world in which Hans and Rachel used to live. Rachel's departure removes one major structural feature from that world, and Hans enters into a downward spiral.

As a corrective to this descent into a netherland, Hans seeks out simpler things. One of these is cricket, a sport at which he was good as a boy and which he discovers members of communities quite different from the one he and Rachel inhabited playing with passionate decorum in New York's outer boroughs. The first time he turns up at the Staten Island Cricket Club, Hans hears a lecture from one of the other players on how 'cricket, more than any sport is . . . a lesson in civility' (15), and how important it is for those playing – immigrants, members of the lower orders – to keep this lesson in mind. The speaker is Khamraj 'Chuck' Ramkissoon. Soon, between flying to London for demoralising weekends with Rachel and Jake, Hans finds himself spending time with Chuck, listening to his plans, visiting obscure and polyglot areas of Brooklyn and Queens, and trying to keep abreast of Chuck's various complicated deals and personal entanglements. In Hans's unhappy state of aftermath and dislocation, Chuck's energies and appetites are a saving grace.

Hans is all the more conscious of Chuck's friendship because he is seeing it in retrospect. We first hear of Chuck when Hans receives the shocking news of his murdered body being found. Recollections of their camaraderie constitute a memorial. And if the tone is not particularly elegiac, the memories perform the function of elegy in preserving the spirit of the deceased. Here, too, the continuing presence of something lost informs Hans's awareness of his recent life and times. In detailing Chuck's unpredictable, risky, liberated, not entirely lawful way of life – such a contrast to that of a company man – Hans is obviously paying tribute to an individual unique both for his wayward schemes and scams and for his lack of secrecy and stealth. But in doing so, Hans is also tacitly acknowledging the importance of remembering and the faith in constancy and attachment which remembrance enacts. Chuck has kept Hans living in the city, and has ensured that the city has remained alive for him, a healing gift all the more noteworthy considering the ease with which it transcends conventional inhibitions of race and class. As a minor character observes of him, Chuck is 'a rare bird' (251).

Part of Chuck's appeal, and an important element in his restorative presence, is his focus on the future. The principal expression of this focus is his scheme to convert a disused airfield into a venue for world cricket. His vision of the place seems to combine Broadway with the United Nations. On the one hand, such grandiosity denotes imagination and possibility, and in those ways is consistent with Chuck's high-flier persona, his overall belief that there is nothing to stop him, his translation of the foundational American belief in life, liberty and the pursuit of happiness. On the other hand, the project is fraught with legal difficulties, and as such is representative of what might be called Chuck's regular jobs working for unsavoury Russians and in illegal gambling. The airfield is a kind of no-man's-land, more redolent of aftermath than of renewal. Besides, whatever Chuck's plans for marketing the game, it is the game itself that matters to him, just as it matters to Hans.

For both men, cricket acts as a means of connection – with each other, with their past and their homes. Here again, a principle of continuity is renewed. Revisiting his pre-American life is for Hans, in particular, essential to the return to self-possession, on which he must embark if he is to have a future. And though Chuck's behaviour in every other sphere has a certain touch of the piratical and swashbuckling about it, he willingly submits to cricket's protocols and perfectly understands the need to do so. The game embodies a sense of balance, of partnership, of different and complementary kinds of pairings and oppositions, of individuality in the service of more than oneself, all of which give rise to images of harmony, equilibrium and self-containment. All that fall are wickets, and they are easily set up again. Chuck believes that 'all people . . . are at their most civilized when they're playing cricket' (211). And Hans sees in the game the dream of an ethic, where players are 'men imagining an environment of justice' (121). It might even be thought that cricket adds to *Netherland*'s aesthetic appeal, given the narrative's back and forth momentum, its unexpected swerves and breaks, and its dual conceptions of duration and open-endedness.

And it is with two images of continuation and balance that the novel concludes. One of these images is provided by the here and now. Hans is restored to Rachel and Jake and all three are on top of the world at the London Eye. But this moment of completeness gives way to Hans's memory of himself and his late mother approaching Manhattan on the Staten Island ferry with the World Trade Center towering before them. It is the first time in the novel that those buildings are mentioned, and the sleight of artistic hand with unites them and their resonances of loss and woe to the present moment and its turning wheel creates a fitting sense of recuperation in a world where the alternative seems such an active possibility – a world where, as Chuck's murder makes clear, the disequilibrium of sudden violence and wasteful death can come all too close to home.

Supplementary Reading

Benjamin Kunkel, 'Men in White', *London Review of Books*, vol. 30, no. 14 (17 July 2008), pp. 20–2

Zadie Smith, 'Two Paths for the Novel', *New York Review of Books*, vol. 58, no. 18 (11 November 2008), pp. 89–94

Brian G. Caraher, 'Netherland', *Estudios Irlandeses*, no. 6 (2011), pp. 165–7

Jeff Hill, 'The American Dream of Chuck Ramkissoon: Cricket in Joseph O'Neill's *Netherland*', *Journal of Sport History*, vol. 37, no. 2 (Summer 2010), pp. 219–34

Also Published in 2008

Sebastian Barry, *The Secret Scripture*; Michael Harding, *Bird in the Snow*; William King, *Leaving Ardglass*; Joseph O'Connor, *Redemption Falls*; David Park, *The Truth Commissioner*; James Ryan, *South of the Border*

2009

Colum McCann, *Let the Great World Spin*

Dubliner Colum McCann (b. 1965) features Ireland prominently in his highly regarded short stories – of which he has published two collections – but his novels have consistently dealt with international settings and themes. These range from being on the road in the US and Mexico in Songdogs *(1995) to the past and present of New York's subterranean life in* This Side of Brightness *(1998). And they include a fictionalised biography of Rudolf Nureyev –* Dancer *(2003) – and* Zoli *(2006), a life of a Roma poet set in mid-twentieth-century central Europe. The protagonists of these works are outsiders and boundary-crossers whose lives are romances of appetite and energy and whose stories McCann tells in a style buoyed up by a sense of wonder.*

A spinning world – great or not as it may be; and as this novel indicates, it is great in many ways and also small in many other ways – is an image of poise and persistence. These qualities are also exemplified by Philippe Petit, who on the morning of 7 August 1974 carried out his famous high-wire walk between the two towers of the World Trade Center. This event acts as the fulcrum of *Let the Great World Spin*, its composure and daring a symbolic rectification of the day's other more mundane challenges and falls from grace – the occasions of mourning, fatal collisions, incarcerations and acts of love which the novel details. Unlike Petit's unique walk in the sky, the stuff of daily life is lowering, produces casualties, entails sacrifices, is redolent of things broken and incomplete. Yet the juxtaposition of the funambulist's exploits with the high costs of living creates an image of all not being lost. The very excess of Petit's performance, the degree of intention and concentration that it requires, redeems the accidental, unforeseen, unconscious drama of the diurnal by its implicit rhetoric of uplift. Even the most marginal and overlooked citizens can be touched by the appeal of Petit's gesture. His accomplishment embodies extreme, though temporary, degrees of isolation and vulnerability, and in doing so transcends them. The downtrodden lift their eyes and experience wonder.

Petit crystallises this novel's sense of the metaphysical but he does not introduce it. Appropriately enough, Petit is kept at a distance, apart from a number of relatively brief forays into his outlook and preparation (inspired by his book, *To Reach the Clouds*). The high-wire walk itself is in the nature of a curtain-raiser attended by all sorts and conditions of New Yorkers on their morning way to work. But the novel's spiritual dimension as such arises from the somewhat offbeat Christianity espoused by Corrigan, a maverick worker-priest. Even in his Dublin adolescence, Corrigan felt inspired not only to tend to the down and out but to share the abjection and abandonment of their alcohol-soaked reality – a spinning world, indeed. Now working with Bronx prostitutes, among whom he lives in almost extravagantly impoverished conditions, he insists that despite, or rather because of, his effectively non-institutional status, he is still a follower of Christ, the man who, as he says, 'never rejected the world' (20), much like Corrigan himself.

When Corrigan's brother, Ciaran, himself at a loose end, joins him in the Bronx, he finds it difficult to accept that it is quite in this fashion and in this place that Corrigan should be doing the Lord's work: 'You could be doing something back home . . . . Up north. Belfast. Something for us. Your own people' (37). Yet it is here that Corrigan's faith is most clearly being tested, not only because of his life amidst the underclass, particularly the mother and daughter team of Tillie and Jazzlyn, but because he also has to acknowledge his own human needs and weaknesses when he falls for Adelita, a Guatemalan nurse. The test is how best to get back up once he has fallen. Rising to the occasion that Adelita presents requires reconfiguring in more intimate and personal terms all the principles of love, grace, faith and survival which give his pastoral presence its objective validity. Corrigan finds such a development very troubling, especially in its implications for his vow of clerical celibacy, and he has to walk something like a moral tightrope while ensuring that he is negotiating the challenge in good faith. And events conspire to deny him lasting fulfilment, although perhaps this outcome is rhetorically fitting, since it speaks to the novel's interest in risk, in crossing over and in potential.

The events in question, which take place later the same day as Petit's walk, may be seen as the antithesis of it. Another driver's careless lane-change causes Corrigan's car to spin out of control, killing him and his passenger, Jazzlyn. The latter is only in the car because her mother, Tillie, has in effect agreed to sacrifice herself by doing the jail-time to which Jazzlyn has been sentenced. Yet this disaster results in Ciaran meeting his wife, who had been travelling with the careless driver. And it also gives rise to an extended passage of testifying on Tillie's part, which leaves no doubt that her fallen state is not her whole story, but rather is a condition that gives rise to a transgressive energy comparable to that of Corrigan's commitment. Indeed, the novel is premised on a tissue of comparative relations between wreckage and restoration, happenstance and design, imbalance and stability, an ensemble of gestures and engagements signifying the restless need to venture human capital. And in order to avoid the risk of tendentiousness or moralising, the novel disperses its episodes and the alignments they produce over a wide range of class, race and gender settings. This narrative strategy foregoes the narrowness of conventional plotting in favour of a looser structure which facilitates a multiplicity of perspectives on the ups and downs of a large cast of characters but which also articulates an economy of possibility.

Such an economy – a system whereby values are traded – envisages its most significant activity to be the reconciliation of differences. Philippe Petit's accomplishment harmonises the most antithetical elements – man and wire, earth and air, insouciance and danger – to create a metaphysic of the physical. Nowhere is this prototype of harmony more significantly deployed in *Let the Great World Spin* than in the sphere of race relations. As will be already evident from the interconnection between Corrigan, Tilly and Jazzlyn, and also between Corrigan and Adelita, the body is of primary importance to the story of possibility which the novel advances. And this story's significance is further highlighted in the relationship which develops over the course of the Petit day between Park Avenue's Claire Soderbergh and Gloria, a Bronx neighbour of Tilly, Jazzlyn and Corrigan. Both Claire and Gloria lost sons in Vietnam, and are members of a group of mourning mothers who awkwardly try bearing witness to each other's grief. Gloria not only succeeds in helping Claire; she also goes on to rescue Tilly's grandchildren, bereft by jail and death (the novel extends its temporal reach to take in the visit of one of those grandchildren, under inhospitable circumstances, to a dying Claire). And, as further evidence of the citizenry's unexpected, unwitting yet unavoidable interconnections, Claire's husband, Solomon, is the judge who jails Tilly and who, later, hears the case against Philippe Petit, arraigned before him on charges of public disorder. The sky is the limit for connectivity's permutations and combinations.

It is this sense of boundless possibility, and of New York as its ground, that the image of the man in the sky initiates and sustains. In that way, the image acts as an antidote for those other things in the sky which will always be associated with the World Trade Center – a source of amazement as opposed to a site of murder, an expression of individual daredevilry instead of a manifestation of impersonal enmity, a tribute to reaching rather than collapsing. And yet, appalling as the attacks of September 11 were, faith in the potential of interconnectedness embraces it as well. Tilly is moved by the poems of Rumi. And this novel's title comes from Tennyson's 'Locksley Hall', a work indebted to the 'Mu'allaqat', a poem from ancient Arabia.

Supplementary Reading

Joseph Lennon, 'Colum McCann', in Michael R. Molino (ed.), *Twenty-First-Century British and Irish Novelists* (Detroit: Thomson Gale, 2003), pp. 181–91
Jennifer Levasseur and Kevin Rabalais, 'Interview with Colum McCann', *Glimmer Train*, no. 69 (2009), pp. 56–73
John Cusatis, *Understanding Colum McCann* (Columbia, South Carolina: University of South Carolina Press, 2011)
Eóin Flannery, *Colum McCann: The Aesthetics of Redemption* (Dublin: Irish Academic Press, 2011)

Also Published in 2009

John Banville, *The Infinities*; Kevin Casey, *A State of Mind*; Jennifer Johnston, *Truth or Fiction*; Claire Kilroy, *All the Names Have Been Changed*; Hugh Maxton, *20/16 Vision*; Peter Murphy, *John the Revelator*

2010

Paul Murray, *Skippy Dies*

Murray (b. 1975), a native of Dublin, is also the author of the novel An Evening of Long Goodbyes *(2003).*

Daniel 'Skippy' Juster is a second-year boarder at Seabrook College, a highly reputed secondary south County Dublin school run by the Paraclete Fathers (modelled, it appears, on Blackrock College, run by the Holy Ghost Fathers). During a doughnut-eating competition with his room-mate, Ruprecht van Doren, Skippy collapses and dies. To this, the novel's opening event, it is tempting to apply the well-known acronym 'gubu' – grotesque, unprecedented, bizarre, unbelievable – adjectives that may also be applied to much of the subsequent action.

Life at Seabrook, which is the novel's main focus, proves particularly susceptible to such epithets for a number of reasons. The school is in nothing like the stable state it claims for itself by virtue of its reputation and tradition. Change is in the air, but the way it is being handled is hamfisted, at best. The old clerical order is passing, its ingrained pastoral values now in such a state of decay as to be a menace to the boys under its care, as is exemplified by Father Green, also known as Père Vert. His charitable ministrations to the lower-class denizens of nearby St Patrick's Villas are further opportunities for sexual predation. The new, lay, regime is headed by Greg Costigan, nicknamed the Automator, a crass autocrat whose understanding of education has nothing to do with pastoral responsibility and everything to do with image and fund-raising, concerns that he articulates in the neologisms and clichés of managerial lingo. The old and new administrative ethos appear to be at odds with each other. At the same time, however, they both are equally and self-servingly indifferent to their effects on the youngsters entrusted to them.

But Seabrook is also on shaky ground on account of these same youngsters. As adolescents undergoing their own state of transition, they naturally display disdain for learning and authority, and their limited attention span is devoted to acting cool, bullying, constructing a plausible heterosexual identity and playing video games. The degree to which they seem ineducable – at least by the school's unreflecting and unchanging methods – is perhaps overstated. But the fact that the main evidence for their self-willed ignorance is found in history class has an obvious resonance, and in addition emphasises the all-consuming character of the present moment in their minds – for which they are not entirely at fault. The only class in which an interest is shown is geography and that is because it is taught by the very attractive Aurelie McIntyre. She is on a brief break from her career in finance, and her allure is also noticed by Seabrook alumnus, failed financial analyst and current Seabrook history teacher, Howard Fallon, with predictable consequences for his relationship with his live-in American partner, Halley.

In many ways, masters and boys resemble each other, though the system in which they are involved will work only if this resemblance is never acknowledged. As a result, school is a place where worlds collide – the different realms of staff and students, those of the old regime and the new, those of an old boy like Howard and the bright young cold-hearted thing, Aurelie, and those of escapists such as Skippy and Ruprecht and their more boastful and aggressive peers. In fact, the institution has many opposing constituent elements, and only nominally contains them, even though its standing among its bourgeois fee-payers rests on the reliability of repetition, the putative safety of a known world and related ideas of the uniform and unchanging. Costigan, in particular, is especially keen to capitalise on such ideas, seeing in whatever merit they might have in themselves a pretext for marketing the Seabrook brand. The school has no centre; instead, it is a constellation of contraries. When things are not actually falling apart, they are threatening to. Farce alternates with entropy, obligation with neglect, growth with coercion, the true story with the cover-up; and *Skippy Dies* elaborates on the erratic coexistence of these polarities with deftly comic aplomb.

The novel's title, however, indicates that its aims are not limited to the somewhat facile institutional targets just mentioned. Skippy's death overshadows all that follows, not only by virtue of its own shocking nature but through the manner in which it came about and how the powers that be deal with it. The youngster's surname does have an unavoidably ironic ring. In a juster world, he would not be treated so belittlingly in life or in death. Alive, he is a scapegoat; in death, an embarrassment. The sexual abuse leading to his killing himself is a perversion of the school spirit with which Skippy, as a member of the swim team, is expected to identify. And the abuse is also a callous betrayal on the part of Roche, the swimming coach – who is punished, if that is the word, by being transferred to a school in Mauritius. Perhaps Skippy is too consistently misfortune's child, not only in being at the mercy of Seabrook's ingeniously wide array of peer pressures but also because his mother has cancer and his father seems a parody of parental incompetence. At the same time, the boy's vulnerability and lack of support – especially with regard to being abused (in a world full of talk, there is nobody he can talk to) – humanises him to a degree attained by only a select handful of the novel's other characters. And if his falling for Lorelei – Lori – Wakeham, a student from the convent next door, is a textbook case of puppy love, it also points to his having a heart, a rare possession at Seabrook.

The possibility of a juster, or at least a less stereotypical, world slowly dawns on Howard Fallon. Known as Howard the Coward, a nickname given him as a result of a schoolboy episode that left a classmate crippled, his story turns out to be a variation on Skippy's. Initially an apparent weakling, he is spurred to take a stand by the administration's self-protective reaction to Skippy's death. He gets himself into further trouble when, in an act of revisionist pedagogy, he takes his class across Dublin to the First World War memorial at Islandbridge. Howard has found himself engaged and stimulated by his preparations to teach the history of the war, and his investment in doing so also creates a belated but thematically effective link with Skippy, whose grandfather served in the conflict. Showing the dead soldier's uniform to his students proves a novel way to get their attention, as well as usefully reminding Howard that history is not a waste of time and Seabrook students are neither to be written off nor taken for granted. Howard's ultimately uncowardly behaviour on various fronts demonstrates the possibility of common purpose, the value in identifying in a non-institutional common heritage, and that on however limited a scale, ostensibly conflicting worlds may be integrated. Not that thoughts of that kind count for anything in the Automator's world. The letter he sends out at the end of term papers over the many cracks that have appeared in the school's fabric, and is a masterpiece of public relations written with a rare expertise in the use of weasel words. On that note the novel ends. Nothing has changed.

By its wide frame of reference – to string theory, Robert Graves's *The White Goddess*, cosmology, for instance – and its depiction of a range of scenarios which includes the teenage drug scene, gated suburban communities and the treatment of immigrant labour, *Skippy Dies* leaves the reader in no doubt that no one version of the fluid and variegated everyday suffices. These and many more seemingly digressive ingredients combine to give the novel a fullness which its individual discourses on their own, whether historical, scientific, pedagogic or even satirical, are not capable of providing. It is tempting to think of Skippy as the un-Harry Potter, for whom magic is the mere touch of Lori's lips. But *Skippy Dies* cannot be as innocent as its hero. If not necessarily in theme, then in range and inventiveness, the whole story is a rebuke not only to the Automator's letter but to everything that authority figure stands for, even if he is allowed to have the last word. Grounded in the crises of transition and development characteristic of adolescence, the novel is in the nature of a report card – unexpectedly well timed to coincide with a fresh set of changes in Irish social reality – on additional, unsuspected manifestations of the same types of crises, as teachers and students, parents and offspring, townies and boarders, bullies and weaklings, and many others in between, stumble through a mismanaged and fragmented present without the remotest idea of what difference their doing so will make to securing a future.

Supplementary Reading

Dan Kois, 'Ghost, Come Back Again', *The New York Times Book Review*, 5 September 2010

Fintan O'Toole, 'Future Fictions', *Princeton University Library Chronicle*, vol. 52, no. 1 (Autumn 2010), pp. 407–18

Also Published in 2010

Emma Donoghue, *Room*; Roddy Doyle, *The Dead Republic*; Hugo Hamilton, *Hand in the Fire*; Neil Jordan, *Mistaken*; Claire Keegan, *Forester*; Patrick McCabe, *The Stray Sod Country*

Bibliographical Note

First editions appear in square brackets or where only one edition is noted. Other editions are those from which citations have been made.

The Country Girls ([London: Hutchinson, 1960] Harmondsworth: Penguin, 1963)

The Hollow Ball ([London: Cassell, 1961] Belfast: Blackstaff, 1990)

The Fugitives ([London: Weidenfeld & Nicolson, 1962] London: Pan, 1976)

Thy Tears Might Cease ([London: Hutchinson, 1963] New York: Signet, 1965)

How It Is (*Comment C'est*) ([Paris: Editions de Minuit, 1961; London: Calder, 1964] New York: Evergreen, 1964)

The Emperor of Ice-Cream ([London: André Deutsch, 1965] Mayflower, 1967)

Langrishe, Go Down (London: Calder & Boyars, 1966)

The Third Policeman (London: Hart-Davis, MacGibbon, 1967)

As Towns with Fire ([London: MacGibbon & Kee, 1968] Belfast: Blackstaff, 1985)

Strumpet City ([London: Hutchinson, 1969] London: Panther, 1971)

Troubles ([London: Cape, 1970] New York: New York Review Books, 2002)

Black List, Section H ([Carbondale, Illinois: Southern Illinois University Press, 1971] Harmondsworth, Penguin, 1996)

The Captains and the Kings ([London: Hamish Hamilton, 1972] London: Coronet, 1973)

An End to Flight (London: Faber & Faber, 1973)

Gone in the Head (London: Routledge & Kegan Paul, 1974)

Stamping Ground ([London: Secker & Warburg, 1975] London: Sphere, 1985)

The Stepdaughter ([London: Duckworth, 1976] New York: Scribner, 1974)

Proxopera ([London: Gollancz, 1977]) *The State of Ireland: A Novella and Seventeen Stories* (Harmondsworth: Penguin, 1982)

Bogmail ([London: Martin Brian & O'Keeffe, 1978] New York: Ticknor & Fields, 1981)

The Pornographer (London: Faber & Faber, 1979)

No Country for Young Men ([London: Allen Lane, 1980] New York: Carroll & Graf, 1980)

Kepler (London: Secker & Warburg, 1981)

In Night's City ([Dublin: Wolfhound, 1982] Champaign, Illinois: Dalkey Archive, 2006)

Cal ([London: Cape, 1983] New York: Braziller, 1983)

A Curious Street ([London: Hamish Hamilton, 1984] New York: Braziller, 1984)

The Killeen ([London: Hamish Hamilton, 1985] New York: Atheneum, 1986)

Open Cut ([London: Heinemann, 1986] London: Sceptre, 1987)

Work and Play ([London: Hamish Hamilton, 1987] New York: Fireside, 1990)

The Silence in the Garden ([London: 1988] New York: Viking, 1988)

Motherland ([London: Chatto & Windus, 1989] London: Picador, 1990)

The Journey Home (London: Viking, 1990)

The Last Shot (London: Faber & Faber, 1991)

The Butcher Boy ([London: Picador, 1992] New York: Delta, 1994)

Paddy Clarke Ha Ha Ha (London: Secker & Warburg, 1993)

A Goat's Song (London: Harvill, 1994)

Hood ([London: Hamish Hamilton, 1995] Los Angeles: Alyson, 1998)

Reading in the Dark ([London: Cape, 1996] New York: Vintage, 1998)

One Day as a Tiger ([London: Chatto & Windus, 1997] London: Vintage, 1998)

The Salesman (London: Secker & Warburg, 1998)

The International (London: Anchor, 1999)

The Pretender ([London: Cape, 2000] London: Vintage, 2001)

The Blue Tango (London: Faber & Faber, 2001)

Authenticity ([London: Faber & Faber, 2002] Minneapolis: Graywolf, 2005)

The Parts (London: Faber & Faber, 2003)

The Master ([London: Picador, 2004] New York: Scribner, 2005)

A Long, Long Way (London: Faber & Faber, 2005)

Julius Winsome (New York: Overlook, 2006)

The Gathering ([London: Cape, 2007] London: Vintage, 2007)

Netherland (New York: Pantheon, 2008)

Let the Great World Spin ([New York: Random House, 2009] New York: Random House, 2010)

Skippy Dies (London: Hamish Hamilton, 2010)

Bibliography

Achilles, Jochen, 'James Plunkett', in Rüdiger Imhof (ed.), *Contemporary Irish Novelists* (Tübingen: Narr, 1990), pp. 41–57

Adelman, Gary, 'Torturer and Servant: Samuel Beckett's *How It Is*', *Journal of Modern Literature*, vol. 25, no. 1 (Fall 2001), pp. 81–92

Alcobia-Murphy, Shane, *What Rough Beasts? Irish and Scottish Studies in the New Millennium* (Newcastle upon Tyne: Cambridge Scholars, 2008)

Alexander, Neal, 'Remembering to Forget: Northern Irish Fiction after the Troubles', in Scott Brewer and Michael Parker (eds), *Irish Literature since 1990: Diverse Voices* (Manchester: Manchester University Press, 2009), pp. 272–83

Allen, Richard C. and Stephen Regan (eds), *Irelands of the Mind: Memory and Identity in Modern Irelands of the Mind: Memory and Identity in Modern Irish Culture* (Newcastle upon Tyne: Cambridge Scholars, 2008)

Arrowsmith, Aidan, 'Plastic Paddy: Negotiating Identity in Second-Generation "Irish-English" Writing', *Irish Studies Review*, vol. 8, no. 1 (April 2000), pp. 35–43

____, 'Inside-Out: Literature, Cultural Identity and Irish Migration to England', in Ashok Bery and Patricia Murray (eds), *Comparing Postcolonial Literatures* (Basingstoke: Macmillan, 2001), pp. 59–69

____, 'Photographic Memories: Nostalgia and Irish Diaspora Writing', *Textual Practice*, vol. 19, no. 2 (Summer 2005), pp. 297–322

Atcheson, James (ed.), *The British and Irish Novel since 1960* (New York: St Martin's Press, 1991)

Balinisteanu, Tudor, *Narrative, Social Myth and Reality in Contemporary Scottish and Irish Women's Writing: Kennedy, Lochhead, Bourke, Ní Dhuibhne and Carr* (Newcastle upon Tyne: Cambridge Scholars, 2009)

Baneham, Sam, 'Aidan Higgins: A Political Dimension', *Review of Contemporary Fiction*, vol. 3, no. 1 (Spring 1983), pp. 168–74

Banville, John, 'A Talk', *Irish University Review*, vol. 11, no. 1 (Spring 1981), pp. 13–17

____, 'Finding the Order of Things', *The Irish Times*, 18 July 1992, Weekend, p. 9

____, 'The Great Tradition', *The Sunday Times*, 21 March 1993, pp. 8–9

____, 'Hitler, Stalin, Bob Dylan, Roddy Doyle . . . and Me', *Hot Press*, vol. 18, no. 19 (5 October 1994), pp. 14–16

____, 'The Personae of Summer', in Jacqueline Genet and Wynne Hellegouarc'h (eds), *Irish Writers and their Creative Process* (Gerrards Cross: Colin Smythe, 1996), pp. 118–23

____, 'Thou Shalt Not Kill', in Paul Brennan and Catherine de Saint Phalle (eds), *Arguing at the Crossroads: Essays on a Changing Ireland* (Dublin: New Island Books, 1997), pp. 133–42

____, 'A World Too Wide', *Irish University Review*, vol. 36, no. 1 (Spring/Summer 2006), pp. 1–8

Barfoot, C.C. and Theo D'haen (eds), *The Clash of Ireland: Literary Contrasts and Connections* (Amsterdam: Rodopi, 1989)

Barrington, Brendan (ed.), *The Wartime Broadcasts of Francis Stuart 1942–1944* (Dublin: Lilliput Press, 2000)

Barry, Kevin, 'Lullabies for Insomniacs: The Writer and Contemporary Irish Society', *Irish Review*, no. 2 (1987), pp. 7–13

Behrend, Hanna, 'James Plunkett's Contribution to Democratic and Socialist Culture', *Zeitschrift für Anglistik und Amerikanistik*, vol. 27, no. 4 (1979), pp. 307–26

Beja, Morris, 'Felons of Our Selves: The Fiction of Aidan Higgins', *Irish University Review*, vol. 3, no. 2 (Spring 1973), pp. 163–78

Bell, Fergus Hanna (ed.), *A Salute from the Banderol: The Selected Writings of Sam Hanna Bell* (Belfast: Blackstaff, 2009)

Bell, Sam Hanna, et al., 'The War Years in Ulster (1939–45): A Symposium', *Honest Ulsterman*, no. 64 (1979), pp. 11–62

Belletto, Stephen, 'Hugo Hamilton', in Michael R. Molino (ed.), *Twentieth-Century British and Irish Novelists* (Detroit: Gale, 2003), pp. 121–9

Bennett, Ronan, 'Don't Mention the War: Culture in Northern Ireland', in David Miller (ed.), *Rethinking Northern Ireland: Culture, Ideology and Colonialism* (London: Longman, 1998), pp. 199–210

Benstock, Shari, 'The Masculine World of Jennifer Johnston', in Thomas F. Staley (ed.), *Twentieth-Century Women Novelists* (London: Macmillan, 1982), pp. 191–217

Bensyl, Stacia, 'Swings and Roundabouts: An Interview with Emma Donoghue', *Irish Studies Review*, vol. 8, no. 1 (April 2000), pp. 73–81

Berensmeyer, Ingo, *John Banville: Fictions of Order* (Heidelberg: Winter Universitätsverlag, 1999)

Blackwood, Caroline, *For All That I Found There* (London: Duckworth, 1973)

Bolger, Dermot (ed.), *Invisible Cities. The New Dubliners: Travels Through Unofficial Dublin* (Dublin: Raven Arts, 1988)

____ (ed.), *Letters from the New Island* (Dublin: Raven Arts, 1991)

____ (ed.), *Ireland in Exile* (Dublin: New Island Books, 1993)

Bolger, Dermot, 'Introduction', *The Picador Book of Contemporary Irish Fiction* (London: Picador [1993] 2000), pp. vii–xxvi

Booker, M. Keith, 'Late Capitalism Comes to Dublin: "American" Popular Culture in the Novels of Roddy Doyle', *ARIEL: A Review of International English Literature*, vol. 28, no. 3 (July 1997), pp. 28–45

Böss, Michael and Éamon Maher (eds), *Engaging Modernity: Readings of Irish*

Politics, Culture and Literature at the Turn of the Century (Dublin: Veritas, 2003)

Bourke, Angela, Siobhán Kilfeather, Maria Luddy, Margaret MacCurtain, Gerardine Meaney, Máirín Ní Dhonnchadha, Mary O'Dowd and Clair Wills (eds), *The Field Day Anthology of Irish Writing, Vols 4 & 5: Irish Women's Writings and Traditions* (Cork: Cork University Press, 2002)

Boylan, Roger, 'Reading Aidan Higgins', *Context*, no. 20 (2007), pp. 1–3

Bradford, Richard, *The Novel Now: Contemporary British Fiction* (Malden, Massachusetts: Blackwell, 2007)

Bradley, Antony and Maryann Gialanella Valiulis (eds), *Gender and Sexuality in Modern Ireland* (Amherst, Massachusetts: University of Massachusetts Press, 1997)

Brannigan, John (ed.), 'The Battle for the GPO: Literary Revisionism in Roddy Doyle's *A Star Called Henry* and Jamie O'Neill's *At Swim Two Boys*', in Munira H. Mutran and Laura P.Z. Izarra (eds), *Kaleidoscopic Views of Ireland* (São Paulo: Universidade de São Paulo, 2003), pp. 115–32

____, 'Northern Irish Fiction: Provisionals and Pataphysicians', in James F. English (ed.), *Concise Companion to Contemporary British Fiction* (Malden, Massachusetts: Blackwell, 2006), pp. 141–63

____, *Race in Modern Irish Literature and Culture* (Edinburgh: Edinburgh University Press, 2009)

Brearton, Fran and Éamonn Hughes (eds), *Last Before America: Irish and American Writing* (Belfast: Blackstaff, 2001)

Brennan, Paul and Catherine de Saint Phalle (eds), *Arguing at the Crossroads: Essays on a Changing Ireland* (Dublin: New Island Books, 1997)

Brewster, Scott, Virginia Crossman, Fiona Becket and David Alderson (eds), *Ireland in Proximity: History, Gender, Space* (London: Routledge, 1999)

Brewster, Scott and Michael Parker (eds), *Irish Literature since 1990: Diverse Voices* (Manchester: Manchester University Press, 2009)

Briggs, Sarah, Paul Hyland and Neil Sammells (eds), *Reviewing Ireland: Essays and Interviews from* Irish Studies Review (Bath: Sulis, 1998)

Brophy, James D. and Raymond J. Porter (eds), *Contemporary Irish Writing* (Boston: Twayne, 1983)

Brouillette, Sarah, 'The Northern Irish Novelist in Ronan Bennett's *The Catastrophist*', *Contemporary Literature*, vol. 48, no. 2 (Summer 2007), pp. 253–77

Brown, Terence, 'Family Lives: The Fiction of Richard Power', in Patrick Rafroidi and Maurice Harmon (eds), *The Irish Novel in Our Time* (Villeneuve d'Asq: Publications de l'Université de Lille III, 1976), pp. 245–53

____, 'Dublin in Twentieth-Century Writing: Metaphor and Subject', *Irish University Review*, vol. 8, no. 1 (Spring/Summer 1978), pp. 7–21

____, *Ireland: A Social and Cultural History 1922–1985* (London: Fontana, 1981; expanded ed., 2004 as *Ireland: A Social and Cultural History 1922–2002*)

____, *Ireland's Literature: Selected Essays* (Dublin: Lilliput Press, 1988)

____, 'Redeeming the Time: John McGahern and John Banville', in Brown, *The Literature of Ireland: Criticism and Culture* (Cambridge: Cambridge University Press, 2010), pp. 225–38

Bruer, Rolf, 'Flann O'Brien and Samuel Beckett', *Irish University Review*, vol. 37, no. 2 (Autumn/Winter 2007), pp. 340–51

Burleigh, David, 'Dead and Gone: The Fiction of Jennifer Johnston and Julia O'Faoláin', in Masaru Sekine (ed.), *Irish Writers and Society at Large* (Gerrards Cross: Colin Smythe, 1985), pp. 1–15

Byrne, James P., Pádraig Kirwan and Michael O'Sullivan (eds), *Affecting Irishness: Negotiating Cultural Identity Within and Beyond the Nation* (New York: Peter Lang, 2008)

Cahalan, James, *Great Hatred, Little Room: The Irish Historical Novel* (Syracuse: Syracuse University Press, 1983)

____, *The Irish Novel: A Critical History* (Dublin: Gill & Macmillan, 1988)

____, *Modern Irish Literature and Culture: A Chronology* (Boston: G.K. Hall, 1993)

____, 'Female and Male Perspectives on Growing up Irish in Edna O'Brien, John McGahern and Brian Moore', *Colby Quarterly*, vol. 31, no. 1 (March 1995), pp. 55–73

____, *Double Visions: Women and Men in Modern and Contemporary Irish Fiction* (Syracuse: Syracuse University Press, 1999)

Cairns, David and Shaun Richards (eds), *Writing Ireland: Colonialism, Nationalism, and Culture* (Manchester: Manchester University Press, 1988)

Callan, Annie, 'Interview with Mary Morrissy', *Glimmer Train*, no. 18 (Spring 1996), pp. 89–103

Carillo, Ester, 'Bleak Cities: Belfast in Maurice Leitch's Novels and Barcelona in the Works of Juan Marsé', in Alan A. Gillis and Aaron Kelly (eds), *Critical Ireland: New Essays in Literature and Culture* (Dublin: Four Courts Press, 2001), pp. 22–9

Carlson, Julia, *Banned in Ireland: Censorship and the Irish Writer* (London: Routledge, 1990)

Carson, Douglas, 'The Antiphon, the Banderol and the Hollow Ball: Sam Hanna Bell 1909–1990', *Irish Review*, no. 9 (Autumn 1990), pp. 91–9

Cleary, Joe, '"Forked-Tongued on the Border Bit": Partition and the Politics of Form in Contemporary Narratives of the Northern Irish Conflict', *South Atlantic Quarterly*, vol. 95, no. 1 (Winter 1996), pp. 227–76

____, *Outrageous Fortune: Capital and Culture in Modern Ireland* (Dublin: Field Day, 2007)

Cliff, Brian and Éibhear Walshe (eds), *Representing the Troubles: Texts and Images, 1970–2000* (Dublin: Four Courts Press, 2004)

Clissmann, Anne, *Flann O'Brien: A Critical Introduction to his Writings* (Dublin: Gill & Macmillan, 1975)

Colletta, Lisa and Maureen O'Connor (eds), *Wild Colonial Girl: Essays on Edna O'Brien* (Madison, Wisconsin: University of Wisconsin Press, 2006)

Connolly, Claire (ed.), *Theorising Ireland* (London: Palgrave, 2002)

Connolly, Joseph, 'Legend and Lyric as Structure in the Selected Fiction of Jennifer Johnston', *Éire-Ireland*, vol. 21, no. 3 (1986), pp. 119–24

Connolly, Peter (ed.), *Literature and the Changing Ireland* (Gerrards Cross: Colin Smythe, 1982)

Conrad, Kathryn, *Locked in the Family Cell: Gender, Sexuality and Political Agency in Irish National Discourse* (Madison, Wisconsin: University of Wisconsin Press, 2004)

____, 'Occupied Country: The Negotiation of Lesbianism in Irish Feminist Narrative', *Éire-Ireland*, vol. 31, nos 1–2 (Summer 2006), pp. 123–36

Corcoran, Neil, *After Yeats and Joyce: Reading Modern Irish Literature* (Oxford: Oxford University Press, 1997)

Cosgrove, Brian, 'Ego Contra Mundum: Thomas Kilroy's *The Big Chapel*', in Patrick Rafroidi and Maurice Harmon (eds), *The Irish Novel in Our Time* (Villeneuve-d'Asq: Publications de l'Université de Lille III, 1976), pp. 297–309

____, 'Roddy Doyle's Backward Look: Tradition and Modernity in *Paddy Clarke Ha Ha Ha*', *Studies*, vol. 85, no. 339 (Autumn 1996), pp. 231–42

____, 'Irish/Postmodern Literature: A Case of Either/Or?' *Studies*, vol. 88, no. 352 (Winter 1999), pp. 381–8

Coughlan, Patricia, 'Irish Literature and Feminism in Postmodernity', *Hungarian Journal of English and American Studies*, vol. 10, nos 1–2 (Spring/Fall 2004), pp. 175–202

____, '"Without a Blink of Her Lovely Eye": *The Pleasure of Eliza Lynch* and Visionary Scepticism', *Irish University Review*, vol. 35, no. 2 (Autumn/Winter 2005), pp. 349–73

____, 'Banville, the Feminine and the Scenes of Eros', *Irish University Review*, vol. 36, no. 1 (Spring/Summer 2006), pp. 81–101

Coughlan, Patricia and Tina O'Toole (eds), *Irish Literature: Feminist Perspectives* (Dublin: Carysfort, 2008)

Craig, Patricia, *Brian Moore: A Biography* (London: Bloomsbury, 2002)

Cronin, Anthony, *A Question of Modernity* (London: Secker & Warburg, 1966)

____, *Heritage Now* (Dingle: Brandon, 1982)

____, *No Laughing Matter: The Life and Times of Flann O'Brien* (London: Grafton, 1989)

____, *Samuel Beckett: The Last Modernist* (London: HarperCollins, 1996)

Cronin, John, '*The Dark* Is Not Light Enough: The Fiction of John McGahern', *Studies*, vol. 58, no. 232 (Winter 1969), pp. 427–32

____, 'John McGahern: A New Image', in Jacqueline Genet and Wynne Hellegouarc'h (eds), *Irish Writers and their Creative Process* (Gerrards Cross: Colin Smythe, 1996), pp. 110–17

Cronin, Michael G. '"He's My Country": Liberalism, Nationalism and Sexuality in Contemporary Irish Gay Fiction', *Éire-Ireland*, vol. 39, no. 4 (Fall/Winter 2004), pp. 257–67

Crotty, Patrick, '"All Toppers": Children in the Fiction of John McGahern', in Elmer Kennedy-Andrews (ed.), *The Irish Novel since the 1960s: A Collection of Critical Essays* (Gerrards Cross: Colin Smythe, 2006), pp. 277–300

Cullingford, Elizabeth, *Ireland's Others: Ethnicity and Gender in Irish Literature and Popular Culture* (South Bend, Indiana: University of Notre Dame Press, in association with Field Day, 2001)

Cusatis, John, *Understanding Colum McCann* (Columbia, South Carolina: University of South Carolina Press, 2011)

Cusick, Christine (ed.), *Out of the Earth: Ecocritical Readings of Irish Texts* (Cork: Cork University Press, 2010)

Davey, Maeve Eileen, '"She Had to Start Thinking Like a Man": Women Writing Bodies in Contemporary Northern Irish Fiction', *Estudios Irlandeses*, no. 5 (2010), pp. 12–24

Davis, Alex, John Goodby, Andrew Hadfield and Eve Patten (eds), *Irish Studies: The Essential Glossary* (London: Arnold, 2003)

Dawe, Gerard, '"My Town": *Proxopera* and the Politics of Remembrance', *Irish University Review*, vol. 38, no. 1 (Spring/Summer 2008), pp. 89–97

Dawe, Gerard and Edna Longley (eds), *Across a Roaring Hill: The Protestant Imagination in Modern Ireland* (Belfast: Blackstaff, 1985)

Deane, Paul, 'The Great Chain of Irish Being Reconsidered: Desmond Hogan's *A Curious Street*', *Notes on Modern Irish Literature*, no. 6 (1994), pp. 39–48

Deane, Seamus, 'Be Assured I am Inventing: The Fiction of John Banville', in Patrick Rafroidi and Maurice Harmon (eds), *The Irish Novel in Our Time* (Villeneuve d'Asq: Publications de l'Université de Lille, 1975), pp. 329–39

____, 'The Artist and the Troubles', in T.P. Coogan (ed.), *Ireland and the Arts* (London: Namara, 1983), pp. 42–50

____, *A Short History of Irish Literature* (London: Hutchinson, 1986)

____, 'Introduction', in *Nationalism, Colonialism and Literature* (Minneapolis: University of Minnesota Press, 1990), pp. 3–19

____, 'Society and the Artist', *Studies*, vol. 79, no. 315 (Autumn 1990), pp. 247–56

____, 'General Introduction', in Deane (ed.), *The Field Day Anthology of Irish Writing*, 3 vols (Derry: Field Day, 1991)

____, *Strange Country: Modernity and Nationhood in Irish Writing since 1790* (Oxford: Clarendon Press, 1997)

Delaney, Paul (ed.), *Reading Colm Tóibín* (Dublin: Liffey Press, 2008)

Dell'Amico, Carol, 'Anne Enright's *The Gathering*: Trauma, Testimony, Memory', *New Hibernia Review*, vol. 14, no. 3 (2010), pp. 59–74

Devine, Kathleen, 'Form, Theme and Genre: The Importance of *Catholics* in Brian Moore's Work', in Elmer Kennedy-Andrews (ed.), *The Irish Novel since the 1960s: A Collection of Critical Essays* (Gerrards Cross: Colin Smythe, 2006), pp. 215–46

Devine, Paul, 'Style and Structure in John McGahern's *The Dark*', *Critique*, vol. 21, no. 1 (1979), pp. 49–58

D'haen, Theo, 'Des Hogan and Ireland's Post-Modern Past', in Joris Duytschaever and Geert Lernout (eds), *History and Violence in Anglo-Irish Literature* (Amsterdam: Rodopi, 1988), pp. 79–83

D'haen, Theo and José Lanters (eds), *Troubled Histories, Troubled Fictions: Twentieth-Century Anglo-Irish Prose* (Amsterdam: Rodopi, 1995)

D'hoker, Elke, *Visions of Alterity: Representation in the Works of John Banville* (Amsterdam: Rodopi, 2004)

___, 'Self-Consciousness, Solipsism, and Storytelling: John Banville's Debt to Samuel Beckett', *Irish University Review*, vol. 36, no. 1 (Spring/Summer 2006), pp. 68–80

___, 'The Unreliable Ripley: Irony and Satire in Robert McLiam Wilson's *Ripley Bogle*', *Modern Fiction Studies*, vol. 53, no. 3 (Fall 2007), pp. 460–77

___, Raphaël Ingelbien and Hedwig Schwall (eds), *Irish Women Writers: New Critical Perspectives* (New York: Peter Lang, 2010)

DiBattista, Maria. 'Joyce's Ghost: The Bogey of Realism in *Amongst Women*', in Karen Lawrence (ed.), *Transcultural Joyce* (Cambridge: Cambridge University Press, 1998), pp. 21–36

Donnelly, Brian, 'The Big House in the Recent Novel', *Studies*, vol. 64, no. 254 (Summer 1975), pp. 133–42

___, 'Roddy Doyle: From Barrytown to the GPO', *Irish University Review*, vol. 30, no. 1 (Spring/Summer 2000), pp. 17–31

Donoghue, Denis, *Irish Essays* (Cambridge: Cambridge University Press, 2011), pp. 215–44

Donoghue, Emma, 'Noises from Woodsheds: Tales of Irish Lesbians 1886–1989', in Íde Carroll and Eoin Collins (eds), *Lesbian and Gay Visions of Ireland* (London: Cassell, 1995), pp. 158–70

___, 'Fictions and Frictions', *Irish Journal of Feminist Studies*, vol. 2, no. 2 (1997), pp. 109–11

Donovan, Katie, A.N. Jeffares and Brendan Kennelly (eds), *Ireland's Women: Writings Past and Present* (London: Kyle Cathie, 1994)

Doyle, Roddy, 'Green Yodel No. 1', in Andrew Higgins Wyndham (ed.), *Re-Imagining Ireland* (Charlottesville, Virginia: University Press of Virginia, 2006), pp. 69–71

Dunleavy, J.E. and R. Lynch, 'Contemporary Irish Women Novelists', in James Atcheson (ed.), *The British and Irish Novel since 1960* (London: Macmillan, 1991), pp. 93–108

Dunn, Douglas (ed.), *Two Decades of Irish Writing* (Cheadle Hulme: Carcanet, 1975)

Duytschaever, Joris and Geert Lernout (eds), *History and Violence in Anglo-Irish Literature* (Amsterdam: Rodopi, 1988)

Edge, Sarah, 'Representing Gender and National Identity', in David Miller (ed.), *Rethinking Northern Ireland: Culture, Ideology and Colonialism* (London: Longman, 1998), pp. 211–27

Elborn, Geoffrey, *Francis Stuart: A Life* (Dublin: Raven Arts, 1990)

Estévez-Saá, José Manuel, 'An Interview with Joseph O'Connor', *Contemporary Literature*, vol. 46, no. 2 (Summer 2005), pp. 161–75

Esty, Joshua, '"Monstrous Fruit": Excremental Vision in Postcolonial Irish and African Fiction', in Glenn Hooper and Colin Graham (eds), *Irish and Postcolonial Writing* (Basingstoke: Palgrave Macmillan, 2002), pp. 127–41

Eyler, Audrey S., *Celtic, Christian, Socialist: The Novels of Anthony C. West* (Rutherford, New Jersey: Fairleigh Dickinson University Press, 1993)

Farquharson, Danine and Sean Farrell (eds), *Shadows of the Gunman: Violence and Culture in Modern Ireland* (Cork: Cork University Press, 2008)

Ferriter, Diarmaid, *The Transformation of Ireland 1900–2000* (London: Profile, 2004)

Fitzgerald-Hoyt, Mary, 'The Influence of Italy in the Writings of William Trevor and Julia O'Faoláin', *Notes on Modern Irish Literature*, no. 2 (1990), pp. 61–7

____, *William Trevor: Re-Imagining Ireland* (Dublin: Liffey Press, 2003)

Flannery, Eoin, *Versions of Ireland: Empire, Modernity and Resistance in Irish Culture* (Newcastle upon Tyne: Cambridge Scholars Press, 2006)

____, 'Rites of Passage: The Liminal in Colum McCann's *Songdogs* and *This Side of Brightness*', *Irish Studies Review*, vol. 16, no. 1 (Spring 2008), pp. 1–17

____, *Ireland and Postcolonial Studies: Theory, Discourse, Utopia* (Basingstoke: Palgrave Macmillan, 2009)

____, *Colum McCann and the Aesthetics of Redemption* (Dublin: Irish Academic Press, 2011)

Fletcher, John, *The Novels of Samuel Beckett* (London: Chatto & Windus, 1970, 2nd ed.)

Fogarty, Anne, 'Uncanny Families: Neo-Gothic Motifs and the Theme of Social Change in Contemporary Irish Women's Fiction', *Irish University Review*, vol. 30, no. 1 (Spring/Summer, 2000), pp. 59–81

____, 'Deliberately Personal? The Politics of Identity in Contemporary Irish Women's Writing', *Nordic Irish Studies*, no. 1 (2002), pp. 1–17

Foster, John Wilson, *Forces and Themes in Ulster Fiction* (Dublin: Gill & Macmillan, 1974)

____, 'Irish Fiction 1965–1990', in Seamus Deane (ed.), *The Field Day Anthology of Irish Writing*, 3 vols (Derry: Field Day, 1991), III, pp. 937–43

____, *Colonial Consequences: Essays in Irish Literature and Culture* (Dublin: Lilliput Press, 1991)

____, *Between Shadows: Modern Irish Writing and Culture* (Dublin: Irish Academic Press, 2009), pp. 57–89, 101–17

Foster, R.F., "'We Are All Revisionists Now'", *The Irish Review*, no. 1 (1986), pp. 1–5

——, "'Something of Us Will Remain': Sebastian Barry and Irish History', in Christina Hunt Mahony (ed.), *Out of History: Essays on the Writings of Sebastian Barry* (Dublin: Carysfort, 2006), pp. 183–97

——, *Luck and the Irish: A Brief History of Change 1970–2000* (London: Allen Lane, 2007)

——, "'Changed Utterly'? Transformation and Continuity in Late Twentieth-Century Ireland', *Historical Research*, vol. 80, no. 209 (August 2007), pp. 419–41

——, 'The Novelist's Nose: The Progress and Uses of Irish Fiction', *Princeton University Library Chronicle*, vol. 52, no. 1 (Autumn 2010), pp. 25–42

Fournier, Suzanne J. 'Structure and Theme in John McGahern's *The Pornographer*', *Éire-Ireland*, vol. 22, no. 1 (Spring 1987), pp. 139–49

Frawley, Oona, *Irish Pastoral: Nostalgia and Twentieth-Century Irish Literature* (Dublin: Irish Academic Press, 2005)

Frehner, Ruth, *The Colonizer's Daughter: Gender in the Anglo-Irish Big House Novel* (Tübingen: Franacke, 1999)

Freyer, Grattan, 'Change Naturally: The Fiction of O'Flaherty, O'Faoláin, McGahern', *Éire-Ireland*, vol. 18, no. 1 (Spring 1983), pp. 138–44

Furomoto, Toshi, George Hughes, Chizuko Inoue, James McElwain, Peter McMillan and Tetsuro Sano (eds), *International Aspects of Irish Literature* (Gerrards Cross: Colin Smythe, 1996)

Gallagher, Michael Paul, SJ, 'The Novels of John Broderick', in Patrick Rafroidi and Maurice Harmon (eds), *The Irish Novel in Our Time* (Villeneuve d'Asq: Publications de l'Université de Lille III, 1976), pp. 235–43

——, 'Religion as Favourite Metaphor: Moore's Recent Fiction', *Irish University Review*, vol. 18, no. 1 (Spring/Summer 1988), pp. 50–8

Garfitt, Roger, 'Constants in Contemporary Irish Fiction', in Douglas Dunn (ed.), *Two Decades of Irish Writing: A Critical Survey* (Cheadle Hulme: Carcanet, 1975), pp. 207–41

Garrett, Robert F., *Trauma and History in the Irish Novel: The Return of the Dead* (Basingstoke: Palgrave Macmillan, 2011)

——, 'John McGahern's *Amongst Women*: Representation, Memory and Trauma', *Irish University Review*, vol. 35, no. 1 (Spring/Summer 2005), pp. 121–35

Gauthier, Tim, 'Identity, Self-Loathing and the Neocolonial Condition in Patrick McCabe's *The Butcher Boy*', *Critique: Studies in Contemporary Fiction*, vol. 44, no. 2 (Winter 2003), pp. 196–211

Genet, Jacqueline (ed.), *The Big House in Ireland: Reality and Representation* (Dingle: Brandon, 1991)

——, *Rural Ireland, Real Ireland* (Gerrards Cross: Colin Smythe, 1996)

Genet, Jacqueline and Wynne Hellegouarc'h (eds), *Irish Writers and their Creative Process* (Gerrards Cross: Colin Smythe, 1996)

Gibbons, Luke, *Transformations in Irish Culture* (Cork: Cork University Press in association with Field Day, 1996)

Gillis, Alan A. and Aaron Kelly (eds), *Critical Ireland: New Essays in Literature and Culture* (Dublin: Four Courts Press, 2001)

Gilsenan, Irene and Carmen Zamorano Llena (eds), *Redefinitions of Irish Identity: A Postnationalist Approach* (Oxford: Peter Lang, 2010)

Glitzen, Julian, 'The Truth-Tellers of William Trevor', *Critique*, vol. 21, no. 1 (August 1979), pp. 59–72

Goetsch, Paul, 'Brian Moore's Canadian Fiction', in Heinz Kosok (ed.), *Studies in Anglo-Irish Literature* (Bonn: Bouvier Verlag, 1982), pp. 345–56

Goodby, John, 'Bhabha, the Post/Colonial and Glenn Patterson's *Burning Your Own*', *Irish Studies Review*, vol. 7, no. 1 (April 1999), pp. 65–72

Goodby, John and Jo Furber, '"A Shocking Libel on the People of Donegal"? The Novels of Patrick McGinley', in Elmer Kennedy Andrews (ed.), *The Irish Novel since the 1960s: A Collection of Critical Essays* (Gerrards Cross: Colin Smythe, 2006), pp. 189–214

Gorman, Michael, 'Unflinching Fidelity: The Work of John McGahern', *Krino*, no. 4 (Autumn 1987), pp. 82–4

Graecen, Lavinia, *J.G. Farrell: The Making of a Writer* (London: Bloomsbury, 1999; Revised edition, Cork: Cork University Press, 2012)

Graecen, Lavinia, *J.G. Farrell in His Own Words: Selected Letters and Diaries* (Cork: Cork University Press, 2009)

Graham, Colin, '"Liminal Spaces": Post-Colonial Theories and Irish Culture', *The Irish Review*, no. 16 (Autumn/Winter 1994), pp. 29–43

____, 'Subalternity and Gender: Problems of Post-Colonial Irishness', *Journal of Gender Studies*, vol. 5, no. 3 (1996), pp. 363–73

Graham, Colin and Richard Haslam (eds), *Ireland and Cultural Theory: The Mechanics of Authenticity* (Basingstoke: Macmillan, 1998)

Graham, Colin, *Deconstructing Ireland: Identity, Theory, Culture* (Edinburgh: Edinburgh University Press, 1999)

Grant, Patrick, *Literature, Rhetoric and Violence in Northern Ireland 1968–98: Hardened to Death* (Basingstoke: Palgrave, 2001)

Grassi, Samuele, 'Fathers in a Coma: Father–Son Relationships in Neil Jordan's Fiction', *Estudios Irlandeses*, no. 3 (2008), pp. 101–12

Gray, Breda, 'Longings and Belongings – Gendered Spatialities of Irishness', *Irish Studies Review*, vol. 7, no. 2 (August 1999), pp. 193–210

Grennan, Éamon, 'John McGahern: Vision and Revisionism', *Colby Library Quarterly*, vol. 31, no. 1 (March 1995), pp. 30–9

____, '"Only What Happens": Mulling Over McGahern', *Irish University Review*, vol. 35, no. 1 (Spring/Summer 2005), pp. 13–27

Griffin, Susan (ed.) and Introduction, *All a Novelist Needs: Colm Tóibín on Henry James* (Baltimore: Johns Hopkins University Press, 2010), pp. ix–xviii

Guy, Peter D., '"If One Is Lonely One Prefers Discomfort": The Lives of John Broderick', *Studies*, vol. 97, no. 387 (Autumn 2008), pp. 251–62

Haberstroh, Patricia Boyle and Christine St Peter (eds), *Opening the Field. Irish Women: Texts and Contexts* (Cork: Cork University Press, 2007)

Hamilton, Hugo, 'Introduction', in Francis Stuart, *The Pillar of Cloud* ([London: Gollancz, 1948] Dublin: New Island Books, 1994), pp. 1–4

Hand, Derek, *John Banville: Exploring Fictions* (Dublin: Liffey Press, 2002)

____, 'Something Happened: Benedict Kiely's *Nothing Happens in Carmincross* and the Breakdown of the Irish Novel', in Brian Cliff and Éibhear Walshe (eds), *Representing the Troubles: Texts and Images, 1970–2000* (Dublin: Four Courts Press, 2004), pp. 27–38

Hand, Derek (ed.), *Irish University Review*, vol. 36, no. 1 (Spring/Summer 2006), John Banville Special Number

____, *The Irish Novel* (Cambridge: Cambridge University Press, 2011)

Hansson, Heidi, '"To Say I": Female Identity in *The Maid's Tale* and *The Wig My Father Wore*', in Elmer Kennedy-Andrews (ed.), *The Irish Novel since the 1960s: A Collection of Critical Essays* (Gerrards Cross: Colin Smythe, 2006), pp. 137–49

____, 'Anne Enright and Postnationalism in the Contemporary Irish Novel', in Scott Brewster and Michael Parker (eds), *Irish Literature since 1990* (Manchester: Manchester University Press, 2009), pp. 216–31

Hargreaves, Tamsin, 'Women's Consciousness and Identity in Four Irish Women Novelists', in Michael Kenneally (ed.), *Cultural Contexts and Literary Idioms in Contemporary Irish Literature* (Gerrards Cross: Colin Smythe, 1988), pp. 290–305

Harmon, Maurice, 'Generations Apart: 1925–1975', in Patrick Rafroidi and Maurice Harmon (eds), *The Irish Novel in Our Time* (Villeneuve-d'Asq: Publications de l'Université de Lille III, 1976), pp. 49–65

____, 'The Era of Inhibitions: Irish Literature 1920–1960', in Masaru Sekine (ed.), *Irish Writers and Society at Large* (Gerrards Cross: Colin Smythe, 1985), pp. 31–41

____, 'The Achievement of Francis Stuart', in Barbara Brown (ed.), *Maurice Harmon: Selected Essays* (Dublin: Irish Academic Press, 2006), pp. 82–94

Harte, Liam, 'A Kind of Scab: Irish Identity in the Writings of Dermot Bolger and Joseph O'Connor', *Irish Studies Review*, vol. 20, no. 3 (Autumn 1997), pp. 17–22

Harte, Liam and Michael Parker (eds), *Contemporary Irish Fiction: Themes, Tropes, Theories* (Basingstoke: Macmillan, 2000)

Harte, Liam and Lance Pettit, 'States of Dislocation: William Trevor's *Felicia's Journey* and Maurice Leitch's *Gilchrist*', in Ashok Bery and Patricia Murray (eds), *Comparing Postcolonial Literatures* (London: Macmillan, 2000), pp. 70–80

Harte, Liam, 'History, Text and Society' in Colm Tóibín's *The Heather Blazing*, *New Hibernia Review*, vol. 6, no. 4 (Winter 2002), pp. 55–67.

____, '"The Endless Mutations of the Shore": Colm Tóibín's Marine

Imaginary.' *Critique: Studies in Contemporary Fiction*, vol. 51, no. 4 (2010), pp. 333–49.

____, 'History Lessons: Postcolonialism and Seamus Deane's *Reading in the Dark*', *Irish University Review*, vol. 30, no. 1 (Spring/Summer 2000), pp. 149–62

____, 'Mourning Remains: Unresolved Trauma and Survival in Anne Enright's *The Gathering*', *LIT: Literature Interpretation Theory*, vol. 21, no. 3 (July–September 2010), pp. 187–204

Haslam, Richard, '"The Pose Arranged and Lingered Over": Visualizing the "Troubles"', in Liam Harte and Michael Parker (eds), *Contemporary Irish Fiction: Themes, Tropes, Theories* (Basingstoke: Macmillan, 2000), pp. 192–212

____, 'Critical Reductionism and Bernard MacLaverty's *Cal*', in Brian Cliff and Éibhear Walshe (eds), *Representing the Troubles: Texts and Images, 1970–2000* (Dublin: Four Courts Press, 2004), pp. 39–54

Healy, Dermot, 'Towards *Bornholm Night-Ferry* and *Texts for the Air*: A Re-reading of Aidan Higgins', *Review of Contemporary Fiction*, vol. 3, no. 1 (1983), pp. 181–92

Heaney, Liam, 'Science in Literature: John Banville's Extended Narrative', *Studies*, vol. 85, no. 340 (Winter 1996), pp. 362–9

Herr, Cheryl, 'The Erotics of Irishness', *Critical Inquiry*, vol. 17, no. 1 (Autumn 1990), pp. 1–34

Herron, Tom, 'ContamiNation: Patrick McCabe and Colm Tóibín's Pathographies of the Republic', in Liam Harte and Michael Parker (eds), *Contemporary Irish Fiction: Themes, Tropes, Theories* (Basingstoke: Macmillan, 2000), pp. 168–91

____, 'Derry *Is* Donegal: Thresholds, Vectors, Limits in Seamus Deane's *Reading in the Dark*', *Études Irlandaises*, vol. 29, no. 2 (Fall 2004), pp. 165–83

Hicks, Patrick, 'The Failure of Parenting and the Success of Love in Robert McLiam Wilson's *Ripley Bogle* and *Eureka Street*', *Irish Studies Review*, vol. 16, no. 2 (May 2008), pp. 131–41

Higdon, David Leon, 'Brian Moore, *I Am Mary Dunne*, Momento Ergo Sum', in Higdon, *Shadows of the Past in Contemporary British Fiction* (Athens, Georgia: University of Georgia Press, 1984), pp. 63–82

Higgins, Aidan, *Windy Arbours: Collected Criticism* (Normal, Illinois: Dalkey Archive, 2005)

____, 'The Heroe's [sic] Potion: Chaos or Anarchy in the Cultic Twilight', *The Review of Contemporary Fiction*, vol. 3, no. I (Spring 1983), pp. 108–14

____, 'Tired Lines, or Tales My Mother Told Me', in John Ryan (ed.), *A Bash in the Tunnel: James Joyce by the Irish* (Brighton: Clifton Books, 1970), pp. 55–60

Hill, Jeff, 'The American Dream of Chuck Ramkissoon: Cricket in Joseph O'Neill's *Netherland*', *Journal of Sports History*, vol. 37, no. 2 (Summer 2010), pp. 219–34

Hogan, Desmond, *The Edge of the City: A Scrapbook 1976–91* (Dublin: Lilliput Press, 1993)

Holland, Siobhan, 'Re-citing the Rosary: Women, Catholicism and Agency in Brian Moore's *Cold Heaven* and John McGahern's *Amongst Women*', in Liam Harte and Michael Parker (eds), *Contemporary Irish Fiction: Themes, Tropes, Theories* (Basingstoke: Macmillan, 2000), pp. 56–78

——, 'Tact and Tactics: A Case for Matrifocality in *Amongst Women*', in Alan Marshall and Neil Sammells (eds), *Irish Encounters: Poetry, Politics and Prose* (Bath: Sulis, 1998), pp. 115–26

Holmsten, Elin, *Liminal Borderlands in Irish Literature and Culture* (Oxford: Peter Lang, 2008)

Hooper, Glenn and Colin Graham (eds), *Irish and Postcolonial Writing* (Basingstoke: Palgrave Macmillan, 2002)

Hooper, Glenn and Colin Graham, 'Troublesome Tales: J.G. Farrell and the Decline of Empire', in Glenn Hooper and Colin Graham (eds), *Irish and Postcolonial Writing* (Basingstoke: Palgrave Macmillan, 2002), pp. 222–49

Hopper, Keith, *Flann O'Brien: A Portrait of the Artist as a Young Post-Modernist* (Cork: Cork University Press, 1995; 2nd ed. 2009)

——, 'Cultural Crisis Then and Now: Science, Literature, and Religion in John Banville's *Doctor Copernicus* and *Kepler*', *Critique: Studies in Contemporary Fiction*, vol. 39, no. 2 (1998), pp. 176–92

Horton, Patricia, '"Absent from Home": Family, Community and National Identity in Patrick McCabe's *The Butcher Boy*', *Irish Journal of Feminist Studies*, vol. 3, no. 1 (December 1998), pp. 75–93

Houston, Nainsí J. *How Irish Women Writers Portray Masculinity* (Lewiston, New York: Mellen, 2006)

Hughes, Éamonn (ed.), *Culture and Politics in Northern Ireland 1960–1990* (Buckingham: Open University Press, 1991)

Hughes, Éamonn, '"Lancelot's Position": The Fiction of Irish-Britain', in A. Robert Lee (ed.), *Other Britain, Other British: Contemporary Multicultural Fiction* (London: Pluto Press, 1995), pp. 142–60

——, '"Town of Shadows": Representations of Belfast in Recent Fiction', *Religion and Literature*, vol. 28, nos 2/3 (Summer/Autumn, 1996), pp. 141–60

——, '"All That Surrounds Our Lives": Time, Sex and Death in *That They May Face the Rising Sun*', *Irish University Review*, vol. 35, no. 1 (Spring/Summer 2005), pp. 147–63

——, '"How I Achieved This Trick": Representations of Masculinity in Contemporary Irish Fiction', in Elmer Kennedy-Andrews (ed.), *The Irish Novel since the 1960s: A Collection of Critical Essays* (Gerrards Cross: Colin Smythe, 2006), pp. 119–36

Imhof, Rüdiger, '*The Newton Letter* by John Banville: An Exercise in Literary Derivation', *Irish University Review*, vol. 13, no. 2 (1983), pp. 162–7

____, 'Bornholm Night-Ferry and Journal to Stella: Aidan Higgins's Indebtedness to Swift', Canadian Journal of Irish Studies, vol. 10, no. 2 (1984), pp. 5–13

Imhof, Rüdiger and Jürgen Kamm, 'Coming to Grips with Aidan Higgins', Études Irlandaises vol. 9 (1984), pp. 145–60

Imhof, Rüdiger, '"Little Bit of Ivory, Two Inches Wide": The Small World of Jennifer Johnston's Fiction', Études Irlandaises, vol. 10 (1985), pp. 129–44

____, 'Swan's Way, or Goethe, Einstein, Banville: The Eternal Recurrence', Études Irlandaises, vol. 12, no. 2 (1987), pp. 113–29

____, 'German Influences on John Banville and Aidan Higgins', in Wolfgang Zack and Heinz Kosok (eds), Literary Interrelations: Ireland, England and the World (Tübingen: Narr, 1987), pp. 335–47

____, John Banville: A Critical Introduction (Dublin: Wolfhound Press, 1989)

____, 'How It Is on the Fringes of Irish Fiction', Irish University Review, vol. 22, no. 1 (Spring/Summer 1992), pp. 151–67

____, 'Post-Joycean Experiment in Recent Irish Fiction', in Barbara Hayley and Christopher Murray (eds), Ireland and France, A Bountiful Friendship: Literature, History and Ideas (Gerrards Cross: Colin Smythe, 1992), pp. 124–36

____, 'In Search of the Rosy Grail: The Creative Process in the Novels of John Banville', in Jacqueline Genet and Wynne Hellegouarc'h (eds), Irish Writers and their Creative Process (Gerrards Cross: Colin Smythe, 1996), pp. 123–38

Imhof, Rüdiger (ed.), Contemporary Irish Novelists (Tübingen: Narr, 1990)

Imhof, Rüdiger, 'Proust and Contemporary Irish Fiction', in Joseph McMinn (ed.), The Internationalism of Irish Literature and Drama (Gerrards Cross: Colin Smythe: 1992), pp. 255–60

____, The Modern Irish Novel: Irish Novelists after 1945 (Dublin: Wolfhound Press, 2002)

Ingman, Heather, 'Nature and Gender in Jennifer Johnston: A Kristevan Reading', Irish University Review, vol. 35, no. 2 (Autumn/Winter 2005), pp. 334–48

____, Twentieth-Century Fiction by Irish Women: Nation and Gender (Aldershot: Ashgate, 2007)

Innes, C.L., The Devil's Own Mirror: The Irishman and the African in Modern Literature (Washington, DC: Three Continents Press, 1990)

Jackson, Ellen-Raissa, 'Gender, Violence and Hybridity: Reading the Postcolonial in Three Irish Novels', Irish Studies Review, vol. 7, no. 2 (August 1999), pp. 221–31

Jackson, Tony E., 'Science, Art and the Shipwreck of Knowledge: The Novels of John Banville', Contemporary Literature, vol. 38, no. 3 (Fall 1997), pp. 510–33

Jeffers, Jennifer, The Irish Novel at the End of the Twentieth Century: Gender, Bodies and Power (New York: Palgrave, 2002)

Johnson O'Brien, Toni and David Cairns (eds), *Gender in Irish Writing* (Milton Keynes: Open University Press, 1991)

Kamm, Jürgen, 'Jennifer Johnston', in Rüdiger Imhof (ed.), *Contemporary Irish Novelists* (Tübingen: Narr, 1990), pp. 193–206

Kearney, Richard, 'A Crisis of Imagination: An Analysis of a Counter-Tradition in the Irish Novel', *The Crane Bag*, vol. 3, no. 1 (1979), pp. 390–402

____, *The Irish Mind: Exploring Intellectual Traditions* (Dublin: Wolfhound Press, 1985)

____, *Transitions: Narratives in Modern Irish Culture* (Dublin: Wolfhound Press, 1987)

Kearney, Richard (ed.), *Across the Frontiers: Ireland in the 1990s* (Dublin: Wolfhound Press, 1988)

Kearney, Richard, *Postnationalist Ireland: Politics, Culture, Philosophy* (London: Routledge, 1997)

____, *Navigations: Collected Irish Essays 1976–2006* (Dublin: Lilliput Press, 2006)

Keating-Miller, Jennifer, *Language, Identity and Liberation in Contemporary Irish Literature* (Basingstoke: Palgrave Macmillan, 2009)

Kelly, Aaron, 'Reproblematizing the Irish Text', in Aaron Kelly and Alan Gillis (eds), *Critical Ireland: New Essays in Literature and Culture* (Dublin: Four Courts Press, 2001), pp. 124–32

____, '*Terror*-torial Imperatives: Belfast and Eoin McNamee's *Resurrection Man*', in Nicholas Allen and Aaron Kelly (eds), *The Cities of Belfast* (Dublin: Four Courts Press, 2003), pp. 168–82

____, *Twentieth-Century Irish Literature* (Basingstoke: Palgrave Macmillan, 2008)

Kemp, Peter, 'The Fight against Fantasy: Iris Murdoch's *The Red and the Green*', *Modern Fiction Studies*, vol. 15, no. 3 (1969), pp. 403–15

Kenneally, Michael (ed.), *Cultural Contexts and Literary Idioms in Contemporary Irish Literature* (Gerrards Cross: Colin Smythe, 1988)

Kennedy-Andrews, Elmer, 'Benedict Kiely's Troubles Fiction: From Post-colonial to Postmodern', *Irish University Review*, vol. 30, no. 1 (Spring/Summer 2000), pp. 98–119

____, 'Antic Dispositions in Some Recent Irish Fiction', in Fran Brearton and Éamon Hughes (eds), *Last Before America: Irish and American Writing* (Belfast: Blackstaff, 2001), pp. 121–41

____, *Fiction and the Northern Ireland Troubles: (De-)constructing the North* (Dublin: Four Courts Press, 2003)

Kennedy-Andrews, Elmer (ed.), *The Irish Novel since the 1960s* (Gerrards Cross: Colin Smythe, 2006)

Kenner, Hugh, *Samuel Beckett: A Critical Study* (Berkeley, California: University of California Press, 1968, 2nd ed.)

Kenner, Hugh, *A Colder Look: The Modern Irish Writers* (New York: Knopf, 1983)

Kenny, John, 'The Novels of Patrick McGinley', *Ropes: Review of Postgraduate Studies*, no. 1 (Galway: Department of English NUIG, 1993), pp. 20–7

——, 'Irish Writing and Writers: Some Recent Irish Writing', *Studies*, vol. 87, no. 348 (Winter 1998), pp. 422–30

——, 'After the News: Critiquing the Irish Novel since the Sixties', *The Irish Review*, no. 25 (Winter/Spring 1999–2000), pp. 62–74

——, '"No Such Genre": Tradition and the Contemporary Irish Novel', in P.J. Mathews (ed.), *New Voices in Irish Criticism* (Dublin: Four Courts Press, 2000), pp. 45–52

——, *John Banville* (Dublin: Irish Academic Press, 2009)

Keown, Edwina and Carol Taaffe (eds), *Irish Modernism: Origins, Contexts, Publics* (New York: Peter Lang, 2010)

Kiberd, Declan, *Inventing Ireland* (Cambridge, Massachusetts: Harvard University Press, 1995)

——, 'John McGahern's *Amongst Women*', in Maria Tymoczko and Colin Ireland (eds), *Language and Tradition in Ireland: Continuity and Displacement* (Amherst, Massachusetts: University of Massachusetts Press, 2003), pp. 195–213

——, *The Irish Writer and the World* (Cambridge: Cambridge University Press, 2005)

——, 'Fallen Nobility: The World of John McGahern', *Irish University Review*, vol. 35, no. 1 (Spring/Summer 2005), pp. 164–74

——, 'The Art of Science: Banville's *Doctor Copernicus*', in Elmer Kennedy-Andrews (ed.), *The Irish Novel since the 1960s: A Collection of Critical Essays* (Gerrards Cross: Colin Smythe, 2006), pp. 173–88

——, 'Growing up Absurd: Edna O'Brien and *The Country Girls*', in Nicholas Allen and Eve Patten (eds), *That Island Never Found: Essays and Poems for Terence Brown* (Dublin: Four Courts Press, 2007), pp. 107–21

Kiely, Benedict, *Counties of Contention: A Study of the Origins and Implications of the Partition of Ireland* (Cork: Mercier Press, 1945 (2nd ed. 2004))

——, *A Raid into Dark Corners and Other Essays* (Cork: Cork University Press, 1999)

Kiely, Kevin, *Francis Stuart: Artist and Outcast* (Dublin: Liffey Press, 2007)

Killeen, Terence, 'Versions of Exile: John McGahern's *The Leavetaking*', *Canadian Journal of Irish Studies*, vol. 17, no. 7 (July 1991), pp. 69–78

Kilroy, Thomas, 'Teller of Tales', *The Times Literary Supplement* (17 March 1972), pp. 301–2

——, 'The Irish Writer: Self and Society 1950–1980', in Peter Connolly (ed.), *Literature and the Changing Ireland* (Gerrards Cross: Colin Smythe, 1982), pp. 175–87

——, 'The Autobiographical Novel', in Augustine Martin (ed.), *The Genius of Irish Prose* (Cork: Mercier Press, 1985), pp. 65–75

Kingston, Madeline, *Something in the Head: The Life and Work of John Broderick* (Dublin: Lilliput Press, 2004)

Kingston, Madeline (ed.), *Stimulus of Sin: Selected Writings of John Broderick* (Dublin: Lilliput Press, 2007)

Kirkland, Richard, *Literature and Culture in Northern Ireland since 1965: Moments of Danger* (Harlow: Longman, 1996)

_____, 'Bourgeois Redemption: The Fictions of Glenn Patterson and Robert McLiam Wilson', in Liam Harte and Michael Parker (eds), *Contemporary Irish Fiction: Themes, Tropes, Theories* (Basingstoke: Macmillan, 2000), pp. 213–31

_____, 'The Spectacle of Terrorism in Northern Irish Culture', *Critical Survey*, vol. 15, no. 1 (2003), pp. 77–90

Kirkpatrick, Kathryn J. (ed.), *Border Crossings: Irish Women Writers and National Identities* (Tuscaloosa, Alabama: University of Alabama Press, 2000)

Klein, Bernard, *On the Uses of History in Recent Irish Writing* (Manchester: Manchester University Press, 2007)

Knowles, Nancy, 'Empty Rhetoric: Argument by Credibility in Patrick McGinley's *Bogmail*', *English Language Notes*, vol. 39, no. 3 (2002), pp. 79–87

Knowlson, James, *Damned to Fame: The Life of Samuel Beckett* (London: Bloomsbury, 1996)

Kosok, Heinz (ed.), *Studies in Anglo-Irish Literature* (Bonn: Bouvier Verlag, 1982)

Kosok, Heinz 'The Novels of Jennifer Johnston', in Maria Diedrich and Christopher Schöenich (eds), *Studien für Englischen und Amerikanischen Prosa nach dem Ersten Weltkrieg: Festschrift für Kurt Otten zum 60. Geburtstag* (Darmstadt: Wissenschaftliche Buchgesellschaft, 1986), pp. 98–111

Kreilkamp, Vera, *The Anglo-Irish Novel and the Big House* (Syracuse: Syracuse University Press, 1998)

Krystek, Izabela, 'Looking for the Self: Dermot Healy's *A Goat's Song* as an Irish Tragedy of Indecision', in Liliana Sikorska (ed.), *Ironies of Art/Tragedies of Life* (Frankfurt: Peter Lang, 2005), pp. 177–94

Ladrón, Marisol Morales, 'Representations of Motherhood in Emma Donoghue's *Slammerkin*', *Irish University Review*, vol. 39, no. 1 (Spring/Summer 2009), pp. 107–21

Laing, Kathryn, Sinéad Mooney and Maureen O'Connor (eds), *Edna O'Brien: New Critical Perspectives* (Dublin: Carysfort, 2006)

Lanters, José, *The 'Tinkers' in Irish Literature: Unsettled Subjects and the Construction of Difference* (Dublin: Irish Academic Press, 2008)

_____, 'Jennifer Johnston's Divided Ireland', in C.C. Barfoot and Theo D'haen (eds), *The Clash of Ireland: Literary Contrasts and Connections* (Amsterdam: Rodopi, 1989), pp. 209–22

Laplace, Philippe and Éric Tabuteau (eds), *Cities on the Margin, on the Margin of Cities: Representations of Urban Space in Contemporary Irish and British Fiction* (Besançon: Presses Universitaires Franc-Comtoises, 2003)

Larsen, Max Deen, 'Saints of the Ascendancy: William Trevor's Big House Novels', in Otto Rauchbauer (ed.), *Ancestral Voices: The Big House in Anglo-Irish Literature* (Hildesheim: Olms, 1992), pp. 257–77

Lee, J.J., *Ireland 1912–1985: Politics and Society* (Cambridge: Cambridge University Press, 1989)

Lehner, Stefanie, *Subaltern Ethics in Contemporary Scottish and Irish Literature: Tracing Counter-Histories* (New York: Palgrave Macmillan, 2011)

Leith, Linda, 'Subverting the Sectarian Heritage: Recent Novels of Northern Ireland', *Canadian Journal of Irish Studies*, vol. 18, no. 2 (December 1992), pp. 88–106

Lennon, Joseph, 'Colum McCann', in Michael R. Molino (ed.), *Twenty-First-Century British and Irish Novelists* (Detroit: Thomson Gale, 2003), pp. 181–91

Lernout, Geert, 'Looking for Pure Visions', *Graph*, no. 1 (October 1986), pp. 12–16

Levasseur, Jennifer and Kevin Rabalais, 'Interview with Colum McCann', *Glimmer Train*, no. 69 (2009), pp. 56–73

Lernout, Geert, 'Looking for Pure Visions', *Graph*, no. 1 (October 1986), pp. 12–16

Lloyd, David, *Anomalous States: Irish Writing and the Post-Colonial Moment* (Dublin: Lilliput Press, 1993)

Longley, Edna, *The Living Stream: Literature and Revisionism in Ireland* (Newcastle upon Tyne: Bloodaxe, 1994)

Longley, Edna and Declan Kiberd, *Multi-Culturalism: The View from the Two Irelands* (Cork: Cork University Press in association with The Centre for Cross Border Studies, Armagh, 2001)

Lubbers, Klaus, '"Balcony of Europe": The Trend Towards Internationalization in Recent Irish Fiction', in Wolfgang Zack and Heinz Kosok (eds), *Literary Interrelations: Ireland, England and the World* (Tübingen: Narr, 1987), pp. 235–47

____, 'John Broderick', in Rüdiger Imhof (ed.), *Contemporary Irish Novelists* (Tübingen: Narr, 1990), pp. 79–91

Lynch, Vivian Valvano, 'Seamus Deane's *Reading in the Dark* Yields "a door into the light"', *Working Papers in Irish Studies*, no. 3 (2000), pp. 16–22

MacAnna, Ferdia, 'The Dublin Renaissance: An Essay on Modern Dublin and Dublin Writers', *Irish Review*, no. 10 (Spring 1991), pp. 14–30

Magee, Patrick, *Gangsters or Guerrillas? Representations of Irish Republicans in 'Troubles Fiction'* (Belfast: Beyond the Pale, 2001)

Magennis, Caroline, '". . . that great swollen belly": The Abject Maternal in Some Recent Northern Irish Fiction', *Irish Studies Review*, vol. 18, no. 1 (February 2010), pp. 91–100

____, *Sons of Ulster: Masculinities in the Contemporary Northern Irish Novel* (New York: Peter Lang, 2010)

Maher, Éamon, *John McGahern: From the Local to the Universal* (Dublin: Liffey Press, 2003)

Maher, Éamon, Grace Neville and Eugene O'Brien (eds), *Modernity and Postmodernity in a Franco-Irish Context* (Frankfurt: Peter Lang, 2008)

Maher, Éamon and Eugene O'Brien, *Breaking the Mould: Literary Representations of Irish Catholicism* (Bern: Peter Lang, 2011)

Mahon, Peter, 'Lacanian "Pussy": Towards a Psychoanalytic Reading of Patrick McCabe's *Breakfast on Pluto*', *Irish University Review*, vol. 37, no. 2 (Autumn/Winter 2007), pp. 441–71

____, *Violence, Politics and Textual Interventions in Northern Ireland* (Basingstoke: Palgrave Macmillan, 2010)

Mahony, Christina Hunt, *Contemporary Irish Literature: Transforming Tradition* (New York: St Martin's Press, 1998)

Mahony, Christina Hunt (ed.), *Out of History: Essays on the Writings of Sebastian Barry* (Dublin: Carysfort, 2006)

Martin, Augustine, 'Inherited Dissent: The Dilemma of the Irish Writer', *Studies*, vol. 54, no. 213 (Spring 1965), pp. 1–20

Martin, Augustine (ed.), *The Genius of Irish Prose* (Dublin: Mercier Press, 1984)

Martin, Augustine, Review of Francis Stuart, *The Pillar of Cloud* and *Redemption*, in Martin, *Bearing Witness: Essays on Anglo-Irish Literature* (Dublin: University College Dublin Press, 1996), pp. 157–9

____, Review of Edna O'Brien, *Time and Tide*, in Martin, *Bearing Witness: Essays on Anglo-Irish Literature* (Dublin: University College Dublin Press, 1996), pp. 159–62

Mastin, Antoinette M., 'Stephen Dedalus in Paris? Joycean Elements in Julia O'Faoláin's *Three Lovers*', *Colby Quarterly*, vol. 30, no. 4 (December 1994), pp. 244–51

McCarthy, Conor, 'Ideology and Geography in Dermot Bolger's *The Journey Home*', *Irish University Review*, vol. 27, no. 1 (Spring/Summer 1997), pp. 98–110

____, *Modernisation, Crisis and Culture in Ireland 1969–1992* (Dublin: Four Courts Press, 2000)

McCarthy, Dermot, 'Belfast Babel: Postmodern Lingo in Eoin McNamee's *Resurrection Man*', *Irish University Review*, vol. 30, no. 1 (Spring/Summer 2000), pp. 132–48

____, *Roddy Doyle: Raining on the Parade* (Dublin: Liffey Press, 2003)

____, *John McGahern and the Art of Memory* (Oxford: Peter Lang, 2010)

McCartney, Anne, *Francis Stuart: Face to Face. A Critical Study* (Belfast: Institute of Irish Studies, 2000)

McCormack, W.J. (ed.), *A Festschrift for Francis Stuart on His Seventieth Birthday* (Dublin: Dolmen Press, 1972)

McCormack, W.J. *The Battle of the Books: Two Decades of Irish Cultural Debate* (Dublin: Lilliput Press, 1986)

McGahern, John, 'The Church and its Spire', in Colm Tóibín (ed.), *Soho Square 6* (London: Bloomsbury, 1993), pp. 16–27

____, 'Reading and Writing', in Jacqueline Genet and Wynne Hellegouarc'h (eds), *Irish Writers and their Creative Process* (Gerrards Cross: Colin Smythe, 1996), pp. 103–9

McGlynn, Mary M., *Narratives of Class in New Irish and Scottish Literature: From Joyce to Kelman, Doyle, Galloway and McNamee* (Basingstoke: Palgrave Macmillan, 2008)

McGrath, Niall, 'Glenn Patterson: Interview with Niall McGrath', *Edinburgh Review*, no. 93 (1995), pp. 41–50

McIlroy, Brian, 'Pattern in Chaos: John Banville's Scientific Art', *Colby Quarterly*, vol. 31, no. 1 (March 1995), pp. 74–80

MacKenna, Dolores, *William Trevor: The Writer and His Work* (Dublin: New Island Books, 1999)

MacKillop, James, 'The Hungry Grass: Richard Power's Pastoral Elegy', *Éire-Ireland*, vol. 18, no. 3 (Fall 1983), pp. 86–99

McMahon, Seán, 'Town and Country', *Éire-Ireland*, vol. 6, no. 1 (Spring 1971), pp. 120–31

____, 'Anglo-Irish Attitudes: The Novels of Jennifer Johnston', *Éire-Ireland*, vol. 10, no. 3 (Autumn 1975), pp. 137–41

____, 'The Realist Novel after the Second World War', in Augustine Martin (ed.), *The Genius of Irish Prose* (Dublin and Cork: Mercier Press, 1985), pp. 145–54

____, *Sam Hanna Bell: A Biography* (Belfast: Blackstaff, 1999)

McMinn, Joseph, 'Contemporary Novels on the 'Troubles', *Études Irlandaises*, vol. 5 (1980), pp. 113–21

____, *John Banville: A Critical Study* (Dublin: Gill & Macmillan, 1991)

McMinn, Joseph (ed.), *The Internationalism of Irish Literature and Drama* (Gerrards Cross: Colin Smythe, 1992)

McMinn, Joseph, *The Supreme Fictions of John Banville* (Manchester: Manchester University Press, 1999)

McSweeney, Kerry, 'Brian Moore's Grammars of Emotions', in McSweeney, *Four Contemporary Novelists* (Kingston and Montreal: McGill-Queen's University Press, 1983), pp. 55–99

Mianowski, Marie, 'Down-and-Outs, Subways and Suburbs: Subversions in Robert McLiam Wilson's *Ripley Bogle* and Colum McCann's *This Side of Brightness*', in Ciaran Ross (ed.), *Sub-Versions: Trans-National Readings of Modern Irish Literature* (Amsterdam: Rodopi, 2010), pp. 87–100

Middleton, Tim, 'Joseph O'Connor', in Michael R. Molino (ed.), *Twenty-First-Century British and Irish Novelists* (Detroit: Gale, 2003), pp. 271–8

Mikowski, Sylvie, 'Le Roman de Dublin: Nouvelles Figurations', *Études Irlandaises*, vol. 32, no. 2 (Autumn 2007), pp. 139–53

____, 'Reimagining the Irish Historical Novel in Roddy Doyle's *A Star Called Henry* and Joseph O'Connor's *Star of the Sea*', in John Strachan and Alison O'Malley-Younger (eds), *Ireland: Evolution and Revolution* (New York: Peter Lang, 2010), pp. 183–92

Mills, Richard, '"Closed Places of the Spirit": Interview with Maurice Leitch',
    Irish Studies Review, vol. 6, no. 1 (April 1998), pp. 63–8
____, '"All Stories are Love Stories": Robert McLiam Wilson Interviewed', *Irish
    Studies Review*, vol. 7, no. 1 (April 1999), pp. 73–7
____, '"Nothing Has to Die". Interview with Glenn Patterson', *Writing Ulster*,
    no. 6 (1999), pp. 113–29
Molloy, F.C., 'The Novels of John McGahern', *Critique*, vol. 19, no. 1 (1977),
    pp. 5–27
____, 'The Search for Truth: The Fiction of John Banville', *Irish University
    Review*, vol. 11, no. 1 (1981), pp. 29–51
____, 'Autobiography and Fiction: Francis Stuart's *Black List, Section H*',
    Critique: Studies in Contemporary Fiction, vol. 25, no. 2 (Winter 1984),
    pp. 115–24
____, 'The Life of Francis Stuart: Questions and Some Answers', *Biography: An
    Interdisciplinary Quarterly*, vol. 10, no. 2 (Spring 1987), pp. 129–41
____, 'A Life Reshaped: Francis Stuart's *Black List, Section H*', *Canadian Journal
    of Irish Studies*, vol. 14, no. 2 (January 1989), pp. 37–47
Monteith, Sharon, Jenny Newman and Pat Wheeler, *Contemporary British and
    Irish Fiction: An Introduction through Interviews* (London: Arnold, 2004)
Morrison, Kristin, *William Trevor* (New York: Twayne, 1993)
____, 'Child Murder as Metaphor of Colonial Exploitation in Toni Morrison's
    Beloved, *The Silence in the Garden* and *The Killeen*', in Toshi Furimoto,
    George Hughes, Chizuko Inoue, James McElwain, Peter McMillan and
    Tetsuro Sano (eds), *International Aspects of Irish Literature* (Gerrards
    Cross: Colin Smythe, 1996), pp. 292–300
Morrissy, Mary, 'Interview', *Studies*, vol. 87, no. 347 (Autumn 1998), pp. 240–4
Morse, Donald E., Csilla Bertha and István Pálffy (eds), *A Small Nation's
    Contribution to the World: Essays on Anglo-Irish Literature and Language*
    (Gerrards Cross: Colin Smythe, 1993)
Mortimer, Mark, 'The World of Jennifer Johnston: A Look at Three Novels',
    The Crane Bag, vol. 4, no. 1 (1980), pp. 88–94
Murphy, Neil, *Irish Fiction and Postmodernist Doubt* (Lewiston, New York:
    Mellen, 2004)
Murphy, Neil (ed.), *Aidan Higgins: The Fragility of Form* (Champaign, Illinois:
    Dalkey Archive, 2010)
Murray, Patrick, 'Athlone's John Broderick', *Éire-Ireland*, vol. 27, no. 4 (Winter
    1992), pp. 20–39
Murray, Tony, 'Curious Streets: Diaspora, Displacement and Transgression in
    Desmond Hogan's London Narratives', *Irish Studies Review*, vol. 14, no.
    2 (May 2006), pp. 239–53
Natterstad, J.H. 'Francis Stuart: The Artist as Outcast', in Heinz Kosok (ed.),
    Studies in Anglo-Irish Literature (Bonn: Bouvier Verlag, 1982), pp. 338–44
Ní Anluain, Clíodhna (ed.), *Reading the Future: Irish Writers in Conversation
    with Mike Murphy* (Dublin: Lilliput Press, 2000)

Niel, Ruth, 'Speech and Silence: Beyond the Religious in Brian Moore's Novels', in Donald E. Morse, Csilla Bertha and István Pálffy (eds), *A Small Nation's Contribution to the World: Essays on Anglo-Irish Literature and Language* (Gerrards Cross: Colin Smythe, 1993), pp. 161–74

Norquay, Glenda and Gerry Smyth, 'Waking Up in Different Places: Contemporary Irish and Scottish Fiction', in Glenda Norquay and Gerry Smyth (eds), *Across the Margins: Cultural Identity and Change in the Atlantic Archipelago* (Manchester: Manchester University Press, 2002), pp. 154–70

O'Brien, George, 'Irish Fiction since 1966: Challenge, Themes, Promise', *Ploughshares*, vol. 6, no. 1 (1980), pp. 138–59

____, 'John Banville: Portraits of the Artist', in James D. Brophy and Éamon Grennan (eds), *New Irish Writing: Essays in Memory of Raymond J. Porter* (Boston: Twayne, 1989), pp. 161–73

O'Brien, George (ed.) and Introduction, *Colby Quarterly*, vol. 31, no. 1 (March 1995), pp. 5–23

O'Brien, George, 'The Aesthetics of Exile', in Liam Harte and Michael Parker (eds), *Contemporary Irish Fiction: Themes, Tropes, Theories* (Basingstoke: Macmillan, 2000), pp. 35–55

____, 'The Elephant of Irish Fiction', *Irish Review*, no. 30 (Spring/ Summer 2003), pp. 134–9

O'Brien, Kathleen, 'Contemporary *Caoineadh*: Talking Straight Through the Dead', *Canadian Journal of Irish Studies*, vol. 32, no. 1 (2006), pp. 56–63

O'Connell, Mark, 'The Weight of Emptiness: Narcissism and the Search for the Missing Twin in John Banville's *Birchwood* and *Mefisto*', *Irish University Review*, vol. 40, no. 2 (Autumn/Winter 2010), pp. 129–47

O'Connell, Shaun, 'Door Into the Light: John McGahern's Ireland', *Massachusetts Review*, vol. 25, no. 2 (Summer 1984), pp. 255–68

____, 'Brian Moore's Ireland: A World Well Lost', *Massachusetts Review*, vol. 29, no. 3 (Autumn 1988), pp. 539–55

O'Connor, Joseph, 'Introduction', in Dermot Bolger (ed.), *Ireland in Exile* (Dublin: New Island Books, 1993), pp. 11–18

____, 'Questioning our Self-Congratulations', *Studies*, vol. 87, no. 347 (Autumn 1998), pp. 245–51

O'Connor, Maureen, '"Becoming Animal" in the Novels of Edna O'Brien', in Christine Cusick (ed.), *Out of the Earth: Ecocritical Readings of Irish Texts* (Cork: Cork University Press, 2010), pp. 151–77

____, *The Female and the Species: The Animal in Irish Women's Writing* (Oxford: Peter Lang, 2010)

O'Connor, Sarah, *No Man's Land: Irish Women and the Cultural Present* (New York: Peter Lang, 2011)

O'Connor, Theresa, 'History, Gender and the Postcolonial Condition: Julia O'Faoláin's Comic Rewriting of *Finnegans Wake*', in O'Connor (ed.), *The Comic Tradition in Irish Women Writers* (Gainesville, Florida: University Press of Florida, 1996), pp. 124–48

O'Connor, Theresa (ed.), *The Comic Tradition in Irish Women Writers* (Gainesville, Florida: University Press of Florida, 1996)

O'Donoghue, Jo, *Brian Moore: A Critical Study* (Dublin: Gill & Macmillan, 1990)

O'Faoláin, Julia, 'Irish Innocence', Review of Bernard MacLaverty's *Lamb* (*New York Times Book Review*, 2 November 1980), pp. 13, 22

___, 'The Imagination as Battlefield', in Paul Brennan and Catherine de Saint Phalle (eds), *Arguing at the Crossroads: Essays on a Changing Ireland* (Dublin: New Island Books, 1997), pp. 24–43

___, 'The Furies of Irish Fiction', *Graph* (3rd Series), vol. 3, no. 1 (Spring 1998), pp. 6–11

O'Grady, Timothy, 'Memory, Photography, Ireland', *Irish Studies Review*, vol. 14, no. 2 (May 2006), pp. 255–62

O'Kane Mara, Miriam, 'Reading the Landscape for Clues: Environment in *Paddy Clarke Ha Ha Ha*', in Christine Cusick (ed.), *Out of the Earth: Ecocritical Readings of Irish Texts* (Cork: Cork University Press, 2010), pp. 178–88

O'Keeffe, Timothy (ed.), *Myles: Portraits of Brian O'Nolan* (London: Martin Brian & O'Keeffe, 1973)

Olsson, Anders, 'The Broken Place: Memory, Language, Tradition, and Storytelling in Colm Tóibín's Texts', in Hedda Friberg, Irene Gilsenan Nordin and Lene Yding Pedersen (eds), *Recovering Memory: Irish Representations of Past and Present* (Newcastle upon Tyne: Cambridge Scholars), pp. 128–48

Ó Nualláin, Ciarán, *The Early Years of Brian O'Nolan/Flann O'Brien/Myles na gCopaleen* (Dublin: Lilliput Press, 1998)

O'Reilly, Edouard Magessa, *Samuel Beckett:* Comment C'est/How It Is: *A Critical-Genetic Edition* (New York: Routledge, 2001)

Osborough, W. Nial, 'Another Country, Other Days: Revisiting Thomas Kilroy's *The Big Chapel*', *Irish University Review*, vol. 32, no. 1 (Spring/Summer 2002), pp. 39–67

O'Toole, Fintan, 'Going West: The Country versus the City in Irish Writing', *The Crane Bag*, vol. 9, no. 2 (1985), pp. 111–16

___, *A Mass for Jesse James: A Journey through 1980's Ireland* (Dublin: Raven Arts, 1990)

___, 'Everybody's Doing It', *The Irish Times*, 12 May 1990

___, *Black Hole, Green Card: The Disappearance of Ireland* (Dublin: New Island Books, 1994)

___, *The Ex-Isle of Erin: Images of a Global Ireland* (Dublin: New Island Books, 1997)

___, *The Lie of the Land: Irish Identities* (London: Verso, 1997)

___, 'Future Fictions', *Princeton University Library Chronicle*, vol. 52, no. 1 (Autumn 2010), pp. 407–18

Paratte, Henri-Dominique, 'Conflicts in a Changing World: John McGahern', in Patrick Rafroidi and Maurice Harmon (eds), *The Irish Novel in Our Time*

(Villeneuve d'Asq: Publications de l'Université de Lille III, 1976), pp. 311–27

Parker, Michael, *Northern Irish Literature 1956–1975. Vol 1: The Imprint of History* (Basingstoke: Palgrave Macmillan, 2007)

____, *Northern Irish Literature 1975–2000. Vol 2: The Imprint of History* (Basingstoke: Palgrave Macmillan, 2007)

____, 'Shadows on a Glass: Self-Reflexivity in the Fiction of Deirdre Madden', *Irish University Review*, vol. 30, no. 1 (Spring/Summer 2000), pp. 82–102

Parkin, Andrew, 'Shadows of Destruction: The "Big House" in Contemporary Irish Fiction', in Michael Kenneally (ed.), *Cultural Contexts and Literary Idioms in Contemporary Irish Literature* (Gerrards Cross: Colin Smythe, 1988), pp. 306–28

Paschel, Ulrike, *'No Mean City?' The Image of Dublin in the Novels of Dermot Bolger, Roddy Doyle and Val Mulkerns* (Frankfurt: Peter Lang, 1998)

Patten, Eve, 'Women and Fiction 1985–1990', *Krino*, nos 8/9 (1990), pp. 1–7

____, 'Fiction in Conflict: Northern Ireland's Prodigal Novelists', in Ian Bell (ed.), *Peripheral Visions: Images of Nationhood in Contemporary British Fiction* (Cardiff: University of Wales Press, 1995), pp. 128–48

____, 'Contemporary Irish Fiction', in John Wilson Foster (ed.), *The Cambridge Companion to the Irish Novel* (Cambridge: Cambridge University Press, 2006), pp. 259–75

Patterson, Glenn, 'Writing the Troubles', in Brian Cliff and Éibhear Walshe (eds), *Representing the Troubles: Text and Images, 1970–2000* (Dublin: Four Courts Press, 2004), pp. 15–18

____, *Lapsed Protestant* (Dublin: New Island Books, 2006)

Paulin, Tom, 'A Necessary Provincialism: Brian Moore, Maurice Leitch, Florence Mary McDowell', in Douglas Dunn (ed.), *Two Decades of Irish Writing* (Cheadle Hulme: Carcanet, 1975), pp. 242–56

____, Review of *The Pornographer*, *Encounter*, vol. 52, no. 1 (January 1980), pp. 60–1

Peach, Linden, *The Contemporary Irish Novel: Critical Readings* (Basingstoke: Palgrave Macmillan, 2004)

____, *Contemporary Irish and Welsh Women's Fiction: Gender, Desire and Power* (Cardiff: University of Wales Press, 2007)

Pelan, Rebecca, *Two Irelands: Literary Feminisms North and South* (Syracuse, New York: Syracuse University Press, 2005)

Pelaschiar, Laura, *Writing the North: The Contemporary Irish Novel in Northern Ireland* (Trieste: Edizioni Parnaso, 1998)

____, 'Transforming Belfast: The Evolving Role of the City in Northern Irish Fiction', *Irish University Review*, vol. 30, no. 1 (Spring/Summer 2000), pp. 117–31

Pernot-Deschamps, Marguerite, *The Fictional Imagination of Neil Jordan, Irish Novelist and Film Maker: A Study of Literary Style* (Lampeter: Mellen, 2009)

Pierce, David, *Light, Freedom and Song: A Cultural History of Modern Irish Writing* (New Haven, Connecticut: Yale University Press, 2005)

Pierce, Michael, 'Reconsidering Dermot Bolger's Grotesquery: Class and Sexuality in *The Journey Home*', *Irish University Review*, vol. 40, no. 2 (Autumn/Winter 2010), pp. 86–106

____, *Writing Ireland's Working Class: Dublin after O'Casey* (Basingstoke: Palgrave Macmillan, 2011)

Plunkett, James, *The Gems She Wore: A Book of Irish Places* (London: Hutchinson, 1978)

____, *The Boy on the Back Wall and Other Essays* (Dublin: Poolbeg, 1987)

Popot, Raymonde, 'Edna O'Brien's Paradise Lost', in Patrick Rafroidi and Maurice Harmon (eds), *The Irish Novel in Our Time* (Villeneuve d'Asq: Publications de l'Université de Lille III, 1976), pp. 255–83

Quinn, Antoinette, 'A Prayer for My Daughters: Patriarchy in *Amongst Women*', *Canadian Journal of Irish Studies*, vol. 17, no. 1 (July 1991), pp. 78–90

Quinn, Deirdre and Sharon Tighe-Mooney (eds), *Essays in Irish Literary Criticism: Themes of Gender, Sexuality and Corporeality* (Lewiston, New York: Mellen, 2008)

Rafroidi, Patrick and Maurice Harmon (eds), *The Irish Novel in Our Time* (Villeneuve d'Asq: Publications de l'Université de Lille III, 1976)

Randolph, Jody Allen, *Close to the Next Moment: Interviews from a Changing Ireland* (Manchester: Carcanet, 2010)

Rauchbauer, Otto (ed.), *Ancestral Voices: The Big House in Anglo-Irish Literature* (Hildesheim: Olms, 1992)

Reynolds, Margaret and Jonathan Noakes, *Roddy Doyle: The Essential Guide* (London: Vintage, 2004)

Richards, Shaun, 'Northside Realism and the Twilight's Last Gleaming', *Irish Studies Review*, vol. 1, no. 2 (1992), pp. 18–20

Richtarik, Marilynn and Kevin Chappell, 'An Interview with Glenn Patterson', *Five Points*, vol. 13, no. 2 (2009), pp. 44–56

Rickard, John S., *Irishness and (Post)modernism* (Lewisburg, Pennsylvania: Bucknell University Press, 1994)

Robinson, Paul N. 'Brian Moore's *Catholics*: "The Stone's in the Midst of All"', in Joseph McMinn (ed.), *The Internationalism of Irish Literature and Drama* (Gerrards Cross: Colin Smythe, 1992), pp. 271–6

Roche, Anthony (ed.), *Irish University Review*, vol. 30, no. 1 (Spring/Summer 2000), Contemporary Novel Issue

Rogers, Lori, *Feminine Nation: Performance, Gender and Resistance in the Works of John McGahern and Neil Jordan* (Lanham, Maryland: University Press of America, 1998)

Rolston, Bill, 'Mothers, Whores and Villains: Images of Women in Novels of the Northern Ireland Conflict', *Race and Class*, vol. 31, no. 1 (July 1989), pp. 41–57

Rooks-Hughes, Lorna, 'The Family and the Female Body in the Novels of Edna O'Brien and Julia O'Faoláin', *Canadian Journal of Irish Studies*, vol. 22, no. 2 (December 1996), pp. 83–97

Ross, Ciaran (ed.), *Sub-versions: Trans-national Readings of Modern Irish Literature* (Amsterdam: Rodopi, 2010)

Rosslyn, Felicity, 'The Importance of Being Irish: Jennifer Johnston', *Cambridge Quarterly*, vol. 32, no. 3 (2003), pp. 239–49

Rubenstein, Michael, 'A Fountain of Nationality: Haunted Infrastructure in Flann O'Brien's *The Third Policeman*', in Rubenstein, *Public Works: Infrastructure, Irish Modernism and the Postcolonial* (South Bend, Indiana: University of Notre Dame Press, 2010), pp. 93–129

Ryan, John (ed.), *A Bash in the Tunnel: James Joyce by the Irish* (Brighton: Clifton Books, 1970)

Ryan, Mary, 'A Feminism of Their Own? Irish Women's History and Contemporary Irish Women's Writing', *Estudios Irlandeses*, no. 5 (2010), pp. 92–101

Ryan, Ray (ed.), *Writing in the Irish Republic: Literature, Culture and Politics 1949–1999* (Basingstoke: Macmillan, 2000)

Ryan, Ray, *Ireland and Scotland: Literature and Culture, State and Nation, 1966–2000* (Oxford: Oxford University Press, 2002)

Sailer, Susan Shaw (ed.), *Representing Ireland: Gender, Class, Nationality* (Gainesville, Florida: University Press of Florida, 1997)

Sampson, Denis, 'A Note on John McGahern's *The Leavetaking*', *Canadian Journal of Irish Studies*, vol. 11, no. 2 (December 1976), pp. 61–5

Sampson, Denis (ed.), *Canadian Journal of Irish Studies*, vol. 7, no. 2 (December 1991), Special John McGahern Number

Sampson, Denis, *Outstaring Nature's Eye* (Washington DC: Catholic University of America Press, 1993)

___, '"Home, A Moscow of the Mind": Notes on Brian Moore's Transition to North America', *Colby Quarterly*, vol. 31, no. 1 (March 1995), pp. 46–54

___, *Brian Moore: The Chameleon Novelist* (Toronto: Doubleday, 1998)

___, '"The Day Set Alight in the Mind": Notes on John McGahern's Late Style', *Irish University Review*, vol. 39, no. 1 (Spring/Summer 2007), pp. 122–9

Scanlan, Margaret, *Traces of Another Time: History and Politics in Postwar British Fiction* (Princeton, New Jersey: Princeton University Press, 1990), pp. 23–83

___, 'Eoin McNamee's *Resurrection Man*', in Scanlan, *Plotting Terror: Novelists and Terrorists in Contemporary Fiction* (Charlottesville, Virginia: University Press of Virginia, 2001), pp. 37–56

Schirmer, Gregory A. *William Trevor: A Study of His Fiction* (London: Routledge, 1990)

Schoenberger, Nancy, *Dangerous Muse: The Life of Lady Caroline Blackwood* (New York: Doubleday, 2001)

Schrank, Berenice (ed.), *Canadian Journal of Irish Studies*, vol. 22, no. 2 ('Edna O'Brien Special Issue') (December 1996)

Schumacher, Jeanette, 'Uncanny Doubles: The Fiction of Anne Enright', *New Hibernia Review*, vol. 9, no. 3 (Autumn 2005), pp. 107–22

Schwall, Hedwig, 'The Working-Class Hero's View on 20th-Century Ireland in Recent Historical Novels', *BELL: Belgian Essays on Language and Literature* (2001), pp. 123–38

____, 'Fictions about Factions: An Analysis of Neil Jordan's *Sunrise with Sea Monster*', *Nordic Irish Studies*, no. 1 (2002), pp. 31–50

Schwerter, Stephanie, 'Peacefire: Belfast between Reality and Fiction', *Canadian Journal of Irish Studies*, vol. 33, no. 2 (2007), pp. 19–27

____, 'Transgressing Boundaries: Belfast and the "Romance-Across-the-Divide"', *Estudios Irlandeses*, no. 2 (2007), pp. 173–82

Shaffer, Brian W., *A Companion to the British and Irish Novel 1945–2000* (Malden, Massachusetts: Blackwell, 2005)

Shea, Thomas F., 'Patrick McGinley's Impressions of Flann O'Brien: *The Devil's Diary* and *At Swim-Two-Birds*', *Twentieth Century Literature*, vol. 40, no. 2 (Summer 1994), pp. 272–81

____, 'More Matter with More Art: Typescript Emendations in Patrick McGinley's *Bogmail*', *Canadian Journal of Irish Studies*, vol. 23, no. 2 (December 1997), pp. 23–37

____, 'Patrick McGinley's Appropriation of Cuchulainn: *The Trick of the Ga Bolga* (1985)', *New Hibernia Review*, vol. 5, no. 3 (Autumn 2001), pp. 114–27

____, 'Patrick McGinley's Alternating Current: Allusive Electricity in *The Last Soldier's Song*', *New Hibernia Review*, vol. 13, no. 1 (Spring 2009), pp. 109–24

Sheehan, Ronan, 'Novelists on the Novel: Interview with John Banville and Francis Stuart', *The Crane Bag*, vol. 3, no. 1 (1979), pp. 408–16

Sheehy Skeffington, Owen, 'The McGahern Affair', *Censorship*, no. 2 (Spring 1966), pp. 27–30

Sherry, Ruth, 'How is Irish Writing Reviewed?', *Cyphers*, no. 31 (1991), pp. 5–11

Skelton, Robin, 'Aidan Higgins and the Total Book', in Skelton, *Celtic Contraries* (Syracuse: Syracuse University Press, 1990), pp. 211–23

Sloan, Barry, 'The Remains of Protestantism in Maurice Leitch's Fiction', in Elmer Kennedy-Andrews (ed.), *The Irish Novel since 1966: A Collection of Critical Essays* (Gerrards Cross: Colin Smythe, 2006), pp. 247–61

Smith, James M., 'Retelling Stories: Exposing Mother Ireland in Kathy Prendergast's *Body Map Series* and Mary Leland's *The Killleen*', in Jennifer Grinnell and Alston Connelly (eds), *Re/Dressing Cathleen: Contemporary Works from Irish Women Artists* (Boston: McMullen Museum of Art, 1997), pp. 42–51

____, 'Remembering Ireland's Architecture of Containment: Telling Stories in *The Butcher Boy* and *States of Fear*', *Éire-Ireland*, vol. 36, nos 3–4 (Fall–Winter 2001), pp. 11–30

Smyth, Gerry, 'The Psychotic Tradition: Insanity and Fantasy in the Contemporary Irish Novel', in Alan Marshall and Neil Sammells (eds), *Irish Encounters: Poetry, Politics and Prose* (Bath: Sulis, 1998), pp. 152–64

___, *The Novel and the Nation: Studies in the New Irish Fiction* (London: Pluto Press, 1997)

___, 'The Right to the City: Re-presentations of Dublin in Contemporary Irish Fiction', in Liam Harte and Michael Parker (eds), *Contemporary Irish Fiction: Themes, Tropes, Theories* (Basingstoke: Macmillan, 2000), pp. 13–34

___, 'Shite and Sheep: An Ecocritical Perspective on Two Recent Irish Novels', *Irish University Review*, vol. 30, no. 1 (Spring/Summer 2000), pp. 163–78

___, *Space and the Irish Cultural Imagination* (Basingstoke: Palgrave, 2001)

St Peter, Christine, 'Jennifer Johnston's Irish Troubles', in Toni O'Brien Johnson and David Cairns (eds), *Gender in Irish Writing* (Milton Keynes: Open University Press, 1991), pp. 112–27

___, *Changing Ireland: Strategies in Contemporary Women's Fiction* (New York: Palgrave, 2000)

___, 'Petrifying Time: Incest Narratives from Contemporary Ireland', in Liam Harte and Michael Parker (eds), *Contemporary Irish Fiction: Themes, Tropes, Theories* (Basingstoke: Macmillan, 2000), pp. 125–44

Strachan, John and Alison O'Malley-Younger (eds), *Ireland: Evolution and Revolution* (New York: Peter Lang, 2010)

Strobl, Gerwin, '"Chronicle of a Death Foretold": J.G. Farrell's *Troubles* and the Unravelling of the Union', in Alan Marshall and Neil Sammells (eds), *Irish Encounters: Poetry, Politics and Prose* (Bath: Sulis, 1998), pp. 127–36

Strongman, Luke, 'Toward an Irish Literary Postmodernism: Roddy Doyle's *Paddy Clarke Ha Ha Ha*', *Canadian Journal of Irish Studies*, vol. 23, no. 1 (July 1997), pp. 31–40

Stuart, Francis, 'The Soft Centre of Irish Writing', in William Vorm (ed.), *Paddy No More* (Portmarnock: Wolfhound, 1977), p. 7

Sullivan, Robert, *A Matter of Faith: The Fiction of Brian Moore* (London: Greenwood, 1996)

Swann, Joseph, 'Banville's Faust: *Doctor Copernicus*, *Kepler*, *The Newton Letter* and *Mefisto* as Stories of the European Mind', in Donald E. Morse, Csilla Bertha and István Pálffy (eds), *A Small Nation's Contribution to the World: Essays on Anglo-Irish Literature and Language* (Gerrards Cross: Colin Smythe, 1993), pp. 148–60

Taaffe, Carol, *Ireland Through the Looking-Glass: Flann O'Brien, Myles na gCopaleen and Irish Cultural Debate* (Cork: Cork University Press, 2008)

Thompson, Helen (ed.), *The Current Debate about the Irish Literary Canon: Essays Reassessing* The Field Day Anthology of Irish Writing (Lewiston, New York: Mellen, 2006)

Tigges, Wim, 'Ireland in Wonderland: Flann O'Brien's *The Third Policeman* as a Nonsense Novel', in C.C. Barfoot and Theo D'haen (eds), *The Clash of*

Ireland: Literary Contrasts and Connections (Amsterdam: Rodopi, 1989), pp. 195–208

Tóibín, Colm, *Martyrs and Metaphors* (Dublin: Raven Arts, 1987)

——, 'New Ways of Killing Your Father', *London Review of Books*, vol. 15, no. 22 (18 November 1993), pp. 3–6

Tóibín, Colm (ed.) and Introduction, *Soho Square* 6 (London: Bloomsbury, 1993), pp. 8–9

Tóibín, Colm, 'Foreword', in Francis Stuart, *Black List, Section H* (Dublin: Lilliput Press, 1995)

Tóibín, Colm (ed.) and Introduction, *The Penguin Book of Irish Fiction* (London: Viking, 1999), pp. ix–xxxiv

Tóibín, Colm, 'Issues of Truth and Invention', Review of Brendan Barrington (ed.), *The Wartime Broadcasts of Francis Stuart 1942–1944*, *London Review of Books*, vol. 23, no. 1 (4 January 2001), pp. 3–11

——, 'Writing the Troubles', in Brian Cliff and Éibhear Walshe (eds), *Representing the Troubles: Texts and Images, 1970–2000* (Dublin: Four Courts Press, 2004), pp. 23–6

Toolan, Michael J. 'John McGahern: The Historian and the Pornographer', *Canadian Journal of Irish Studies*, vol. 7, no. 2 (December 1991), pp. 39–55, John McGahern Special Number

Trevor, William, *A Writer's Ireland: Landscape in Literature* (London: Thames & Hudson, 1984)

——, *Excursions in the Real World* (London: Hutchinson, 1993)

Tucker, Amanda, '"Our Story is Everywhere": Colum McCann and Irish Multiculturalism', *Irish University Review*, vol. 40, no. 2 (Autumn/Winter 2010), pp. 107–27

Tynan, Maeve, '"Everything is in the Way the Material Is Composed": Joseph O'Connor's *Star of the Sea* as Historiographic Metafiction', in Maeve Tynan, Maria Belville and Marita Ryan (eds), *Passages: Movements and Moments in Text and Theory* (Newcastle upon Tyne: Cambridge Scholars, 2009), pp. 79–95

Valente, Joseph, 'Race/Sex/Shame: The Queer Nationalism of *At Swim Two Boys*', *Éire-Ireland* vol. 40, nos 3–4 (Fall/Winter 2005), pp. 58–84

Vance, Norman, *Irish Literature: A Social History* (Dublin: Four Courts Press, 1999)

van der Ziel, Stanley (ed.), *John McGahern. Love of the World: Essays* (London: Faber, 2009)

Wachtel, Eleanor, 'Jennifer Johnston interviewed', *Queen's Quarterly*, vol. 104, no. 2 (1997), pp. 318–29

Wall, Éamonn, 'Aidan Higgins's *Balcony of Europe*: Stephen Dedalus Hits the Road', *Colby Quarterly*, vol. 31, no. 1 (March 1995), pp. 81–7

——, 'The Living Stream: John McGahern's *Amongst Women* and Irish Writing in the 1990s', *Studies*, vol. 88, no. 351 (Autumn 1999), pp. 305–14

——, 'Winds Blowing from a Million Directions: Colum McCann's *Songdogs*', in

Charles Fanning (ed.), *New Perspectives on the Irish Diaspora* (Carbondale, Illinois: Southern Illinois University Press, 2000), pp. 281–8

Walsh, Patrick, '"Something Important Had Changed": Modernisation and Irish Fiction since 1960', in Elmer Kennedy-Andrews (ed.), *The Irish Novel since the 1960s: A Collection of Critical Essays* (Gerrards Cross: Colin Smythe, 2006), pp. 27–49

Walshe, Éibhear (ed.), *Sex, Nation and Dissent in Irish Writing* (Cork: Cork University Press, 1997)

Walshe, Éibhear, '"A Lout's Game": Espionage, Irishness and Sexuality in *The Untouchable*', *Irish University Review*, vol. 36, no. 1 (Spring/Summer 2006), pp. 102–15

____, 'The Vanishing Homoerotic: Colm Tóibín's Gay Fictions', *New Hibernia Review*, vol. 10, no. 4 (Winter 2006), pp. 122–36

Walshe, Éibhear and Gwenda Young (eds), *Molly Keane: Essays in Contemporary Criticism* (Dublin: Four Courts Press, 2006)

Ward, Patrick, *Exile, Emigration and Irish Writing* (Dublin: Irish Academic Press, 2001)

Watt, Stephen, 'The Politics of Bernard MacLaverty's *Cal*', *Éire-Ireland*, vol. 28, no. 3 (Fall 1993), pp. 130–46

____, *Beckett and Contemporary Irish Writing* (Cambridge: Cambridge University Press, 2009)

Weekes, Ann Owens, 'Diarmuid and Gráinne Again: Julia O'Faoláin's *No Country for Old Men* [sic]', *Éire–Ireland*, vol. 21, no. 1 (Spring 1986), pp. 89–102

____, *Irish Women Writers: An Uncharted Tradition* (Lexington, Kentucky: University of Kentucky Press, 1990)

____, *Unveiling Treasures: The Attic Guide to the Published Works of Irish Women Literary Writers* (Dublin: Attic Press, 1993)

____, 'Ordinary Women: Themes in Contemporary Fiction by Irish Women', *Colby Quarterly*, vol. 31, no. 1 (March 1995), pp. 88–99

____, 'Figuring the Mother in Contemporary Irish Fiction', in Liam Harte and Michael Parker (eds), *Contemporary Irish Fiction: Themes, Tropes, Theories* (Basingstoke: Macmillan, 2000), pp. 100–24

____, 'Mary Morrissy', in Michael R. Molino (ed.), *Twenty-First-Century British and Irish Novelists* (Detroit: Gale, 2003), pp. 234–40

Welch, Robert, *Changing States: Transformations in Modern Irish Writing* (London: Routledge, 1993)

Wenzell, Tim, *Emerald Green: An Ecocritical Study of Irish Literature* (Newcastle upon Tyne: Cambridge Scholars, 2009)

White, Caramine, *Reading Roddy Doyle* (Syracuse: Syracuse University Press, 2001)

White, Jerry, 'Europe, Ireland, and Deirdre Madden', *World Literature Today*, vol. 73, no. 3 (Summer 1999), pp. 451–60

White, Roberta, *A Studio of One's Own: Fictional Women Painters and the Art of Fiction* (Madison, New Jersey: Fairleigh Dickinson University Press, 2005)

Wilson, Robert McLiam, 'Sticks and Stones: The Irish Identity', *Grand Street*, no. 62 (Fall 1997), pp. 135–9

Wondrich, Roberta Gefter, '"The Familiar Otherwhere of Art': Awareness, Creation, Redemption. Art and the Artistic Imagination in John Banville's Trilogy of Art', *Prospero*, no. 4 (1997), pp. 94–110

____, 'A Great, Sinister Performer: John Banville, *The Untouchable*', *Canadian Journal of Irish Studies*, vol. 23, no. 2 (1997), pp. 123–9

____, 'Exilic Returns: Self and History Outside Ireland in Recent Irish Fiction', *Irish University Review*, vol. 30, no. 1 (Spring/Summer 2000), pp. 1–16

____, 'The Pain Within: Female Bodies, Illness and Motherhood in Contemporary Irish Fiction', *Textus*, vol. 13, no. 1 (Jan–June 2000), pp. 129–48

____, 'Postmodern Love, Postmodern Death and God-like Authors in Irish Fiction: The Case of John Banville', *Barcelona English Language and Literature Series*, no. 11 (2000), pp. 79–88

____, '"Musing among the Posts": Reflections on the Post-Colonial and some Irish Novels', *Journal of Commonwealth and Postcolonial Studies*, vol. 8, nos 1 & 2 (2001), pp. 59–80

____, 'Survivors of Joyce: Joycean Images and Motifs in Some Contemporary Irish Fiction', *Studies*, vol. 90, no. 358 (Summer 2001), pp. 197–206

York, Richard, 'Jennifer Johnston: Tremors of Memory', in Elmer Kennedy-Andrews (ed.), *The Irish Novel since the 1960s: A Collection of Critical Essays* (Gerrards Cross: Colin Smythe, 2006), pp. 277–300

Young, Barbara Ann, *The Child as Emblem of the Nation in Twentieth-Century Irish Literature* (Lewiston, New York: Mellen, 2006)

Index